D1591747

LAST CALL CHICAGO

A HISTORY OF 1001 LGBTQ-FRIENDLY TAVERNS, HAUNTS & HANGOUTS

RICK KARLIN

&

ST SUKIE DE LA CROIX

RATTLING GOOD YARNS
PRESS

Rattling Good Yarns Press
33490 Date Palm Drive 3065
Cathedral City CA 92235
USA
www.rattlinggoodyarns.com

Library of Congress Control Number: 2022941763

ISBN: 978-1-955826-17-4

First Edition

DEDICATION

This book would not be possible without the support and love of my husband Gregg Shapiro, my son Adam Karlin, and my friends who have listened to me drone on for hours about the subject of Chicago's defunct LGBT bars, offering their own memories of these places. A shout out to my friends from my fearless foursome of my early days out in my twenties, and whom I still count among my best friends, Paul Escriva, Kelvin Harris, and the late Ben Bailey. And to my friends who were not able to complete their journey to gay elderhood. You are, and will continue to be, missed.
—Rick Karlin

For those who are gone, those who are left, and those who have yet to arrive.
—St Sukie de la Croix

The authors also dedicate this book to Frankie Knuckles, the Godfather of House Music

TABLE OF CONTENTS

FOREWORD

This is a Gay Bar Love Story.

We met in a small, 2:00 am mafia gay bar called Shari's at Clark and Surf in 1973. Pep was a popular bartender there at a time when bars were gays' only refuge from an uncaring, or worse, an openly hostile world. We were introduced because Pep's then-boyfriend and I shared the same name, Arthur. I was instantly smitten by this handsome, outgoing, and very funny young Cuban.

He had come to Chicago two years earlier after five years in Miami following a year in Costa Rica. His resourceful, stubborn mother had sent him and his younger sister and brother to escape from her ex-husband's plan to send his children to Russia to study communism. I had come to Illinois in 1972 from teaching in Virginia, on sabbatical for a one-year Master's in Theatre at Northwestern. I had never crossed Howard Street because I was determined to avoid the reviled Chicago of popular culture, the scene of the 1968 Democratic Convention riots. Happily, friends from Northwestern convinced me to visit some gay bars. That eventually led to me spending a few hours every week drinking Schlitz and talking to the Cuban. One evening, October 4, 1973, Pep said, "By the way, I broke up with Arthur today." After letting an appropriate amount of time go by (approximately a minute and a half), I asked, "What are you doing after work tonight?" We went home to my student apartment in Evanston, and Pep never left, beginning a fifty-year first date.

Welcomed into the small, tightly knit society of gay bar employees, I soon adjusted to being called "Junior" or "Number 2." We became regular volunteers at fundraisers for a hoped-for community center or to help a gay friend who had fallen on hard times or who needed bail money because of some police entrapment in Lincoln Park. But, most importantly, we took part in all forms of activism that began in bars, extensions of the work of Mattachine, and other suit and tie groups.

The best example of activism with bars and bar patrons, was the community response to the planned arrival of the Orange Juice Queen, the beautiful but notoriously misguided bigot, Anita Bryant, with her Save Our Children campaign. That day, June 14, 1977, forever changed Chicago gay activism. For the thousands and thousands of us who marched on the Medinah Temple in the open, in the daytime, in the downtown streets, our actions put the lie to the notion that being gay had to be limited to a small nighttime part of gay lives. Instead, protesters locked eyes and arms with each other and found in themselves a new activism, a new freedom in the downtown streets of Chicago. Pep and I were a part of it because, like so many others, we were a part of gay bars.

In the early eighties, before MTV, a customer of Pep's at Alfie's named Rocco presented him with his idea for a new gay bar featuring large screen music videos. He asked Pep if he could take on the task of creating such videos. Pep, who had always secretly wanted to be a DJ, jumped at the opportunity. For the next year and a half, Pep worked every day creating visually exciting pieces from the few films, mostly science fiction, available for rent. Opening night of Sidetrack, April 22, 1982, the bar was so packed we ran out of beer and borrowed some from our friend Chuck Rodocker at Touché. From then on, the bar became a slow but steady juggernaut of growth during often turbulent times. Unfortunately, Rocco passed away that year, and AIDS ravaged our community from the mid-eighties until the arrival of protease inhibitors in 1996. During these unspeakably cruel times, bars, which had been gay folk's only refuge, became simultaneously places of paralyzing fear, fear of possible infection from each other, the only people we believed we could count on in a time when the unofficial government response to the plague was, "It's only fags; let them die."

Bars stepped up, those that remained, and helped fund the new organizations our community founded to take care of our own when no one else would. And as we fought back alongside the remarkable ACT UP warriors, we re-learned over and over and over that the only people we could truly trust were in our own communities.

Mostly created and then exacerbated by AIDS, a new grassroots political activism arose in our community as we were increasingly faced with the cold reality that we were, at best, merely second-class citizens. We could be denied housing and employment as well as the other supposed benefits of citizenship, simply because of who we were. This grassroots ferment focused on efforts to pass a Chicago gay rights ordinance. It was largely non-bar, or even anti-bar as newly minted activists wanted to abandon all old ways, including "top down" bar owners who had often been de facto community leaders.

In preparation for a major rally in Daley Plaza the Sunday before a planned City Council vote, these grassroots leaders were debating asking all the bars to close that Sunday so that people would go to the rally—potentially a major split between bar culture (old ways) and anti-bar culture (new ways). As a young bar owner, I went to a planning meeting, unsure if I would be welcome. When asked my opinion of the "close the bars" proposal, I said, "It's a terrible idea; first, closing bars will not guarantee that patrons will attend the rally, and second, if this is a new day, the start of a new world of activism, why would you want to make enemies with the bar world which has been our community's primary source of funding for every initiative up to now? The moderator said, "Fine! What do YOU suggest?" Completely taken aback and fresh out of ideas or confidence, I reached down deep and somehow pulled a thought out of my butt, "Leave the bars open for people to assemble; ask bar owners to donate money to rent buses; pick up rally goers from the bars; bring them back to the bars after." "Ok," said the moderator, "you're in charge of donations and renting buses. Let's move on with the rest of the meeting." And I thought, "What did my big mouth get me into now?" Well, it all worked. We rented Chicago Transit Authority buses for symbolism, picked up thousands of rally goers, and had enough money to pick up attendees from all the gay religious groups. For so many of us in those almost entirely gay buses, it was the first time we were not in the minority. And that epic split between Chicago gay bars and modern gay activism never happened.

That Chicago gay rights ordinance was voted on three times, finally passing on December 21, 1988. A similar Cook County law passed in 1993, and the State of Illinois version passed in 2005. And, of course, Marriage Equality was signed into Illinois law on November 20, 2013. Through it all, the bars were always there while our armies of activists fought and usually won legislative and judicial victories, places where we could mourn our losses and celebrate our deserved victories. Most of all, bars remain our best places to find community and occasionally a few love stories.

To Sukie and Rick, thank you for your tireless work documenting our Chicago and the nearly lost stories of Chicago gay bars.

—Jose "Pep" Pena and Art Johnston, 2022

Owners of Sidetrack, named the #1 Gay Bar in the U.S. by Yelp in 2021, the Most Popular Bar in Illinois by Buzzfeed, the Most Visited Bar in Chicago by LYFT, and the Best Gay Bar in Chicago by TimeOut.

INTRODUCTION

In *Last Call Chicago*, the authors tried to conjure up the atmosphere of the bars by mentioning events they held, names of DJs, raids, etc. We hope that the listings stimulate your memories of your favorite places.

In 1985, Tom Wilson Weinberg's musical adventure, "The Ten Percent Revue," was first performed. It enjoyed a long off-Broadway run, a national tour, and was recorded. The musical was a positive affirmation of LGBT lives during the AIDS crisis when those of us who were there were caring for friends or attending their funerals. One song in the musical is "Before Stonewall".

> *"There was a time before liberation*
> *When all the witches were mad and moonstruck*
> *When the shrinking and the shocking and the mocking were rife*
> *We still found each other*
> *The ones in the life*
> *There was a time before demonstrations*
> *When the queens and fairies were shy and fearful*
> *We ran and we hid from the fist and the knife*
> *And we still found each other*
> *The ones in the life*
> *Do you know Dorothy?*
> *Do you have the time?*
> *Have you got a light, dear?*
> *Change for a dime?*
> *Do you come here often?*
> *I see what you mean*
> *I know a tavern where we won't be seen"*

Reading LGBT history books, one vein of persecution running through them, is that THEY – the politicians, the medical profession, religions (take your pick) – were hellbent on keeping us apart. That's why they raided our bars. And even private parties in our homes. That's why they put us in jail. It's that innocent childlike idea, "if we can't see the problem, it doesn't exist."

THEY could tolerate the existence of an individual homosexual – the camp waiter, the female impersonator in vaudeville, the limp-wristed confirmed-bachelor uncle. What THEY feared most is that if two homosexuals met, there might be an exchange of ideas. If three homosexuals met ... if four homosexuals met ... if enough homosexuals met, well, that's almost a group. What next? A movement?

THEIR fears were well-grounded. We did become a movement, because as Weinberg said, "We still found each other, the ones in the life ... I know a tavern where we won't be seen"

Prior to the existence of LGBT groups like the Daughters of Bilitis and the Mattachine Society, LGBT folks met in bars, taverns, and saloons – they were the community centers. In Chicago—and other large American cities—these bars were run by mobsters. After prohibition started on January 17, 1920, the mob opened illegal speakeasys effectively taking control of the bar business. That grip on the liquor business continued long after prohibition ended on December 5, 1933. The mob started losing control of Chicago's gay bars in 1973 when US

Attorney James R. Thompson investigated tavern shakedowns. Although, when asked to name the last mob-controlled gay bar in Chicago, bar-owner Charles "Chuck" Renslow said it was the LA Connection opened in 1986. The authors can find no mob connection in that bar.

Whatever the truth, the mob should be thanked for providing LGBT folks in Chicago with a place to meet, exchange ideas, and ultimately fight back. Don't forget, it was a raid on a New York gay bar that started our Gay Liberation movement.

Last Call Chicago contains 1,001 gay, gay-friendly bars, saloons, and taverns – with the occasional restaurant thrown in. Many of these establishments were not exclusively "homosexual haunts." Some, like the South Side Black clubs in the 1930s and 1940s, were all-inclusive, where LGBT folks could dance and even canoodle. Some of the bars listed had gay nights once a week, or once a month. Our selection criteria included establishments where LGBT folks could go, meet others, and be reasonably safe.

Obviously, we have only scratched the surface with our 1,001 bars. The names of most of Chicago's gay-welcoming bars have been lost in the mists of time. By their very nature, they were clandestine and flying under the radar. We are also aware that in this deluge of information, we may have omitted some bars that you know of. We've done the best we could with limited information e.g. Those individuals listed as "bar owners" are not always the actual owners. There are often silent partners, and in the case of mob bars, the bars are in the names of distant family members.

The Wind Up bar was owned by the Capone/Guzik gang. Also, the dates of the openings and closings of bars are often unknown or sketchy. In the profiles, we listed dates when a bar was known as being actively gay or gay-friendly, but not necessarily when it opened and closed – unless specifically mentioned. Therefore, having said all that, we recommend that students of LGBT history use this book only as a starting point for their research.

By design, this book focuses on one area, Chicago and its surrounding suburbs. The authors encourage those familiar with other cities to attempt a similar endeavor. Much of our history is written on bar napkins and scribbled on matchbook covers, just waiting to be discovered.

"Since at least the 1940s, gay establishments have served as a safer sanctuary and haven for LGBT people. Entering these places meant a respite from the closet. There, those who had been shunned by family, friends, communities, employers, landlords, or the state could make temporary residence. For some, it was more of a home than they had ever known.

"Even the very real risk of raids, harassment and exploitation did not deter queer people from patronizing these places. Access to them could be a matter of life and death; the effects of depression and anxieties waiting in the outside world were too much to bear for some people shut out by their families or towns. Gay bars and clubs helped combat isolation. They forged community." — Julio Capó, Jr.

Julio Capó, Jr. is Associate Professor of History and Public Humanities at Florida International University, author of "Welcome to Fairyland: Queer Miami before 1940".

Numbered

2Bears Tavern
1140 W. Wilson Ave.
Circa: 2022

Opened March 2022.

11 Fantasies
5232 N. Sheridan Rd.
Circa: 1981

The grand opening of 11 Fantasies took place on October 31, 1981, with a Halloween party.

21 Club (Legacy)
3042 W. Irving Park Rd
Circa: 1961-2000s

This was listed as the oldest gay-owned bar in the city in October 1992 when owner Woodrow "Woody" Moser died. He was survived by his lover of 33 years, Jose "Joe" Rodriguez, who took over management of the bar. Over the years, the bar attracted mostly blue-collar, older, gay men.

The 21 Club was one of the first Chicago gay bars to "come out" and advertise in a gay publication. Its ads started to appear in the *Mattachine Midwest Newsletter* in early-1970. The bar was also known for having a buzzer on the door, as did the nearby lesbian bar, Lost and Found.

In April 1969, the 21 Club celebrated the grand opening of El Salon de Crystal, a new fine dining area in the bar. The dining area came and went over the years but was eventually replaced by a pool table.

On September 20, 1969, the cops raided the 21 Club. Twelve men were arrested for indecency. Moser bailed all his customers out of jail. He then started a defense fund, holding a benefit cocktail party on October 12. One of those in the bar the night it was raided was a son of Mayor Richard J. Daley. He was not arrested or charged, and the raids on gay bars stopped for a while.

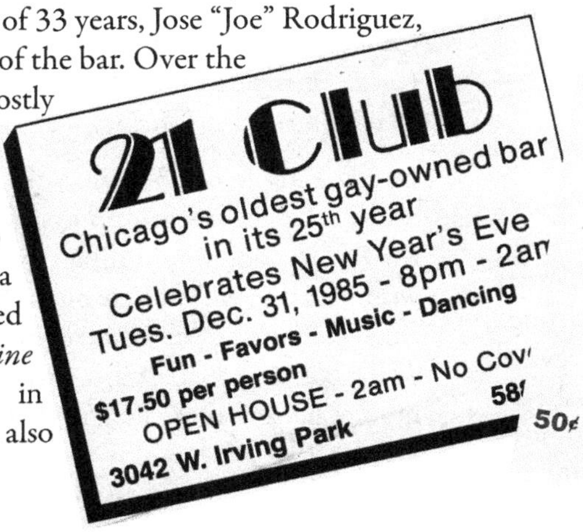

In June 1972, the 21 Club was completely remodeled, as it was again in July 1992. The 1972 remodel included a limited-edition wallpaper mural by caricaturist, Al Hirschfeld, featuring celebrities (Marilyn Monroe, Lucille Ball, Charlie Chaplin) at a nightclub. It took up one entire wall of the dance floor.

On May 11, 1974, the 21 Club held a benefit for Beckman House, the new gay

21 Club

Chicago's oldest gay-owned bar in its 25th year

Celebrates New Year's Eve
Tues. Dec. 31, 1985 - 8pm - 2am
Fun - Favors - Music - Dancing
$17.50 per person
OPEN HOUSE - 2am - No Cover
3042 W. Irving Park

OPEN
THE **21** CLUB
3042 West Irving Park Road

PARTY TIME
EVERYDAY
8 P.M. to 11 P.M.

50¢
• All single mixed drinks
• Manhattans
• Martinis, etc.

center; they raised $500. Patrons were entertained by Aunt Lena and her original 21 Club Adorables.

In 1976, *Gay Chicago Magazine* described the 21 Club as having a "popular jukebox, small dance area." The club was famous for its Friday night fish fry from 8:00 p.m. to midnight and free Sunday "all you can eat" buffet at 8:00 p.m.

In October 1988, the bar changed its name to Legacy 21, after the 21 Club in New York City brought a lawsuit for trademark infringement.

In February 1994, a young Honey West performed at Legacy 21 in a benefit for Chicago House, a residential home for people impacted by HIV/AIDS.

In October 1998, Legacy 21 began featuring gay rock 'n' roll bands when Lair DeFever-Scott brought his Queer Fest America acts to the club. He said that Legacy 21 was the only gay bar that would book them. Scott's ex-husband, Alan Tomasello, was the doorman at Legacy and introduced him to the club's owner. Bands that performed there include Rash, Monkey Paw, and Lair & The Chamber Boys.

In April 2003, Legacy 21 hosted Latin drag king Andres De Los Santos (AKA Aurora Pineda Zarate) and His Flavored Entourage with DJ Wanda.

38
Roseland/South Side
Circa: 1950s

One of the bar's regulars remembered, "Back in the '50s, there was a real swinging one on Roseland. It was called the 38. It was in a residential neighborhood, and there was a church on the other corner. It was a very, very strange group of people. As it got later, all the neighborhood people evaporated, and more and more gay people came in. Sometimes on weekends, you needed a shoehorn to get in there. It was run by an Italian woman, Lucille, and she must have weighed 300 and something-odd lbs. She was pregnant one time, and she had the baby, and no one even noticed. And her husband was built like a pencil. On Fridays, or one night during the week, she would make big pots of spaghetti and you could eat to your heart's content. It was fun, but it only lasted a couple of years. The area started changing."

115 Bourbon St.
3359 W. 115th St., Merrionette Park
Circa: 2013

In July 2013, 115 Bourbon St., the South Side's largest entertainment complex, hosted "The Queens are Back," a huge drag show featuring: Lindsay Devereaux, Serina Devine, Lindsay Bryant, Jazzelle Boyette, Theresa Dawn, Tina Roberts, Velicity Metropolis, Sassy Trade, Angelique Munro, Butter Scotch, Mystique Summers, Chris Ruhu, Myke Kagan, and Lori Dinovo.

131 Club
13126 S. Western Ave., Blue Island
Circa: 1984-1990

The 131 Club was owned by Larry Panice and billed as "Blue Island's Party Bar for Gay Men and Women." It opened around Gay Pride 1984. The lip-sync contests held every Sunday were a highlight. Chuck Udell was one of the popular bartenders there.

This location was later the Edge, Club Krave, and Clubhouse Players.

The Southside's Newest Bar Is The
131 Club
ENTERTAINMENT
WEDNESDAY NIGHTS
10 pm & MIDNIGHT
Open 6 pm daily
131 Club
13126 S. Western
Blue Island
388-8272

152 Club
152 W. North Ave.
Circa: 1950

161 Club
161 W. Harrison St.
Circa: 1980

In the October 31, 1980, issue of *GayLife,* there's a photograph of the Under Construction party with DJ Frankie Knuckles, attended by hundreds of people. On November 7, 1980, American R&B singer, Geraldine Hunt, performed her hit song, "Can't Fake the Feeling," at the 161 Club.

169 Club
169 W. Division St.
Circa: 1963-1969

Called the "One-Sixty-Nine Club" in the 1968-1969 *Damron Guide.* It was run by Howie and Bert, who also managed Alameda and the Place.

Buddy King told the authors, "The One-Sixty-Nine was really ramshackle. It had broken floors so that sometimes people on the dance floor would disappear through the floor, and there would be bricks tossed through the front window from time to time. And the police would come in during the night and go up to the bar, and the bartender would go to the cash register, take money, hand it to them, and they would leave."

307 Club
307 State St., Calumet City
Circa: 1963-1966

One patron remembered, "Living as a gay woman in the '50s and '60s was more difficult than people today can understand. One woman in the south suburbs was fed up with the city, tired of the fear, and sick of having no place local that they could call their own. That woman was Tocci and in 1963, she opened her first bar, the 307 Club at 307 State St. in Calumet City, along with her friend Blossom. The trouble with the club was that it was open to anybody, so while it was a place to go for women like us, it was also considered a good place by 'redneck' types. There were regular customers of both genders there.

"The 307 Club had a nice homey atmosphere complete with peanut shells thrown on the floor and barrels of pickles, but after 2 1/2 years Tocci moved."

Tocci's next blue-collar lesbian bar was the Hideaway.

411 Club
411 E. 63rd St.
Circa: 1989

The 411 Club was a gay/straight bar most likely owned by Texan Jerry Chamblis, who is thought to have also owned an earlier bar called the Sculpture Room. Details are hazy. The bar first appeared in the *Gay Chicago Magazine* bar listings in 1989, though it's known that it was open before that. The 411 was a jazz club and reputedly a favorite of Mayor Harold Washington.

In 1992, six men robbed the 411 Club. The armed robbery occurred just after midnight, September 20, and ended in the murder of manager, John "Johnny" Conley. The suspects allegedly targeted the 411 Club because it was a gay establishment.

430
43rd St.
Circa: 1948

One former patron told the authors, "There were four apartments above the club, and my grandmother lived in that building. There was a pawn shop, then the 430. That was about 1948. A lot of people say it was an undercover gay bar. There were people there that you could meet, but it wasn't an all-out gay bar because you had men and women, you had Blacks and Whites, so it was all undercover."

644 Club
644 N. State St
Circa: 1981

In the January 1981 *Gay Chicago Magazine*, a notice about the bar touted that, "Corky's back on State Street." No other mentions can be found. Shortly before this, it was known as CC's. Corky, a bar personality and bartender, also served up the cocktails at the Ritz on State St., and Mike's Aragon Lounge.

720 Club
720 N. Wells St.
Circa: 2007

Dance music artist, Kristine W, performed at the 720 Club in September 2007. Her 1994 hit, "Feel What You Want," became a gay anthem in the LGBT dance clubs.

This was also the location of Cairo.

905 Club
905 W. Belmont Ave.
Circa: 1980-1995

This was a straight neighborhood bar with an early-morning drinking crowd. It opened at 7 a.m. Then, in 1980, a popular bartender in the community, a lesbian known as Dago Rose, took it over. Supposedly the first day she walked in, she slammed a baseball bat down on the bar and said, "Anybody who wants to live, leaves now." And from that day on it was a queer bar. Joey Santiago and Jack Jorenson were early bartenders.

It was known as Dago Rose's Hideaway or D'Rose's Hideaway from 1980-81. It was later known as Jimmy's 905 with bartenders Jim Asta, Jan Howard, and Johnny Lait. Earlier, Jim Asta owned the Frog Pond, where Dago Rose had been a popular bartender. She later bartended at Act III and Big Red's. Bartender/female impersonator, Jan Howard performed in drag at many bars and clubs, including the Baton, John L's, Harlequin's, Knight Out, and Mama Jan's.

Photo by Dan Di Leo
How many fingers do you see? asks D'Rose's Hideaway bartender Joey Santiago. Two? Good! Then you can have another drink.

In the July 31, 1991, issue of *Nightlines*, Mother Superior reported in her column, "The 905 Club is causing problems for many of the businesses on Belmont near Clark and, although it's a gay club, gay business owners along Belmont are the one's filing the complaints. The Central Lakeview Council is trying to work with these people to close the place, so keep your eyes open."

1002
1002 N. Clark St.
Circa: 1975-1980

The 1002 was a gay men's bar. The bar's motto was, "If you can't get it here, you can't get it anywhere!" In early 1976, it offered free Sunday afternoon buffets and a champagne raffle on Saturday nights. On May 12, 1976, the bar hosted a Mr. 1002 contest; the winner was Don Kyle. Staff members were Chris, Aggie, Toni, Jimmy, Jamie, and Herb. *The Damron Guide* listed the clientele as "rough trade."

GayLife reported in the November 26, 1975, issue, "Charles F. Hunter, chairman of the Northwestern University Radio and TV Department, was murdered November 19 by two men he met at the 1002 Club. He was robbed and thrown from a third-story window of the Lakeshore Hotel."

1450 East
1450 E. Algonquin Rd., Schaumburg
Circa: 1994-1995

In February 1994, the 1450 East was advertised as, "The most talked about new suburban gay bar." At the grand opening, singer, record producer, and DJ, Cajmere (AKA Green Velvet), and singer, Dajae, were scheduled to perform. Honey West was the opening act – she was supposed to sing one song, but when the stars of the show didn't appear, she ended up performing an impromptu set. Rumors of the club closing were squashed in May 1995 when an ad appeared in *Gay Chicago Magazine* that read, "Some dirty rat has been spreading LIES! WE ARE OPEN!" It's not certain if it was slated to be a gay bar from the beginning or if they added a gay night. By the time the bar closed, it was gay just one night a week.

1912 Lounge
2002 S. Wentworth Ave.
Circa: 2016

CRUSH Chicago 2016 was a karaoke/dance party on weekends, designed for "alternative women," and was LGBT inclusive. The bar held many events for women, though gay men were welcomed.

3160 Club
3160 N. Clark St.
Circa: 2006-2014

The 3160 Club was owned by Jim Flint – who also owned the Baton, Annex 2 & 3, and Redoubt – and managed by Dan

Neniskis. It was a piano bar with occasional drag shows and other entertainments. Jeremy Rill and Ben Hartman were the entertainers at the grand opening on January 23, 2006. In April 2009, Rudy de la Mor, a popular cabaret entertainer, performed. He was so popular that he returned in May 2010. Mark Farris, "Chicago's favorite piano man," performed showtunes and played requests from the crowd. In July 2011, Pop Goes the Gio performed there – singer, songwriter, Gio Shamoun, and six members of his "Variety Dance Show" covered three decades of dance hits. Many drag queens performed at the 3160 Club, including Aurora Sexton and Tajma Hall, in December 2007. The bar closed on Tuesday, July 29, 2014.

Prior to the 3160 Club, this location was the home of Annex 3, and before that, it was Teddies. After the 3160 closed, Shakers on Clark opened at this address.

A

A-Frame
1622 Plainfield Rd., Joliet
Circa: 1983

Pat Harris was co-owner of this bar/club for gay men. However, by October 1983, Club Illusions was at this location. It's unclear whether the name changed or whether the bar came under new management.. This was also the location of Continental Club West and Club Illusions.

AA Meat Market
2933 N. Lincoln Ave.
Circa: 1989–1994

Prior to opening as the AA Meat Market leather bar, this location was an actual meat market (butcher shop). In

December 1989, the bar was opened by co-owners, William Payne and Jim Green. It served food and was known for its hamburgers. Upstairs was the AA Prime Leather and Video store – it closed in February 1994.

The back room had a dress code; leather or shirtless. In January 1991, Marc Treelisky became the owner. He was formerly the bar's manager. Payne and Green moved to Key West, Fla.

The clientele at the AA Meat Market were gay men, but in February 1992, they hosted a Ms. Leather Contest. Other contests at the bar included Satan's Black Leather in November

1991, Drummer Boy in July 1992, Full Moon Jockstrap in October 1992, and the annual Mr. AA Meat Market.

Bartenders included Harry Shattuck, Ted R. Jones, JR Kleysteuber, Butch Toland, John Ortiz Jr., and Frank Kellas. Orville "Butch" von Toland also worked at the Manhandler, North End, and the Pelican. Ortiz was the manager at Hev'in, and Frank Kellas was the last owner of the Gold Coast.

Abbey Pub
3420 W. Grace St.
Circa: 1984–2015

The clientele on any night depended upon the band performing. However, a lot of gay bands and solo artists performed there. They included Ripley Caine, Ellen Rosner, and queer female rock trio, Hunter Valentine. In February 2009, the Abbey Pub hosted the Broken Hearts Burlesque Ball, and in August 2011, Queerpocalypse, a dance party billed as "an epic battle against gender conformity through performance." The venue closed in 2015 after a fire.

This was also the location of One More Time.

Abby's Jungle Club
5 W. Erie St.
Circa: 1940s

Thought to have been owned by Abby Davis, it was described as a "storefront joint" and was known as a late-night spot, catering to entertainers, mostly dancers, and strippers.

Aces & Queens
6263 N. Clark St.
Circa: 1998

Aces & Queens was owned by Lilliana Cruz. She also owned the Rainbow Rooms. It was a short-lived bar, more of a neighborhood dive than a lesbian bar. It was popular with postal workers in the evenings. One reason suggested for its failure was that the owner couldn't get rid of the straight clientele.

Act III
855 W. Belmont Ave.
Circa: 1985–1986

Act III was owned by Steve and Sheila. Popular bartenders were Dago Rose, Tony Espozita, and Danniel Lambert (the Dragon Lady). Prior to ACT III, Lambert worked at the Frog Pond and was also the manager of the New Lite Factory. In June 1985, an ad for Act III in *Gay Chicago Magazine* read, "Wear your 'Alive with Pride in '85' button and get $1.00 well or wine drinks."

Adron's
41 S. Harlem Ave., Forest Park
Circa: 1972–1976

In July 1975, Chuck Unser took over as manager of Adron's, a gay men's bar. In the July 18, 1975, edition of *GayLife*, Adron's is described thus, "The psycha-disco dance floor is now going strong at Adron's Lounge in Forest Park. It's set apart from the main bar, with sound pouring in from the ceiling and lights you wouldn't believe." On October 31, 1975, Adron's held a costume party with a 1st prize of a three-day trip to Las Vegas.

This was also the location of Bus Stop Lounge and Nutbush City Limits..

AKA Nightclub
6259 N. Broadway
Circa: 1989–1990

A gay/straight punk dance club.

Alameda
5210 N. Sheridan Rd.
Circa: 1969–1977

Burt Springer
ALAMEDA CLUB
5210 N. SHERIDAN
OPEN AT 12 NOON   334-6280

The Alameda was popular with gay men. An ad in the December 1973 issue of the *Mattachine Midwest Newsletter* reads, "The New Alameda featuring Mr. Skip Arnold." Arnold was a well-known female impersonator who celebrated his 51st birthday at the bar in 1973. Arnold also appeared in 1968 at the Chesterfield. The bar also featured popular DJs Peter Lewicki and Michael Graber. In addition to female impersonators and DJs, the bar had go-go-boys.

According to performer Diana McKay (born Dion Walton II), "It was run by Southern country people, and they wouldn't hire me as a regular performer because I was Black, but the customers found out and they started picketing the place and calling them up on the phone and arguing with them until they finally had to give in and hire me. I was there for one or two years and then they closed."

According to one patron, "One side of the room was the bar, then you went hrough another section of the wall, the other side was the dance floor, and they had the jukebox in the middle of the bar. The bar was occasionally raided." One such raid occurred in the early hours of October 9, 1969.

By 1977, the bar was listed in *The Damron Guide* as being known for rough trade. As reported in the St Sukie de la Croix's book *Chicago After Stonewall*, it was run by Howie and Bert, who previously operated Club 69 and the Place.

Alfie's
900 N. Rush St.
Circa: 1976-1980

The grand opening of this popular gay men's bar was in July 1976. Danny Reilly owned the bar, also Le Pub, and the Brownstone.

Alfie's was an upscale cabaret bar, which also featured dancing. Among the performers were Roberta Whitehall, Nancy Erickson, and Star Kissed: A Tuna Band (Karin PattyDukeEllington Pritikin, Eileen Krauss, Toni Armstrong Jr., Vicki Lucas, and Edie Rosner). The bar featured Rita the Shopping Bag Lady (she sang, played piano, and carried a Fiorucci shopping bag), Carolyn Ford, and most famously, Brian Lasser and Karen Mason, who went on to be New York cabaret headliners and, for Mason, a Broadway star.

In August 1980, Alfie's celebrated its 4th anniversary with a chic champagne toast from Hedda Lettuce. Two months later, Alfie's was closed after an investigation by the IRS uncovered tax irregularities.

Allegro International
2828 N. Clark St. (in Century Mall)
Circa: 1980

This was also the location of Century Disco and Siegelman's Allegro.

Aloha Bikini Lounge
3702 N. Halsted St.
Circa: 1994

This was a short-lived gay men's bar that barely lasted four months. It was owned by Dr. Steve Rempas, who also owned the Loading Dock, Loading Zone, Ozone, Men's Room, and Halsted's. It opened in August 1994 and closed the following November. After the grand opening, Doug Allen wrote in his Culture Shock column in *Gay Chicago Magazine*, "Made it to the Aloha Bikini Bar for the grand opening. The drinks were good, but the cardboard hula girls have to go!"

In 1977, this was the location of the Vista Hermosa, a Latino gay bar, then the Loading Dock. Shortly after the Aloha Bikini Lounge closed, it became Cell Block.

Aloha Lounge
3321 N. Clark St.
Circa: 1960s

This was a gay men's bar. Much later, in the 1980s, this was the location of People Like Us, Chicago's first stand-alone LGBT bookstore.

Amadeus
1640 N. Damen Ave.
Circa: 1993

This was also the location of Mad Bar.

Amazing Grace Tap
1656 W. Grace St.
Circa: 1993

Amen Corner
731 E. 75th St.
Circa: 1982-1984

A popular South Side Black gay men's bar.

Amen Corner
8105 S. Cottage Grove Ave.
Circa: 1984-1985

A popular South Side Black gay men's bar.

This was also the location of Willie's Lounge.

Angel's Palace
6319 W. Roosevelt Rd., Berwyn
Circa: 2018

The grand opening of this Latin bar was in February 2018.

This location was formerly home to Antronio's.

Annabelle's
1801 W. North Avenue
Circa: 1944

This was a lesbian bar owned by Ruth Gemende. It closed in 1944.

MAYOR TAKES LICENSES FROM TWO TAVERNS

Mayor Kennelly yesterday revoked the licenses of two taverns on the recommendation of Police Commissioner O'Connor. One was Annabelle's at 1801 North av., licensed to

Annex
2863-2865 N. Clark St.
Circa: 1965-1977

The Annex was a mostly gay men's bar owned by Nick Dallesandro. Rossee, a coat check girl at the bar, remembered, "That one was definitely syndicate owned. Nick Dallesandro was a typical Italian. His wife, Shirley, ran the bar and shared the profits between cops and Nick's "silent partners."

National drag legend, Skip Arnold, performed his hilarious songs and comedy routines at the Annex in 1965, also later at the Chesterfield and the Alameda. At the Annex, Arnold recorded a vinyl 45 R.P.M. EP of his act with a pianist, bassist and drummer. The A-Side was called "Welcome to Fairyland" and the B-Side "Snow White vs. the Watch Queen."

One customer remembered, "I met Sal Mineo and Tony Curtis in there. It was a place they frequented when they were in town. Sal Mineo was very, very cute at that time."

In a 1974 landmark case, the Annex had its license saved by the Illinois Appellate Court after more than five years of legal battling. In a March 27 ruling, the court held that the City of Chicago was unjustified in revoking the license on the grounds of "deviate sexual acts" and selling liquor to a minor.

The revocation was based on a police raid on August 20, 1968, when the city charged that customers were lewdly fondling each other, and that one bartender made lewd contact with another. The appeals court ruled that the conduct alleged, even if it occurred, did not constitute "deviate sexual conduct" under the law, and that in any event, the evidence did not support a finding that the acts had occurred.

On the night of the raid, there were 15-40 women in the bar. The bartenders that night were Dwight Menard and David Towell, and the bouncer was Michael Casabianca.

Annex 2
430 N. Clark St
Circa: 1981-1983

The Annex 2 opened on July 27, 1981. It was owned by Jim Flint. Among the events held there was the Mr. Annex 2 Contest in the Disco Room on April 29, 1983. In July 1983, it was one of three bars, Baton, and Redoubt (all owned by Flint), to celebrate Jim Flint's birthday with a fundraiser for the Greater Chicago Gay & Lesbian Democrats. In March 1983, the bar advertised a "Truck Stop T Dance" with hot food, hot men, and hot music by DJ Roger Winans. In October 1982, the Chicago Knight Motorcycle Club kicked off its annual Toys for Tots charity drive with a cocktail party at Annex 2. Every Friday, Tony Zito played the piano. In *GayLife* on Friday, September 18, 1981, Ron Helizon reported, "Ikey, formerly of His 'n' Hers, is now serving your favorite pick-me-ups at Annex 2."

This was also the location of Baton Show Lounge, Ramrod, Loft, Sundays, and Punch's.

Annex 3
3160 N. Clark St.
Circa: 1986-2005

The Annex 3 opened on August 27, 1986. This was a piano bar/cabaret and, on weekends, a sports bar. Among the performers were pianist Tony Zito and comedienne Laura Conter. On opening night, the bartenders were Joseph LoPresti, Ikey, and Walt Kohler. It became home to the Royal Imperial Sovereign Barony of the Windy City, hosting drag shows starring Yazmina Couture, Countess I of the Gold Coast, Marquessa I Lady Chanel Exotique, Blondina, and Empress II Fabiola (born Rene Van Hulle). Van Hulle also bartended, as he did in many other bars, including the Lucky Horseshoe Lounge, Broadway Limited, and Nutbush. Rhodesia was another popular bartender.

On January 24, 1992, the Bunker opened in the bar's basement.

In August 1989, the Annex 3 was also a gathering place for the Asians and Friends. December 2002, the Royal Imperial Sovereign Barony of the Windy City held its "Snowball 2002," featuring entertainment by members of the Barony and special guests. It was hosted by the Grand Marquis II Sierra Montana. Admission was a $5 donation. Proceeds benefited the American Liver Foundation, Lesbian Community Cancer Project, Gerber/Hart Library, Leather Archives and Museum, and Equality Illinois Education Fund.

This was also the location of the 3160 Club, Shakers on Clark, and Teddie's.

Annex Buffet
2840 S. State St.
Circa: 1934

The Annex Buffet was a Black pansy parlor in Bronzeville on the South Side. It was opened on October 25, 1934, by Bernie Lustgarten and Arnold Meyer. The club offered milk-fed fried chicken and unusual entertainment under the stars in an open-air garden. The star of the show was Chicago-born female

impersonator, "The Sepia Mae West," (Samuel Fouche). Other acts on the bill were risqué singer Bertha "Chippie" Hill, William Holmes, and Ida Mae Maples' Merry Makers. On October 25, 1934, Lustgarten and Meyer opened the "indoor" Annex Buffet at 2300 S. State St.

In the spring of 1935, Samuel Fouche moved on and was replaced by another Sepia Mae West (Dick Barrow).

Annex Buffet
2300 S. State St.
Circa: 1934

This is the second incarnation of the Annex Buffet.

Another Place
7300 S. Cottage Grove Ave.
Circa: 1969–1975

Customer Ray Thomas related, "We went there and danced, and they were doing mixes with just two turntables and the monitor control, also every Sunday, they had the Gregory someone's Revue. And it was drag queens like Lady Victoria and Miss Santana (she had a ten-inch dick) and a few other ones that I don't quite remember. This was all Black, completely Black. The drag queens, every very single one of them, was Black. They did a lot of Diana Ross, and I would sit there and be totally amazed. In awe of all of it."

Another customer, Craig Anderson, recalled, "Around 1969, there was, at the corner of 73rd and Cottage Grove, Another Place. Douglas Middleton and John Boyd were the owners. It was kind of divey. It was one storefront. It had a long bar on the south side wall and booths along the plate glass windows that faced 73rd street. It had windows in the front too, but once it was dark, you couldn't really see inside. The DJ booth was in the back, and it was built on a platform with a window cut out of the brown paneling that lined the walls. Willie Watson was the DJ."

The address later housed a gay bar called the Bitter End.

Another Place
73rd St. and Cottage Grove Ave.
Circa: 1977–1980

Another Place reopened in April 1980 at a new location on 73rd St. and Cottage Grove Ave. The owner was Douglas Middleton, and his staff included the Black gay community's favorite bartender, Mr. Bruce Lockett.

Antronio's
6319 W. Roosevelt Rd., Berwyn
Circa: 2011–2016

Owned by Jose Antonio Casco, who managed Chesterfield's in the McKinley Park neighborhood for ten years. Casco named the bar by combining the Mexican slang term "antro," which means "hip bar," and his middle name. Antronio's was a community center/Mexican restaurant by day and a Latin gay bar at night. Antronio's closed in 2016 when Casco passed away. Aurora Pineda, a longtime community activist, said, "I remember him being welcoming to everyone. Jose created a safe space for everyone in the LGBT community at Antronio's, especially Latino gay men."

This space later housed Angel's Palace.

Anvil (see Granville Anvil)

Aphrodite's
6445 N. Sheridan Rd.
Circa: 1986-1989

Aphrodite's was a restaurant/bar with a mixed clientele. In *Gay Chicago Magazine* of December 8, 1988, Aphrodite's owners were identified as Paul Nakis and Ed Waters. Nakis told the authors, "I used to own Aphrodite. I used to have the South Side Sisters coming in and doing shows once every two months. It was a restaurant/bar, and it was Greek food."

Aquarius
1434 W. Morse Ave.
Circa: 1970-1971

The December 1970 *Mattachine Midwest Newsletter* reported, "The Aquarius, which was opened as a straight bar by Danny from the King's Ransom, is beginning to change over. We hope all will visit this bar ... and help speed the transition."

Archie's Iowa Rockwell Tavern
2600 W. Iowa St.
Circa: 2010-2011

The bar hosted a Queer Social Club for folks in the Humboldt Park/Ukrainian Village neighborhood with "BBQ Grillin' and chillin' with burgers, dogs, and vegetarian options." The bar also offered free pool, board/bar games, sass and two bike racks. In December 2011, three men entered the bar calling patrons "faggots." A physical fight ensued, severely bruising several patrons.

Argyle Show Lounge
1125 W. Argyle St.
Circa: 1950s

This bar was owned by Sid and Millie Schwartz. Chicago LGBT Hall of Fame inductee, female impersonator, Tony Midnite, performed at the bar in the early-1950s. His piano player was William Friedkin, who went on to direct the movies, Boys in the Band, The Exorcist, and The French Connection. At the Argyle, Midnite shared the stage with Gene "Michelle" Michaels. After numerous raids on the Argyle Show Lounge, the State Attorney's office closed it down for good, with the police accusing Midnite of using the microphone as a phallus. He told the authors, "I was doing bumps and grinds and sliding up and down on it."

Tony Midnite

Arrows
Wabash Ave. and Rush St.
Circa: 1950s-1960s

One woman remembered, "I started going to the bars when I was in my 20s, and ... the first lesbian bar that I recall going in was Arrows, down near Wabash and Rush Street. It only lasted a couple of years. It was very formal. There was a bar on the first floor and the second floor was for dancing. Some of the women would come wearing a tux, they would really dress up, and women would dance together. I only went there once or twice. It was a very fancy place."

Artful Dodger Pub
1516 N. Milwaukee Ave.
Circa: 1982-1985

This gay/straight dance club hosted bands, wet T-shirt contests ("Sex Comes to Wicker Park"), and drag shows. An ad reads, "For people who like their art funky and punky." The manager was Mike River. Featured DJs included Erik Hanson, Sparkle and Wendy, and Doug Taylor. In December 1982, the bar hosted a drag show with Dusty, Lacey Steele, Dolores Del Dodger, and Paddy Addy. Sparkle was an in-house performer and presented "A Tribute to Cher" and "It's Gonna Be a Donna Summer" for his birthday. Batteries Not Included also performed at the club.

This was also the location of Dreamerz.

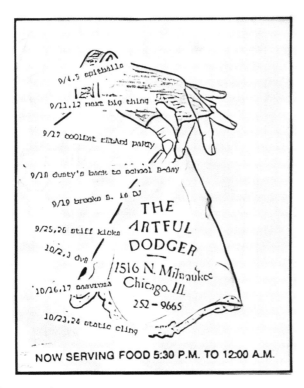

NOW SERVING FOOD 5:30 P.M. TO 12:00 A.M.

@mosphere
5355 N. Clark St.
Circa: 2002-present

Until 2021, @mosphere was owned by Charlie Brown. It held its grand opening in February 2002 that featured DJ Shawn Mock. One of the few dance bars in Andersonville, it also regularly features drag shows with Angelique Munro, Regina Upright, Sassy Trade, Monique Moyet, Marilyn Black, Terri Michaels, Tiger Sky, Wendy Sity, and Summer Breeze. The bar has also hosted benefits for the Legacy Walk, Transformative Justice Law Project of Illinois, and the March 2004 AIDS Foundation of Chicago AIDS Bike Ride kick-off party with Amy Armstrong and Freddy Allen. The bar is now owned by Micah Hilgendorf, who also owns a stake in North End and Lucky Horseshoe Lounge.

Audrey's
Ridgeland at 111th St.
Circa: 1972

Augie's
3729 N. Halsted St.
Circa: 1974-1979

In April 2012, Augie told *Windy City Times*, "I just decided to open the bar because there were no girls' bars. I had just come back from a trip to Puerto Rico, and they had a beautiful girls bar. And that inspired me."

Olga "Augie" Flanigan opened her lesbian bar in 1974. Although, in 1978, ads for the bar read, "FOR BOYS BOYS AND GIRLS."

In March 1979, there was a FOR SALE sign outside of Augie's.

This was also the location for Big Red's, Bobby Love's, Dandy's, In Between, and Norma's.

Augie & CK's
3726 N. Broadway
Circa: 1979-1994

The lesbian club, which opened on June 19, 1979, was formed when two bars merged – Augie's and CK's.

Many have fond memories of the bar, such as this one from Pickles, "I worked at Augie & CK's for about 13 years, so I have quite a few good memories ... every year we would have a Christmas decorating party. It would be on a Monday every year when the bar was closed (you usually had to take the next day off). The staff, their lovers, and all our best customers would help decorate the bar. It would take hours putting up all those lights and hanging all the decorations from the ceiling. Augie wouldn't like us to start drinking till everything was done, because she just knew how we were. And after everything was done, everyone would sit on the dance floor together, and wewould turn all the Christmas lights on and sing a Xmas song."

However, for women of color, it was a different story. On April 10, 1980, the LGBT press reported that about 35 women

Augie

11

picketed Augie & CK's lesbian bar protesting discrimination after the bar allegedly turned away Black and Latino women for having improper IDs.

Sheree Anne Slaughter remembered, "Definitely had problems getting in there. If you knew somebody White, they wouldn't give you such a hard time, but if you just tried to come in by yourself, it was, 'Show me five ID's, your passport, your Visa card, you know anything you got. It was really hard on the Black girls, until after the boycott. And you know how that bar went out ... they went out Black ... (Laughs) ... seriously, you know. But I enjoyed that place, it was a lot of fun. I liked CK, I thought she was a pretty cool woman. I liked the way she dressed."

Carol Kappa, the CK in Augie & CK's, was killed in a tragic accident in the bar. She carried a gun for protection and as she was leaning down to put money in the safe, which was in the floor. The gun fell out of her pocket. It had a faulty safety and the gun discharged, shooting her in the head. She died shortly afterward. In March 1991, it was announced that Cary McNamara was a new co-owner of the bar. The bar closed in February 1994. This location was also Darché's and Charlie's Chicago.

Avalon Nite Club
959 W. Belmont Ave.
Circa: 1987–1995

A bar catering to gay/straight club kids.

This was also the location of Showcase One.

Avenue M
695 N Milwaukee Ave.
Circa: 2008

Avenue M was mostly straight with a gay night.

Avenue Tavern
2914 N. Broadway
Circa: 2003–2020

This was a straight but gay welcoming bar.

This was once the location for Big Daddies Bar & Grill and Bulldog Road.

A-Zone
2129 N. Milwaukee Ave.
Circa: 2002

The A-Zone held weekly gatherings for LGBTQ radicals. They held events such as Thunderpussy and the Queer Family Circus, a queer performance night, and a trans-positive open mic.

Bachelors
444 W. Fullerton Pkwy.
Circa: 1989

Bachelors catered to gay men. This short-lived (open less than six months) bar, owned by Jill Mondelli, was located in the lower level of a high-rise apartment building. It opened onto a small plaza. In July 1989, an ad appeared in *Gay Chicago Magazine* for its Garden Walk of Beer Gardens, describing Bachelors' plaza as, "A sloping courtyard with ivy and flowers leads to this lower-level bar in the midst of Lincoln Park. It was removed from *Gay Chicago Magazine* bar listings in November 1989.

Backstreet
2917 N. Sheffield Ave.
Circa: 1982

This gay men's bar, owned by Phil Insprucker, opened in December 1982 and featured drag shows with Ava-Cado, Hedda Lettuce, Judy Garland, Blanch Hudson, Lisa Loren, and Lauren Hutton. This was also the location of Baskets and Frog Pond.

Badlands
6341 N. Clark St.
Circa: 1990–1995

An ad in the gay press in September 1991, reads, "Join Wacky Wally on Sundays at Badlands." Wally Sprang was a popular bartender, along with Joseph "Texas" Butler and BJ Landry. The owners were Tel and Bill. The bar's slogan was "Where the bad guys hang out."

This was also the location of Dan's on Clark, the Pelican, and Parlour.

Bali Hai
Lake Park Ave. near Hyde Park Blvd.
Circa: 1950s

This bar was mixed gay/straight.

Ballyhoo Café
1942 N. Halsted St.
Circa: 1930s

In the early-1930s, University of Chicago sociologist Ernest Burgess sent his students out to study gay bars. One student visited the Ballyhoo Café and wrote, "There were about 100 queer people in the cafe at the time I arrived – about 75 queer fellows and 25 queer girls. The hostess, dressed in masculine style, was queer as well as the male MC. Their names are Mack and Marge and are quite popular among the group. Mack, who is six foot three inches tall, often did female impersonations. His most popular number was "Alice in the Little Blue Gown." From appearance one could judge some of the fellows were queer. The queer girls could be judged in a like fashion. A few of the queer fellows danced with the queer girls but for the most part the boys danced together – likewise the girls. ... Beer was served at 5 cents a glass – with no cover charge. The queer girls (mentes) who sat next to our table had a large bottle of gin which they drank throughout the whole evening, becoming partially intoxicated."

Banana Tunnel Club
741 S. Western Ave.
Circa: 2001

The grand opening of this Latin bar was in June 2001 and starred the Miss Ketty Show. In December 2001, DJ Zeta and DJ Freddy "Conswing" Santiago provided the music for EL SPECTACULAR show de Veronica Zaid.

Bank Vault
200 State St., Calumet City
Circa: 1975-1985/1990-1995

In the Christopher column of *Chicago GayLife*, he writes, "The only word we now have is that it's called the Vault, it will be located in the infamous row of bars on State Street, and is being opened by Bob, the former owner of Our Place." Located in an old West Hammond Trust and Savings Bank building, the bar had a high ceiling with a balcony. The DJ booth was in an old bank vault. In 1976, *Gay Chicago Magazine* described the bar as, "Medium sized dance floor, disco sound system. Free Sunday salad bar and sandwiches. Free parking in adjacent lot."

In 1977, the Bank Vault owner was Ron Johnson, by 1979, it was Bob Guminey. In November 1978, Angelique De Nuve

won the Miss Bank Vault contest, and the bar hosted regular drag shows with Tamara Lee and the Bank Vault Vultures.

In 1985, the Bank Vault closed for the first time. This location became the Kismet Club, then Ms. Behavin. The grand opening of Double RR Lounge, at this location, was in May 1987. Then again, August 31-September 1, 1990, saw the return of the Bank Vault, with a grand opening featuring the male strip troupe, Headliners of Texas. The bar served a wide range of the gay community, including lesbians and leather. Entertainment in the new Bank Vault ranged from recording artists, video stars, nude model and would-be singer David Burrill, to cabaret singer Rudy de La Mor. In June 1995, the Bank Vault closed, a victim of urban renewal. However, it was not demolished as it's a historical landmark. Jesse James robbed it.

Bar Next Door
1008 N. Clark St.
Circa: 1977-1978

A *GayLife* ad in February 1978 reads, "Your hosts: Dimietrios, Roger, Bob (Lorna) ... and featuring, on weekend mornings, the infamous Precious." Every Wednesday evening, the Bar Next Door hosted a backgammon contest. There were at least three other gay bars on this block.

Baron Lounge
629 N. Clark St.
Circa: 1966-1971

In 1973, US Attorney James R. Thompson (later Governor of Illinois) investigated police shakedowns of bars. Twenty-four Chicago policemen, including Traffic Chief Clarence E. Braasch, were named as members of a police extortion racket that solicited payoffs of hundreds of thousands of dollars from at least 53 taverns in the Near North Side Chicago Avenue district. Many of the bars were gay. The Baron Lounge was one of them.

Baroque
1510 W. 53rd St.
Circa: 1972-1974

This Black bar was first listed in an ad in *Michael's Thing* magazine dated November 9, 1972.

Baskets
2917 N. Sheffield Ave.
Circa: 1982

The grand opening of Baskets was on April 9, 1982. Kris Lee was the manager. A listing in a gay publication notes that "Bloody Marys, Bloody Marias, Screwdrivers and Greyhounds are 50c on Sunday... at Baskets, a new men's bar." Glen "Sudsy" Sudberry tended bar for cocktail hours, and Miguel and TJ took over later in the evening.

This was also the location for Backstreet and the Frog Pond.

Baton Show Lounge
430, then 436 N. Clark St.
Circa: 1969–2019

The Baton Show Lounge opened at 430 N. Clark, then later moved next door to 436. It featured female impersonators and the occasional dancing boy in Las Vegas-style shows, hosted thousands of events, and hundreds of performers have strutted their stuff on the stage over the years. Chili Pepper, Ginger Grant, Mimi Marks, Joanna Caron, Jan Howard, and Audrey Bryant, among them.

Baton owner, Jim "Felicia" Flint, has been a community activist and philanthropist. He was an openly gay candidate for Cook County Commissioner in Chicago in the early 1970s. The show has been featured on numerous television programs, including a February 1979 appearance on the *Phil Donahue Show*. Many of the "girls" have served as top fashion models in the city. It is the pinnacle of drag performing.

Jim Flint also owned and operated numerous other gay bars including the Redoubt, Annex 2 and 3, and the 3160, as well as the Miss Continental contest franchise, the equivalent of the Miss America Pageant for female impersonators.

In addition to drag shows, the Baton has also hosted cabaret and theatrical productions, such as Speak Its Name theater company's June 1981 presentation of *Mad About the Boy*, and benefits to raise money for Mattachine Midwest, ONE of Chicago, Chicago Gay Alliance, Chicago Gay Pride Planning Committee, and Toys for Tots.

The noted Canadian female impersonator, Craig Russell, was at the Baton on July 18, 1973. Russell starred in the movie *Outrageous!*

In 1993, Mayor Richard M. Daley proclaimed March 19th, "James A. Flint Day," in honor of the Baton's 25th anniversary.

In 2019, Flint sold the business to French investor Christophe Chiavazza and moved from Chicago's River North area to the Uptown neighborhood. With that move, what was once the hub of Chicago's bar scene, lost its last gay bar.

The 430 address was also the site of the Loft, Ramrod, Annex 2, Sunday's (Children), and Punch's. The 436 address previously housed Big Basket, Queens Surf, and Sugar Shack. Flint's biography *Jim Flint: The Boy from Peoria* was written by Tracy Baim and Owen Keehnen.

Baton Show Lounge
4713 N. Broadway
Circa: 2019–present

Jim Flint, former Baton owner, was quoted in *Windy City Times*, "Upon learning of my plan to close the club in early 2019, I was approached by several people who wanted me to keep the name and the reputation of the Baton going, so after a lot of thought and consideration, I have agreed to allow them (French investor Christophe Chiavazza) to take it forward."

Flint added that he will be involved with the nightclub in the new location only in an advisory capacity. He would continue to greet guests on the weekends. Moving the Baton from River North to a grittier, up-and-coming neighborhood, the Baton took over the main floor and lower level of a landmark building in the heart of Uptown. The club was shut down for a short time due to the COVID pandemic, but later shows were resumed.

BBC
9 W. Division St.
Circa: 1980

An April 1980 ad touted a "New Wave event."

BBJ's
751 N. Clark St.
Circa: 1983

The bar featured live jazz performances.

Beat Kitchen
2100 W. Belmont Ave.
Circa: 1994–present

A mixed gay/straight music venue. Many LGBT bands played here, including the all-female heavy metal band ½ Mad Poet (Anita Chase, Sheela Reddy, Janet Cramer, and Chandler Marino).

Beauty Bar
1444 W. Chicago Ave.
Circa: 2013

In February 2013, "Beauty and the Beat" was a ladies' night with free manicures and drink specials all night "fo tha ladies."

Bedrock
2856 N. Broadway
Circa: 1989

The weekly gay night at Bedrock started in February 1989 and was gone by June. It was called BENT and often featured male dancers: Terry "Power Tool" Powell, Dick "A Death" O'Day, Tony "The Top Man" Tasso, Tara "Token Female" B. Something, John "Please Sir, I Want Some More" Morehart,

and Scottie "Claussen Pickle" Patrick. BENT also presented shows of questionable taste like *The Karen Carpenter Story*, starring Jeff "top-of-the-world-ma" Lotz as Karen. Also, *Dirty Rotten Diana, a Tribute to Diana Ross*, and *Three Faces of Ethel* starring Karlisa as Ethel Waters, Tracy Turnblad as Ethel Mertz, and Cara as Ethel Merman, with Tony as Jackie Susanne." A popular cocktail concoction was, "The Mermanosa ... A little bit of ETHEL in your glass."

This was also the location of Bubbles.

Beer On Clark
3415 N. Clark St.
Circa: 2013

The bar advertised "Big Man Mondays" on the last Monday of the month.

Belfry
111 W. Hubbard St.
Circa: 1973–1973

In 1973 the *Mattachine Midwest Newsletter* announced, "The Belfry is a new restaurant and bar with your host Mr. Kelly." It was closed less than a month later. Originally owned by Jim Flint, who sold it to Bob Cochran, who eventually converted it to My Brother's Place in 1974.

a nice casual place to meet

THE BELFRY

THE BELFRY
restaurant and bar
111 west hubbard street
chicago
hours: 4 pm to 2 am
for reservations call
321·9039
your host, mr. kelly

Bells
708 or 706 Stateline Rd., Calumet City
Circa: 1959

Owned by a Polish man called Wedge. Co-managed by Bonnie Bey. This bar has only ever been mentioned by one reliable interviewee, who reports it was a lesbian bar.

This was also home to Our Way II (Gallagher's), and the Club.

Benedict's
3937 N. Lincoln Ave.
Circa: 2004

Benedict's was a straight/gay friendly neighborhood saloon that served food.

Benny the Bum's
549 N. Clark St.
Circa: 1940s

Owned by Si and Mollie Ginsberg. Si's brother, Sol, worked the bar and was the business brains behind the enterprise. On Sunday afternoons, they had an amateur drag contest. According to one past customer, "It was just a raunchy, raunchy gay bar, elongated ... there was just open space. Loads of open space, so a lot of people would just be standing around. It wasn't exactly dark, but it wasn't brilliantly lighted either. You felt like a bum if you went in, and you never wore good clothes." Another regular customer remembered drag shows, "On Sunday afternoon they had a drag contest, amateur drag. And you had to move your drinks because the queens would parade on the bar."

The bar closed down in June 1949. One time, the *Chicago Tribune* column Tower Ticker noted, "Benny the Bum's place on N. Clark St., has become the Gayety Café. Vags can now get the bum's rush with a merry laugh."

Bentley's
640 N. State St.
Circa: 1971–1973

Often referred to as Sir Bentley's. Nick Argiris was the assistant manager and a witness in the 1973 trial against Traffic Chief Clarence E. Braasch and 24 others accused of extorting money from gay bars.

Come and See the New Grapes at

Sir Bentlys Pub

Open Daily from 7 AM until 2 AM

640 North State Street   **944-9534**

Berlin
954 W. Belmont Ave.
Circa: 1983–present

The original owners were Tim Sullivan and Shirley Mooney, but Jim Schuman and Jo Webster later bought the bar. Greg Haus has been the DJ for 20+ years and has been joined by

many others. The bar was a focal point for the club scene in Chicago. Many "club kids" and drag queens performed or worked there, including Jo-Jo, Bobby Pins, Silky Jumbo, Miss Foozie, Joan Jett Blakk, and Daisy Mae performing as the Bearded Lady. The bar also featured comics, bands, and singers such as Judy Tenuta, Johnny Dangerous, Cazwell, Pussy Tourette, Patty Elvis, the Del Rubio Triplets, and Valerie James,

as well as male strippers. In the early to mid-'90s, the bar even hosted a C&W night.

A sample of some of the events over the years includes: Instant Heat! a night with the Notorious Male Dancers, New Wave music night, Drag Race – an amateur drag show, "Fashion Obsession" with a fashion show at midnight with bodywear by K.O. Designs and fun fur accessories by Xenophobia, "I Love Leather Obsession" night with a raffle to benefit Open Hand, "Underwear Obsession," a live underwear and lingerie show, with garments provided by Strange Cargo, and in January 1992, "White House or Bust" the formal announcement celebration of the presidential campaign of Joan Jett Blakk. In January 1994, the Gay Metal Society held "Rock Sunday."

Bernie's
48th St. and Damen Ave.
Circa: Unknown

This was a lesbian bar.

Big Basket
436 N. Clark St.
Circa: 1970

RJ Chaffin quoted in *GayLife*, "Chuck Renslow opened the Big Basket. The Basket was the forerunner of today's disco bars, and it featured live music entertainment. After two years, it closed briefly only to rise again as the Sugar Shack. The Sugar Shack was a non-alcohol establishment and lasted only six months or so."

The opening night at the Big Basket, in October 1970, was a benefit for the Chicago Gay Alliance, an offshoot of the Gay Liberation Front. The bar had dancing, live bands, a light show, and a "coffee house room" serving food.

This was also the location of the Baton Show Lounge, and Queen's Surf.

Michelle Fire

Big Chicks
5024 N. Sheridan Rd.
Circa: 1986–present

"Big Chicks is unusual for a Chicago bar. It attracts everyone from twinks to leather dykes, artsy intellectuals to whoo girls,

and is often listed as a "must-visit spot" by travel guides and LGBT publications." Big Chicks (no apostrophe!) boasts both a sidewalk café and a rear beer garden, both of which it shares with neighboring restaurant Tweet, also owned by Michelle Fire. The bar is famous for its free Sunday buffet.

Michelle Fire (born Michelle Feuer) worked at the Loading Dock, Opal Station, and His 'n' Hers. She opened Big Chicks in an art deco building, formerly home to the Sheridan Lounge. At the time, the bar was a hangout for Appalachians living in the SRO across the street. Slowly, as Fire renovated the bar, she built her LGBT following. Fire, a noted artist, hung the work of artist friends and notables such as Diane Arbus and Ed Paschke. Equally comfortable with leather queens and lesbians, as a bartender she always had a following in the community. She eventually took over the neighboring beauty parlor. It served as a salon hosting literary and art events as well as benefits for community groups for everything from local LGBT sports teams to the Homolatte performance series and the Radical Faeries of Chicago.

In July 1996, Kathy Bergquist reported in *Nightlines*, "Anyone who walks into Michelle Fire's generously warm establishment, Big Chicks, will probably also have a memory to savor. Located in Uptown ... Big Chicks is a friendly neighborhood bar with a primarily queer clientele – a queer Cheers, if you will. Usually wall-to-wall, jam-packed with men on Fridays and Saturdays, those who just want to go have a beer and a chat with friends will find the space very conducive to that during the week. While a guys' hang out, there are always a few lesbian faces in the crowd, and unlike some male-oriented venues in town, I've always been made to feel welcome at Big Chicks."

When there was a chance that Big Chicks could lose its liquor license, Tracy Baim reported, in a November 2003 article in *Windy City Times*, on the support from customers, "The outrage was explosive – thousands of emails, hundreds of people at a Nov. 24 rally outside the bar at 5024 N. Sheridan, and a couple hundred more at a hearing Nov. 25 at the city's liquor commission in the basement of the Daley Center."

Big Daddy's
848 N. Clark St.
Circa: 1976-1978

A 1976 description of the bar reads, "This relatively new addition to gay Chicago has established itself with the well-known personalities of the old Jamie's. Conveniently located one block south of Bug House Square."

Bug House Square was an area known for gay hustlers. On November 12, 1976, *GayLife* newspaper described Big Daddy's as a "cruisy bar."

Big Daddies Bar & Grill
2914 N. Broadway
Circa: 1994-2001

Big Daddies Bar & Grill, catering to gay men, opened in April 1994 with Ken Killian as the proprietor. He was formerly the owner of JJ's. According to a *Windy City Times,* December 2001 article, "The recent closing of the Cellblock bar's back room and a rumored raid at the Manhandler had tongues wagging in the community about a possible crackdown on the city's gay sex spaces, but sources at both bars said, in this case, fiction is stranger than truth ... "

"Rumors of a possible crackdown came as some said the incidents were suspiciously close to the November closing of Big Daddies ...

"According to the Chicago Department of Revenue, the bar's license expired on Nov. 15 and owners did not renew it."

The raids on Cell Block and the Manhandler were just rumors.

This was also the location of the Avenue Tavern and Bulldog Road.

Big Jim's
3505 N. Halsted St.
Circa: 2016-2019

This bar opened as an expansion of Little Jim's and did well for three years until the property was sold to Howard Brown Health for its new clinic.

Big Lou's
731 W. North Ave.
Circa: 1940s-1950s

Nab 36 Women, 28 Men in Vice Raid on Tavern

Police arrested 36 women and 28 men early yesterday in a vice raid on Big Lou's tavern, 731 North av., operated by Miss Lou Kane, 41, of 1702 N. La Saile st.

Big Lou's was run by lesbian Lou Kane (born Lucille Kinovsky). One regular described her as "a big dyke who appeared tough but was really a sweetheart." Another that she was "a big blousy White trash type woman." The bar offered music by two Black piano players, Theresa Whitehead and Theury Dry. On February 16, 1952, the bar was raided and closed down with thirty-six women and twenty-eight men arrested.

The *Chicago Tribune* wrote, "Police charged the place is a hangout for perverts. They said the women generally were attired in men's clothing and were dancing together. The men, police said, were consorting with one another."

On February 24, Big Lou lost her license, as did two other nearby gay bars, the Hollywood Bowl, 1300 N. Clark St, and an unnamed tavern at 1942 N. Sedgwick, operated by Mary Anderson.

Big Red's
642 W. Diversey Pkwy.
Circa: 1976-1982

Adrene "Big Red" Perom was a statuesque (nearly 6 feet tall) former model who saved her money and opened a bar. She worked at Flanagan's Pub on Broadway. Wally Thomas drank there and told her he was selling his bar Virgo Out. Big Red bought it and was going to call it the Long and Skinny Bar, because of its shape, and run it as a straight bar. But she inherited a lot of Virgo Out customers. As Big Red herself noted, "I opened in 1976 as a straight bar, but I turned it gay on Valentine's Day of 1977. I closed my eyes and went to the calendar and pointed to a date, and when it turned out to be Valentine's Day, I thought, 'My God, it's the day that represents love, what better day could it be?' It had been a gay bar when I bought it, and the straights in this neighborhood ... I was across the street from a pool room, and the people that were coming in there were garbage. I was having the police two or three times a week and then somebody said, 'Why don't you turn it back to what it was?' And I just never thought of it. You don't wake up one morning and say, 'I'm going to have a gay bar.' So, I turned it, and it was the best thing I ever did. I've enjoyed being a part of this community for all these years. That bar, on Clark and Diversey, closed because of the landlord; he wanted so much rent I would be working for him. It was impossible."

Over the years, Big Red hosted many benefits at this bar, such as the Prince Charles and Lady Diana look-alike contest. However, one of the most popular was the Celebrity Pie Toss – which she inherited from the Butterfly. "In the beginning, the money went to the Rodde Fund, and then after the AIDS crisis came along, I changed that, and I started to do it for Chicago House and DirectAID," Perom was quoted as saying.

Virgo Out and Boys at Sea, were also at this location.

Big Red's
3019 N. Clark St.
Circa: 1982-1985

Adrene "Big Red" Perom's second bar. In March 1983, she started her annual chili cook-off, where cooks competed against each other for making the best chili. That first year, Annie Nelson won the trophy and $50 bar tab. It was a benefit for the Howard Brown Memorial Clinic's AIDS Action Project. In 1985, this incarnation of Big Red's closed after a developer bought the property. It was eventually torn down and replaced by a strip mall.

This was also the location of jock's, the Locker, and Minkee's.

Big Red's
3729 N. Halsted St.
Circa: 1985-1992

This was the third and final incarnation of Big Red's. As with the other two Big Red's, this was a neighborhood bar. Perom continued to hold fundraising events for the community, including the annual pie toss. In November 1988, Rick's Retreat's owner Joe Esposito, and Norm Janis, owner of LA Connection, were among those pied to raise $2,506 for Chicago House and Rodde Center. In 1990, Chicago Molly was the pie toss MC, and the proceeds went to Chicago House and Direct Aid.

Hank Taylor was a bartender there.

Big Red had a loyal following at all three bars and only sold as her health began to fail. "Halsted St. was my last bar, and I sold that December 1, 1992," Big Red told the authors.

Although straight, Adrene "Big Red" Perom" was a beloved member of the Chicago LGBT community. In 1999, she was inducted as a "Friend of the Community" into the Chicago Gay and Lesbian Hall of Fame. She died in August 2000. A month later, a tribute to her was held at El Jardin restaurant, 3335 N. Clark.

This was also the location of Norma's, Bobby Love's, Dandy's, In Between, and Augie's.

Big Wig
1551 W. Division St.
Circa: 2003-2004

Big Wig was a queer-friendly space that hosted occasional LGBT/kink-themed events, such as "Sin City," a pleasure play party to benefit the film *Dominatrix Waitrix,* a sci-fi queer sex movie about a leather-clad amorphous, multi-gendered waitress who preys on her puppet-like customers. It was hosted by Edith Edit and Mistress Minax. Other events included, "Homo Reality," a trance dance party with DJ Pussy Galore, and "Cock," an electro 1980s dance party with DJs Missa Messian and Gigglebyte.

Billy D's
1736 W. Algonquin Rd., Hoffman Estates
Circa: 2004

This was an LGBT-friendly restaurant and bar with karaoke.

Biology Bar
1520 N. Fremont St.
Circa: 2002–2005

In 2005, this straight/LGBT-friendly bar hosted Windy City Black Pride's "Red, White, and Blue" party. The House of Tut and Clubhouse Productions produced many parties at Biology Bar, including a Club LaRay Revival hosted by Otis Mack, Flame Monroe, and Mz. Ruff 'n' Stuff with DJ Ron Carroll.

Birdcage
5310 N. Clark St.
Circa: 2021

The Birdcage was a straight/LGBT-friendly bar with a drag burlesque show. It closed on October 24, 2021.

Bird's Nest
2500 N. Southport Ave.
Circa: 2003

This was once the location of the Lite Factory.

Bistro (AKA Dugan's Bistro)
420 N. Dearborn St.
Circa: 1973–1982

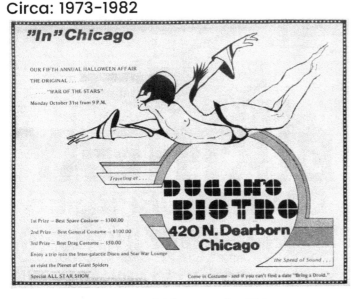

One of the most successful bars on the Chicago gay scene during the disco period was the Bistro. It was owned and operated by Eddie Dugan (born Edward Davison). The bar was designed by Ronn Veltman, among others. Michael O'Callahan and "Peter," who worked on the bar's construction, were bartenders on the opening night. As Chicago's premiere disco, it was consistently featured in news reports and was a must-stop for visiting celebrities, gay and straight.

Lou DiVito became Bistro's main DJ in 1974. An interior decorator, DiVito assisted in designing the club's layout and sound and light systems. Billboard named DiVito, "Best Regional Dee-jay" in 1978 and 1979. As Danny Goss, DiVito's alternate for many years, recalls, "Lou was the first DJ I ever heard mix on the beat and in perfect pitch." DiVito became Chicago radio's first "hot mixer" in 1979, recording mixes for WDAI from his DJ booth.

Each year the club's interior was refreshed in preparation for an anniversary celebration. The club's sixth anniversary featured nine mirror balls and four mortar guns shooting foam stars. "Who else could put a thousand miles of mylar ribbon down the outside of a building and cover a corner with glitter – right across the street from a police station?" quipped impressionist Allan Lozito.

As quoted by the *Chicago Tribune*, "There was a large main floor bar and a raised dance floor. Special effects included a fog machine and a snow machine behind mirrored walls, four ceiling-mounted Nerf cannons, and a state-of-the-art sound and light system."

The Bistro was known for performance artists such as mime and dancer Kim Spaulding, drag and performance artist TL Noble, Vera Vinyl, and most famously, the Bearded Lady (born Robert W. Theiss). Theiss was a large man who performed in full-face make-up and had a wild untrimmed beard. He often wore costumes in layers that he removed as he danced to whatever tunes were playing. He once took a hit of poppers, did a backflip off the small stage, and did a perfect landing on the dance floor in sling-back heels.

Among the performers who appeared at Bistro were Viola Wills, Tiny Tim, Chili Pepper, Sylvester, Linda Clifford, Candi Staton, and practically every disco diva around at the time.

The Bistro closed May 31, 1982, a victim of a redevelopment project, nine years to the day after it opened.

There were numerous complaints about discrimination against women and minorities at the bar, and its license was temporarily revoked. In October 1974, the Illinois Liquor Control Commission settled the case with a promise by the Bistro not to engage in such discrimination, though the bar never admitted ever having done so.

In the June 4, 1982, issue of *GayLife*, Ron Ehemann wrote about the demise of the Bistro. "An era ends – after nine years as one of the flagships of the night, Dugan's Bistro succumbed to the wrecking ball and 'progress.' Whether you were a Bistro Bunnie or not, most everyone had been through the doors. Dignitaries and celebrities, young and old – part of being in gay Chicago involved at least one night at the Bistro. The Bistro had its share of complaints, its share of 'attitude' and its share of controversy. But the Bistro had something else; a mystique and atmosphere, not unlike New York's infamous Studio 54. Though some felt the door policy was too harsh, one thing that was always excluded was depression, Eddie Dugan knew how to throw a party. Contributing to the success of the Bistro were hundreds of employees over the years – dedicated people who worked while we partied ... much of the energy and creativity came from Tommy Noble, Lou DiVito, and Ronny Veltman. Door policy notwithstanding, the Bistro was one of those rare places where gay and non-gay merged."

Bistro Too
5015 N. Clark St.
Circa: 1987–1992

Many of the same people involved in Bistro and Paradise were also on the creative team of Bistro Too. It was to be a joint venture between Charles "Chuck" Renslow and Eddie Dugan, but Dugan passed away April 10, 1987 – though his parents attended the opening night at Bistro Too on September 26, 1987. One of its popular events was Drag Queen Wrestling. Some of the wrestlers included Mildred Fierce, Zulu the Zebra Woman, Diesel Debbie, and Helen Killer. Steve "Killer" told the authors, "I was Helen Killer, the blind wrestler. They would lead me on, then when I was in the ring, suddenly I could see! I wrestled against Tina, against the Bride of Doom, against Mad Mary Kay, and against Mildred Fierce. ... We had a good time at Bistro Too."

Inside the Bistro Too

Among some of the regular performers were drag act Memory Lane, Shelly DeWinter, TL Noble, the Chicago Meatpackers strippers, Tamara Lee, Viv Vashawn, and Candi Staton. Celebrity guests included Boy George, Lynn Lavner, the Village People, Hazell Dean, and Thelma Houston. Mondays were women's night, entitled Club Mondo Lezbo. In February 1993, it even hosted "Chicago's Country Dance" with David Boyer and DJ Ron Goodman.

This was also the location of the Chicago Eagle and, at times, a part of Man's Country bathhouse.

Bitter End
7300 S. Cottage Grove Ave.
Circa: 1980-1982

In 1981, at this Black gay men's bar, the DJ was Maurice Strickland, and the bartender was Bruce Lockett.

This was also the location of Another Place.

BJ's
3231 N. Clark St.
Circa: 1980-1986

BJ's was a neighborhood bar with a small dance floor and rear garden where barbecues were often held on weekends. The food was prepared by James Earl Botrager, who once co-owned David's Place.

BJ's was owned by Rick Jones; he later brought in Steve Picon as a partner. In May 1984, they converted the lower level into a leather bar for the weekend. They renamed it B'Low Blow, to capitalize on the leathermen in town for International Mr. Leather. It served as a back room of sorts. Popular DJs included Larry Brewer, Billy Albiez, Tom Parks, and Chipper. Don "Wheezy" Crenshaw was one of the bartenders – he also bartended at Cheeks, Company, Manhandler, and Pelican.

This was also the location of Odyssey and Ruthie's.

Black Orchid Lounge
230 W. North Ave.
Circa: 2000-2001

This short-lived nightclub brought in some top-name entertainers, including Cyndi Lauper, Rita Moreno, Michael Feinstein, and Jennifer Holliday. It was not particularly gay, but depending upon the entertainer, could draw a large gay crowd.

Black Orchid Nightclub
Rush St.
Circa: 1956-1957

Not a gay club, but Christine Jorgensen performed at the Black Orchid. On December 1, 1952, a front-page article in the *New York Daily News* read, "Ex-GI Becomes Blonde Beauty:

Operations Transform Bronx Youth," and George/Christine Jorgensen was outed as the first person in the world to change sex. On July 3, 1956, she opened at the Black Orchid Nightclub. She described her act to Robert Wiedrich of the *Chicago Tribune*, "It's a philosophical comedy number which shows life is full of changes. It's brilliant. If you're going to be what people consider a star, you've got to live the part. The idea of being the girl next door is silly."

In November 1957, TC Jones, described by the *Chicago Tribune* as the "Last of the female impersonators in the grand style," performed at the Black Orchid. The newspaper described Jones as "a perfect lady until the final minute of his act, when he whips off his wig to reveal a shining bald dome that would put Yul Brynner's to shame." In his act, Jones portrayed Tallulah Bankhead, Katherine Hepburn, Bette Davis, and other femmes.

Black Tulip
2024 W. Roscoe St.
Circa: 1989

Extremely short-lived bar. It was first listed in *Gay Chicago Magazine* in September 1989, and its last listing was in early November of that same year. In October, a cabaret revue, "Bombay Pete" debuted.

Blue Dahlia
5640 North Ave.
Circa: 1955–1979

The Blue Dahlia was a club showcasing female impersonators. An ad in June 1971 read, "See Maria Montez "The Latin Dream" parade his/her stuff on the stage at the Blue Dahlia."

One regular explained, "They were in drag, but all of the songs, they sang, there was no records only an orchestra in the background."

Blue Max
7414 W. Madison St., Forest Park
Circa: 1996

This was also the location of Hard Wood.

Blue Moon
6238 N. Broadway
Circa: 1989

It was first listed in *Gay Chicago Magazine* in February 1989. By April 9, it was off the list.

Blue Parrot
1128 W. Granville Ave.
Circa: 1984–1985

The Blue Parrot, a gay men's bar, opened in December 1984 with a Christmas tree trimming party and an ad reading, "The back bar you've heard so much about is now open. Cum see for yourself."

However, the grand opening was in February 1985.

Blue Pub
3100 W. Irving Park Rd.
Circa: 1965–1987

The Blue Pub was a piano bar famous for "The Two Black Georgia's." A regular at the bar, Old Marlene, told the authors, "There was Georgia Owens and Georgia White. Georgia White was a thin woman that used to forget wearing underpants, and she'd pull up her dress and show everything that God gave her. That's the way it was! She was at Louis Gages, and the Blue Pub. ... Georgia White died of a massive heart attack, she had cirrhosis of the liver.

"So then we got the other Georgia [Owens]. She worked in a lot of gay bars over her lifetime. She was a jazz pianist. She didn't stay at the Blue Pub long. When she came in, they had to have a mic for her because she didn't have a voice, whereas Georgia White you could hear her every place."

Dr. Thomas Erwin Gertz recalled the Blue Pub, "The guys would get in there and get a couple of drinks. They would sit around that bar and some of them would even sit on the bench with Georgia and say let's do 'Hello Dolly' and how about 'Sound of Music' and we would just ask for a song and Georgia would just do them and, of course, when she had a few drinks, she would do *Bye Bye Blackbird*. ... Back your ass against the wall, here I come balls and all, bye bye cherry.' Well, when she did that, you could be walking down the street outside and it sounded like a choral group inside."

Blue Trax
2210 S. Michigan Ave.
Circa: 1986

The bar featured a 600 square foot dance floor.

Bobby Love's
3729 N. Halsted St.
Circa: 2000–present

Bobby Love's opened in July 2000 as a cocktail and piano bar, like its predecessor, Dandy's. However, it soon gained a huge following with karaoke by Creagh and drag shows starring Roberta Lovella (born Robert Love), and his host of drag queens, such as Regina Upright, Paula Sinclaire, Cherise Pretty, and Honey Dew. In July 2007, Bobby Love's hosted Honey West and strippers and cream.

This was also the location of Big Red's, Norma's, Dandy's second location, In Between, and Augie's.

Bob's Bistro A Go-Go
Location unknown
Circa: 1966

Bogart's
Ontario St. at N. Fairbanks Ct.
Circa: 1975

Bohemia
Dearborn St. and Division St.
Circa: 1950s-1960s

Old Marlene described, "A block down the street from the old Haig, then you turn in and there was the old Bohemia, and it had female/male prostitutes, you name it, it had everything under creation, from millionaires to street people. Gay male prostitutes, it was the most fun bar in the city of Chicago, and we never got raided ... I shouldn't say never, but very rarely did we get raided. Two brothers owned it and the nephew was the manager; he was a real good man. They were Jewish. And the nephew, we all gave blood for his wife. We had to lay off the sauce, but we laid off the sauce to give blood to his wife because his wife needed blood. That bar was there for years; that was a living institution. That had everything in there, nowadays you don't have a bar like that."

Boiler Room
2210 N. California Ave.
Circa: 2010

The Boiler Room held a Big Gay Brunch with dancing on the back patio to DJ Josie Bush, and Butch Sassidy and the Come Dance Kid.

Bonanza
7641 S. Halsted St.
Circa: 1960s

A Black club where gay celebrity Wilbur "Hi-Fi" White performed.

Bonsai Bar & Lounge
3503 N. Halsted St.
Circa: early 2000s-2020

A small storefront restaurant and bar specializing in Asian cuisine. It had a small but devoted following with gay men until it closed during the COVID pandemic of 2020-2021.

Boobs Draw Too
5834 W. Grand Ave.
Circa: 1986

Boobs Draw Too started out as a straight bar run by a lesbian couple, Barb Holzafal and Marion. It was straight because Marion was born and grew up in the area and had a son. When Marion passed away, in early 1986, Barb turned the bar gay and named it after her nickname, Boobs.

The grand opening was on May 31, 1986, with three guest bartenders: Dago Rose and David from Big Red's and Danniel from Act III. It closed six months later.

Boombala
2950 N. Lincoln Ave.
Circa: 1987-1990

Boombala was a short-lived cabaret bar owned by Mary Ann Johnson. It was described in the gay press in September 1989 as, "Located on busy and booming north Lincoln Avenue. Boombala is a quiet, intimate retreat, bedecked in heavenly swathes of white cloth, small white tables and chairs, and a long white bar. Entering, one feels instantly removed from whatever world we left. Singers, musicians, and comedians are all featured there, weekdays and weekends."

Among those who performed at Boombala's were Mary Lynn Morrison and Bill Muzzillo, Judy Tenuta, and Joanne Pallato and the Willie Pickens Trio.

Boopsie's
42nd St. and Harlem Ave., Stickney
Circa: 1973-1976

When the liquor laws were changed so that 19-year-olds could drink alcohol, the *Chicago Gay Crusader* reported that, in October 1973, Boopsie's posted a sign that read, "19 year old chickens welcome." The following month, the publication described the bar, "It's remarkably friendly, and seldom will someone walk in and be ignored ... the drag shows aren't bad."

Bottom Lounge
1375 W. Lake St.
Circa: 2013-present

Mostly straight, but occasionally hosts LGBT events. The Bottom Lounge was described in *Nightspots* as being a "fierce party space that is inclusive and empowering to queer folks and allies of all ages, gender identities, races, and sexual identities." In April 2013, the bar hosted Queer Dance, a benefit for About Face Theatre's youth-driven play, *What's the T*

Boys At Sea
642 W. Diversey Pkwy.
Circa: 1973-1975

Boys at Sea was a gay men's bar owned by John Britt, who also owned the Wooden Barrell Pub.

At various times, this location was also Virgo Out and Big Red's.

JERRY, STELLA AND TERRY, are the three healthy bartenders at the BOYS AT SEA

Bradberry
7101 N. Clark St.
Circa: 1972-1974

This was a syndicate-run lesbian bar. It was most likely owned by the same outfit that owned Chez Ron, another lesbian bar. Shortly after the bar opened, in November of 1972, there was a fire. Its reopening was reported in the *Mattachine Midwest Newsletter* in October 1973, but by August of 1974, the *Chicago Gay Crusader* reported, "News is that Bradberry is bad news for our sisters. Strike it from your list. They don't want our business."

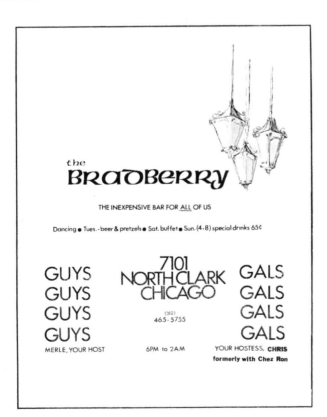

the BRADBERRY

THE INEXPENSIVE BAR FOR ALL OF US

Dancing • Tues.-beer & pretzels • Sat. buffet • Sun. (4-8) special drinks 65¢

GUYS
GUYS
GUYS
GUYS

7101
NORTH CLARK
CHICAGO
(312)
465-5755

GALS
GALS
GALS
GALS

MERLE, YOUR HOST   6PM to 2AM   YOUR HOSTESS, CHRIS
                                          formerly with Chez Ron

Brando's Speakeasy
343 S. Dearborn St.
Circa: 2008-2012

In March 2012, Brando's hosted a Gay and Lesbian Candidate Meet and Greet, organized by the Coalition for Justice and Respect (CJR), a civil rights organization of African-American same gender loving Black gays and lesbians. The evening featured candidates for county-wide races and local district races for state legislature and statewide races. In February 2008, there was a ladies-only Oscar/L Word Party with DJs Fathom and Kimya.

Bridge
1177 N. Elston Ave.
Circa: 1990

The Bridge advertised in the gay press as a "nightclub and marina."

This was also the location of Fire Island and Scooter's.

Bristol's Nightclub
2986 N. Elston Ave.
Circa: 1992

Broadway Kunfusion
3510 N. Broadway
Circa: 1978-1980

Located in the basement of an apartment building, bartender and personality, Michael K, opened this bar after Carol's in Exile closed. Broadway Kunfusion specialized in theme parties, such as the "Babes on Broadway Revue," starring drag stars Terri Paige – the Pantomime Rage, Mysterious Marilyn, Dynamic Danee, and Diana McKay.

This was also the location of Garland's and Carol in Exile.

Broadway Lady
3714 N. Broadway
Circa: 1976

A lesbian bar.

This was also the location of F-Beat.

Broadway Limited
3132 N. Broadway
Circa: 1976-1980

The bar and dance floor at Broadway Limited was located on the second floor of a small complex of stores called Carmichael Village. To access the bar, patrons entered a courtyard at the back and up a flight of steps between two train cars, which served as a small restaurant. On the second floor there was a small lounge bar, and beyond that, a larger bar and dance area with a stainless-steel floor. It was second only to Bistro as the top dance destination in the city. Among the celebrities who partied at the bar were Chaka Khan and Patti La Belle, who came in after a concert with the Bluebells. In January 1976, Gloria Gaynor performed there.

Many thought the bar was a fire trap. In early January 1976, a concerned reader wrote to *GayLife* newspaper about alleged unsafe conditions; his main concern being fire escapes and fire protection. This, coupled with an article in the *Advocate* about the same bar, caused *GayLife* to investigate. In an article headlined, "Allegations against Broadway Limited found to be untrue," the newspaper lists the fire protections and notes that residents wanting to close the bar down have called out the fire inspectors before.

The club was owned by Mike Siegel and Carey Wallach. The managers were Jack O'Rook, Harry Kuck, James "Boris" Cremeens, Rene Van Hulle, and Bob Levy, and the DJs included Peter Lewicki, Jim Thompson, Grant Smith, Tony Aloia, and Mark Vallese.

After several incidents, including a September 1978 stabbing of Wallach by a patron who was refused entry, and a bombing incident on March 11, 1979, the couple closed the bar because

they got tired of running it. In a letter to the community, they stated, "that gay people have themselves to blame for a good deal of the trouble that befalls them. The problem is, as we see it, you don't put your best foot forward." The letter continued in that vein for several paragraphs.

Broadway Sam's
5346 N. Broadway
Circa: 1970–1975

In November 1972, Broadway Sam's debuted its new solid plexiglass dance floor, twelve-foot wide, twenty-two foot long, with multicolored ceiling lights. The owner/manager was Bob Levy.

In the summer, there were weekly buffet dinners on Sundays at 6 p.m. On May 28, 1973, 250 people turned up at Broadway Sam's for its 2nd Mr. King contest. The winner, chosen from 22 contestants, was 'identified as Bill.'

In October 1975, in *Chicago Gay Crusader*, it was reported that Broadway Sam's had become Bananas, a straight disco.

Brownstone
435 W. Diversey Pkwy.
Circa: 1977–1978

The Brownstone's grand opening was on July 26, 1977. It was billed as "the big sister" of Le Pub and Alfie's, all three owned by Danny Reilly. The Brownstone opened as a bar and after a few months rebranded as a restaurant. The Manila-born manager and chef was Cesar Vera, who also worked at Broadway Sam's, Cheeks, Carol's Speakeasy, Coconuts, Crystal's Blinkers, Loading Zone, and other bars.

Bubba's
5405 W. Addison Ave.
Circa: 1981

On June 15, 1981, Bubba's opened with a show featuring Angelique Du Pray, Sunni Richards, Jan Howard, Mysterious Marilyn, Andrea Cheryl Stevens, and Diana McKay. The MC was Michael "K." The bar was described in the gay press as Chicago's newest and hottest show bar and dance emporium.

Bubbles
2856 N. Broadway
Circa: 1977

The first Mr. Bubbles, Bob Kelble, is flanked by, from left, Chloé, 1st runner-up, Dion; 2nd runner-up, Bob and bar manager, Gene.

Sherman Heinrich

The bar opened on January 6, 1977, with live entertainment in the upstairs lounge.

This was also the location of Bedrock.

Bubbles Bistro
9046 Golf Rd., Niles
Circa: 1984-1985

Bubbles Bistro was in a nearly abandoned shopping mall. The bar had two levels and maybe three bars. On weekends it was packed.

Bubbles Bistro was owned by Malcolm Silverman, who named it after his wife. On October 31, 1985, police entered the bar and allegedly found two underage patrons. Doorman John Chambers and manager Scott Van Berschot were charged with allowing minors in a place where liquor was sold. At a hearing, the bar's liquor license was suspended, but an appeal was filed. On November 8, 1985, police began turning away patrons at the door. Silverman filed a suit against the Village of Niles, alleging the Village and Niles Mayor Nicholas Blase launched a campaign of harassment, in an attempt to close the bar.

An ad in *GayLife* on July 25, 1985, read, "Just a note to say that we are thrilled with your continuing support. This has given us the opportunity to do more for you. Since opening it has been our concept to do more than just open our doors. Bubbles, your bar, is a party bar and a party bar to us consists of having three major parties a month and drink specials during the week... At this time, we would like to dispel any rumors that have arisen since our opening... There have been rumors to the effect that people have been accosted in our parking lot. This is a gross and libelous lie. We have an excellent staff and security patrolling our parking lot. This also dispels the rumor that cars are being vandalized. One of the most absurd rumors we have herd [sic] to date, is that the police officers are beating up gays in the parking lot. Our police department is always welcome at Bubbles. Remember, they have been invited in for your safety.

... Finally, it is not our intention to disassociate ourselves with the lesbian community. However, we are a men's dance bar. We are sorry we had to clear the matters up this way, but we feel that 'people who live in glass houses shouldn't throw stones.'"

In March 1986, an article in *Windy City Times* read, "Bubbles Bistro, the Niles establishment which was allegedly harassed last year because it had a gay and lesbian clientele, was closed last week. Niles Chief of Police Clarence Emrickson said the establishment appears closed, as posters out front note the business has filed for bankruptcy. Owner Malcolm Silverman and manager Scott Van Berschot could not be reached for comment."

Bucks
3439 N. Halsted St.
Circa: 1983-2013

Open 10am daily
Noon Sat., Sun., holidays
Cocktail hr. til 7pm Mon.-Fri.
Tuesday cocktail hr. all night

Buck's

3439 N. Halsted
525-1125

Pig Out!!!
Pig Roast
Saturday, Oct. 20th — 5ish
50¢ Draft Always

This neighborhood bar was opened by John Farquharson in 1983. In 1986 he sold it to Bill Rowe and "Dean." In 1993, William J. "Bill" Rowe, aged 45, died from AIDS complications and his partner, David Hough, took over the bar with "Dean."

Bucks boyz by Sukie

Buck's bartender, Everett "Rex" Shane

Buddies'
3301 N. Clark St.
Circa: 1988-2004

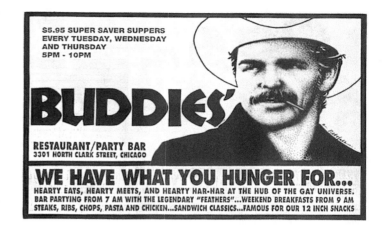

A popular bar and restaurant, Buddies' also served as a quasi-community center, hosting events for a variety of LGBT organizations. Among the groups that held events or meetings there were the Chicago LGBT Hall of Fame, AXIOS!, the organization for LGBT Greeks, Royal Imperial Sovereign Barony of the Windy City, and the Illinois Gay Rodeo Association.

The SheDevils were also in Mardi Gras attire at Buddies', but how could you tell?
Photos by Terry Gaskins

If there were a gay *Cheers*, Bucks was it. Events over the years included an annual winter luau pig roast to benefit Direct Aid, a charity providing funds directly to people impacted by AIDS. On Bucks popular beer garden, *Gay Chicago Magazine* wrote, "A brick patio and awninged cabana make this an unexpected oasis."

One of the popular activities that raised money for Direct Aid was "Chicken Shit Bingo." To play the game, the chickens were placed in a cage atop a bingo board, and whenever a dropping landed on a number, you covered the number on your bingo card. In September 1991, Bucks Chicken Shit Bingo raised $5,219 for Direct Aid.

Bucks closed on April 15, 2013. It was bought by Mark Liberson, who also owns Hydrate, Elixir, and Halsted's. He then opened Replay Lakeview at this location.

Buck's Basement
712 N. Rush St.
Circa: 1992

This was the lower-level bar at Gentry. They tried marketing it as a separate bar for a short time.

Buddies' restaurant was popular, especially for Sunday brunch, and specialized in Southwest cuisine. One feature was a salsa bar. The owners were Marty Enright and George Brophy. The manager was Michael Shimandle, who owned Bughaus and owned or co-owned Bushes and Bulldog Road. Among the many popular bartenders were Ikey, Feathers, Randy Lockhart, and Eio. For a short time, Buddies' basement was a leather bar called Boiler Room.

One of Buddies' advertising slogans was "meet, greet, eat." Partly for those qualities, it was picked in 1999 by *Genre* magazine as one of the nation's "Top 10 Gayest Restaurants." In 2003, Buddies' was inducted into the Chicago LGBT Hall of Fame.

Buddies' closed in 2004 and the owners moved to Tallahassee, Fla. On November 29, 2017, Martin "Marty" Enright died of pancreatic cancer. He was 85.

Bughaus
2570 N. Clark St.
Circa: 1981–1983

Bughaus opened in May 1981. It was owned by Michael Shimandle and Paul Beasley. The bar was popular with local softball league players. It was the permanent home of the Bughaus Bushmen. On August 13, 1981, plainclothes cops arrested a 30-year-old man and charged him with solicitation. A bartender was also charged with keeping a house of prostitution. His case was dismissed.

Stephen Kulieke in *GayLife*, wrote, "According to police reports of the incident, the man charged with soliciting had approached a plainclothes Vice Control Section officer and offered to fellate him for $100. Police maintained that the bartender 'overheard' the alleged transaction and later was directly apprised of it by the plainclothes officer."

Bughaus closed in September 1983.

This was also the location of Take One, Molly's Follies, Pourquoi Pas?, Robert's Lounge, and K's on Clark.

Bugle Boy
3320 N. Halsted St.
Circa: 1992–1993

Bugle Boy was a cabaret bar owned by Tim Carr. In October 1992, prior to opening, the bar held a Halloween party. The following month was the grand opening with Suzy Petri, "the mental dish herself," and Fred Marlman on keyboards performing cabaret songs by Edith Piaf, Patsy Cline, Marlene Dietrich, and James Brown. Other performers at Bugle Boy were Michael Thompson, David Hamilton, Honey West, and

Paige Turner. In September 1993, Tim Carr changed the name of Bugle Boy to Carr's Halsted Street Cabaret after receiving a cease and desist from a clothing company. He almost called the new bar Carr-Tune.

This was also the location of Bushes, Rocks, Niteline, G Spot, Gentry of Halsted, Carr's Halsted Street Cabaret, and Scarlet

Bulldog Road
2914 N. Broadway
Circa: 1984–1991

Woody Lorenz opened Bulldog Road in March 1984. By the following September, Crazy Mary's, a restaurant, was added. One of the attractions at Bulldog Road was movie night, when films such as *Auntie Mame, Who Framed Roger Rabbit*, and *Some Like it Hot*, were shown. Many events were hosted by Bulldog Road, including wet boxer shorts contests, a Strike Against AIDS raffle, and on March 21, 1991, the bar celebrated its 7th anniversary with special guest star Debbie Matt.

Popular bartenders include Robert "Bob" York, David Mitsakopoulos, Michael Koltes, and Feathers. William "Feathers" Gary worked at many bars in Chicago, including the Granville Anvil, Cheeks, Different Strokes, O'Banion's, and Buddies'. Feathers died in November 2013.

This was also the location of Big Daddies Bar & Grill and Avenue Tavern.

Bullfrogs
2916 N. Broadway
Circa: 1993

Bunbury's
725 W. Belmont Ave.
Circa: 1979

Burgundy Inn
2335 N. Clark St.
Circa: 1960s–2005

A restaurant/bar that hosted several LGBT events

Burlington
3425 W. Fullerton Ave.
Circa: 2013–present

A primarily straight bar with a gay night every third Wednesday of the month. In January 2015, "Burly," an alternative queer party, was a tribute to Dolly Parton. It was in honor of Parton's 69th birthday and called "Welcome to Burlywood." *Nightspots* described the clientele as, "queer, gay, lesbian, and otherwise funky and/or bearded individuals."

Burning Spear
7740 S. Stoney Island Blvd.
Circa: 1976

This was also the location of Club 77 and High Chaparrel.

Burton Place
168 W. Burton Pl.
Circa: 1973

A neighborhood bar and restaurant, also the location of Devil's Den.

Burt's Hideaway
317 S. Throop St.
Circa: 1975–1977

In the October 1975 issue of the *Chicago Gay Crusader*, Christopher, in his column, wrote, "Burt's Hideaway, west of the Loop, is now open for business, with booze, sandwiches and so on."

Bushes
3320 N. Halsted St.
Circa: 1976–1986

Co-owned by Michael Shimandle and Paul Beasley, Bushes was one of the first bars on Halsted St. It was a popular stop before heading down to the Hubbard Street bars. A description of the bar in *Gay Chicago Magazine* reads, "A welcome new addition to the Halsted area, this friendly establishment features a contemporary design. In light of their infamous name, the bar's decor is enhanced by special effects including live bushes and plants. The conversational level jukebox features balanced music from classic to rock."

The Bushes was also known for displaying the work of local

artists, such as Bruce Cegur, Bill McGuire, Robert Joel Zaban, and Steve Pickering. It had a reputation as being an upscale bar, kind of preppy.

"When Michael took over the management and designed and built Bushes, he had very little money, so he painted the walls black, he put up mirrors, which made the place look twice as large as it is. He had lamps hanging over the bar and above all, the courtesy of the bartenders was exemplary. You came away feeling better about yourself, just because of the climate they created," reported Phil to the authors.

In September 1983, the bar was sold to Dan Moon and Allen Jernsted, who also owned a popular restaurant, Two Doors South, a few blocks away on Clark St.

This was also the location of Gentry on Halsted, Carr's Halsted Street Cabaret, Bugle Boy, G-Spot, Niteline, Rocks, and Scarlet.

Bus Stop
520 N. Clark St.
Circa: 1982–1984

Bus Stop was managed by Lunde Fisher. It opened on March 27, 1982. A note in the gay press read, "A great place to get wrecked with Zibble, Wayne, and the rest of the staff." On March 6, 1983, the bar hosted a party for the cast members of *42nd Street*. And in May 1984, Bertie Lee and the New Ground, a country and western band, performed at Bus Stop. The bar also featured go-go boys and a free buffet on Sundays. In May 1984, Gary Solin purchased the bar.

This was also the location of St. Regis.

Bus Stop Lounge
41 S. Harlem Ave.
Circa: 1976

This was also the location of Adron's and Nutbush City Limits.

Butterfly
1437 N. Wells St.
Circa: 1976-1979

"CUM"
EXPERIENCE THE
NEW BUTTERFLY
1437 North Wells
787-9202
☆ NEW ENLARGED DANCE AREA ☆
BAR DRINKS 90¢ BEER 50¢
Hours: two to two
FUN ┅ FOOD ┅ DANCING
SUNDAY BRUNCH 12-5 PM

The Butterfly was owned by Leslie and GG. The bar was sometimes called the Iron Butterfly by the customers. Harry Shattuck was a bartender. They initiated the idea of a pie toss as a charitable fundraiser. The first celebrity Pie Toss was held at the Butterfly on May 21, 1977, as a benefit for the Gay/Lesbian Pride Week Committee. The second Pie Toss took place at the same bar on February 15, 1978. The money went to the Frank M. Rodde Memorial Building Fund. Celebrity targets that year included: Big Red, Guy (from the El Dorado), Mother Carol, Grant Ford, Polish Princess (Ron Helizon), Ben Allen, Ralph Paul, Leslie, and Delilah Kenny.

Leslie, one the bar owners, told the authors, "I owned the Butterfly, I was in with my cousin. My cousin Ronnie had a couple of places on Wells Street. He knew I was gay, and he approached me to be his partner. It was a mixed bar, men and women. They had everything coming in, they had straight people, drunks, they had drag queens, gay people, women, men, and it drew all the characters in that bar. We had the Cabaret Players, we put on the USO. show ... we had a guy who was real thin and his name was Rick and he played Frank Sinatra, and we had somebody played Kate Smith, we had the Andrew Sisters. We have a friend who owns Broadway Costumes, and Bob provided us with all these costumes and wigs and put on quite a show. We had a money tree, the branch of a tree in the bar and we gave the money to the campaign against Anita Bryant. We had a stapler and you stapled money to that tree. We had about $3000 that we donated to that. We raised a lot of money in that bar. We did a lot of things, had a lot of potlucks, gave a lot of dinners. I stopped because I was married to it, I did the ordering, I did bartending, I washed the floors, it was terrible, I'm not a drinker, I don't keep late hours, what am I doing with a bar? ... (laughs) ... and I can't stand drunks. But anyway, I had a very good bar."

This was also the location of Our Way on Wells.

Buzz
308 W. Erie St.
Circa: 2002-2006

In 2006, Box Boy Rich presented SLUT-TEA with resident DJ/Producer Teri Bristol. Special guest DJ Luis M and Music Planet recording artist Georgie Porgie. Hosted by Big Scott, JO-L, Heath-Her, Josh, J-Ho, Tee, Teri Yaki, Sal-E, and Bruce Barrios.

This was also the location of Club Inta and Cuvee.

Byfield's
1301 N. State Pkwy., Ambassador Hotel
Circa: 1981-1986

Traditionally, Chicago bars in large hotels have been gathering places for gay men going back to the 1930s and perhaps even before that. Byfield's was a cabaret/show lounge. It was home to noted singer comedienne Pudgy, who got her start in gay bars and was married to a former Mr. Man's Country. Other performers included Tricia Alexander, Lori Noelle, and Judy Tenuta.

Cabaret
15 W. Hubbard St.
Circa: 2006

A mixed gay/straight crowd with an LGBT tea dance on Sundays, "brought to you by Ahhh men!, with DJ Luis M and, from New York, DJ Joe D'Espinosa."

Cabin Inn
3119 S. Cottage Grove Ave.
Circa: 1933–1938

The Cabin Inn was a Black pansy club owned by Nathan "Big Ivy" Ivy, and Jack Hardy. They opened this Bronzeville drag club in 1933. In July 1934, the Cabin Inn featured female impersonator and blues singer Luzetta Hall and Blue and Jean, a two-man dance team who were known as the "Lady and Gentleman of the Carioca" – Jean was a boy in drag.

With Dick "Mae West" Barrow at the helm, the Cabin Inn flourished, adding more female impersonators to their roster, such as Robert "Dixie Lee" Johnson and "Marlene Dietrich."

In October 1935, the Cabin Inn hosted a double wedding: one the genuine article with the nuptials of "midget" dancer "Bullfrog Shorty" Burch to Muriel Borsack, and the other a same-sex wedding between female impersonator Jean Acker and Vernon Long, a man who was, according to the *Chicago Defender*, "a very handsome bridegroom." Mr. Luzetta Hall acted as Jean Acker's "bridesmaid." Guests came from as far away as Philadelphia, Madison, Detroit, and Indianapolis. As the cars pulled up outside the Cabin Inn, the guests alighted

and entered the club on a street lit by "electric candles" and floodlights.

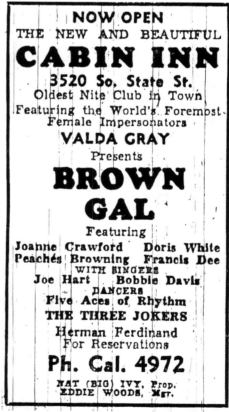

Police raided the "double wedding" and temporarily closed the club. Twelve employees were arrested and charged with obscenity in the Cabin raid: the owners Nat Ivy and Jack

Hardy, bartenders Dewey Parker and Bob Henderson, Carroll Joseph who operated the floodlights, and seven female impersonators, three working at the Cabin and four guests at the wedding. In South State St. court, Judge Eugene McGarry dismissed all the charges, saying, "The testimony does not show any specific violations of ordinance ... It appears that these men were dressed in female clothes. The testimony shows it was a masquerade party. Female impersonators appear on stage every day. In the absence of any such testimony I have no choice but to find the defendants not guilty and that will be the order."

In 1938, the Cabin Inn relocated to 3520 S. State St.

Cabin Inn
3520 S. State St.
Circa: 1938-1940

This was the second incarnation of the Cabin Inn.

Café Ashie (see Star Gaze)

Cafe Topa
3806 N. Ashland Ave.
Circa: 1973

Cairo
720 N. Wells St.
Circa: 1989-1995

One regular remembered, "The downstairs was lined with catacombs, and it had a sunken dance floor. The main floor was a jazz cabaret that served dinner. The second floor eventually

turned into a VIP room, and a few years after the grand opening, the top floor opened, and it was a dance room that played underground music. It was called the Pyramid Room with high ceilings, floor-to-ceiling windows, and a great view of the downtown area. Sunday night was gay night."

Among the cabaret performers were touring artists such as Judy Tenuta and Lea Delaria and local talents such as Alexandra Billings, Charlene Unger (AKA Peter Mohawk), Jamie Baron, Alyn Toler, Nan Mason, and the cast of the campy play *Whatever Happened to be B.B. Jane?*

The owner was Jerry Kleiner, along with sixteen investors. Later it was owned by John Abel and Dan Piedmonte, then two brothers Ron and Al.

Byron Dorsey hosted up in the Pyramid Room with DJs such as Mark Farina, Psycho Bitch, and Teri Bristol. When Glee Club opened, Cairo lost its Sunday night crowd. In March 1993, Cairo ended its gay night promotion.

Cairo was just a few doors north of where the Shanty Inn had been, nearly 50 years earlier.

This was also the location of the 720 Club.

Call
1547 W. Bryn Mawr Ave.
Circa: 2008-present

Originally named Cattle Call, it shortened its name a few months after opening. In August 2017, Chicago's Original Country Dance, hosted by David Boyer, celebrated 30 years of country dance parties in Chicago. Boyer hosted the first "Texas 2-Stepping Night" at Carol's Speakeasy.

Many drag queens have performed at the Call, including Angelique Munro, Ashley Morgan, Miss Foozie, Bianca Chablis Balenciaga, Tina Torch, Delores Van-Cartier, and Viviana Mendez.

The bar also features a long-running celebration of Britney Spears, "It's Britney, Bitch."

In 2011, the Call celebrated Noches De Fuego Latin Nights with the hottest Latin rhythms: salsa, cumbia, merengue, reggaeton and Latin pop.

In October 2014, a musical called, *Witches Among Us,* was staged in the bar.

Candy Store Lounge
6545 W. Roosevelt Rd.
Circa: 1969

Cape Cod Room (Drake Hotel)
Michigan Ave. and Lake Shore Drive
Circa: 1965

Listed in the *Bob Damron Guide* in 1965. At least going back to the 1930s in Chicago, it was common for hotel bars to attract a large gay crowd.

Carnival
2628 N. Halsted St.
Circa: 1979

This was a juice bar for young gay teens.

Also at this location were the Snake Pit, and the Pits.

Carol in Exile
3510 N. Broadway
Circa: 1976-1977

One patron told the authors, it was "an awkward bar, you had to walk down and there were lots of fans and vents above." The grand opening was on October 10-11, 1976. With Mother Carol (born Richard Farnham) as host, it featured stage shows with Tillie the Dirty Old Lady. Many interviewed remember Carol as "...a terrible drunk. Carol was just a party girl, party girl."

The bar is most notable for one of its bartenders, Frank "Punkin" Rodde III, who was found dead from multiple stab wounds in the bathtub of his apartment. His fellow bartenders acted as pallbearers. A much-beloved member of the community, a fund was started in his name to raise money to open a gay community center.

It was also the location of Broadway Kunfusion and Garland's.

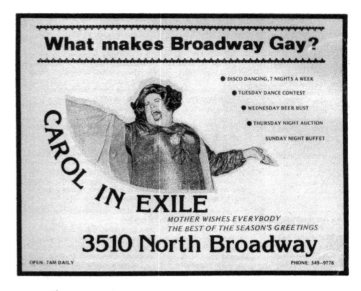

Carol's Coming Out Pub
2519 N. Halsted St.
Circa: 1972-1976

The earliest bar hosted by Mother Carol (born Richard Farnham). In 1976, *Gay Chicago Magazine* wrote of Carol's Coming Out Pub, "Popular jukebox, small dance area, live shows and go-go boys featured occasionally. Games room annex and beer garden."

Carol's Pub bartender, Rick

Steve "Missie" Allman, a popular bartender, told the authors, "Mother Carol was outrageous. Big, heavy, in drag, she always had her tongue sticking out; she looked like the cover of that Rolling Stones album."

This was later the location of Little Bits.

Carol's Speakeasy
1355 N. Wells St.
Circa: 1978–1991

Carol's Speakeasy was presided over by Mother Carol (born Richard Farnham). Fred Kramer and Roger Hickey were the co-owners. Although Mother Carol died less than a year after the bar opened, on September 30, 1979, it continued operating for more than a decade, with Cesar Vera managing, followed by David Boyer. The bar's logo of a tongue sticking out of red lips was a depiction of Farnham's signature move while performing.

The bar featured a large dance floor and a back room. The dance floor was augmented with a light and laser show with visual programming by Grant Smith and DJs Joel Levin and Larry Fox. Rumor had it that there were tunnels leading to neighboring buildings, in case of police raids.

Personal appearances by recording stars such as Linda

Clifford, Limahl from London, Izora Armstead of Weather Girls, and Bronski Beat were featured. In addition to hosting benefits for such charities as Horizons Community Services, Howard Brown Memorial Clinic, and the Illinois Gay & Lesbian Task Force, the bar also welcomed local politicians, such as aldermanic candidate Ron Sable, and screened movies such as *The Times of Harvey Milk*.

The club also featured male strippers, held regular leather nights and weekly C&W dances, with free lessons offered. Country recording star Dena Kaye was a regular performer.

Carol's Speakeasy had an amazing lineup of talented DJs in 1979: Peter Lewicki (Thursdays), Frankie Knuckles (Fridays), Greg Collier (Saturdays), and Mike Graber (Sundays). Saturday afternoons featured a roller-skating party, and Sunday featured shows by the Bearded Lady (born Robert W. Theiss). The Bearded Lady performed at many clubs, including Le Trolls, Bistro, Center Stage, and Coconuts. Carol's Speakeasy was renovated in 1979 with a new lighting system and a larger dancefloor.

In 1980, a "Punk Out" party starred performers with names such as Mysterious Marilynn, Mary Ann Mouthful, Diana Hutton, and Cotton Candy. By 1982, the club featured video screens with VJ Grant Smith and DJ Joel Levin. Later DJs included Mark Vallese and Larry Fox.

CAROL'S SPEAKEASY

WANTED
Clip For Reward
Reward - Free cocktail Saturday, Jan. 26
Last seen in the vincity of
Carol's Speakeasy
1355 N. Wells St.
Special: This Saturday — Jelly Beans - 75¢
Whatever your type — You'll find him at Carol's
944-4226

Carol's Speakeasy, 1355 N. Wells St., is running a "Name the Back Bar Contest" now through April 20.

MARCH PLANNED TO PROTEST POLICE VIOLENCE, TACTICS
Photo by David Veltkamp

Nursing Mother Carol back to health are, from left to right, Dennis Lopez, columnist Richard Cooke, Bill Maggio and Jim Thompson.
Photo by David Veltkamp

THE BIG TOP IS COMING

OUR MOVIE
SILVER STREAK
AUGUST
14, 15, & 16
Carol's
Speakeasy
Restaurant/Disco
1355 North Wells   Chicago

An infamous September 12, 1985, police raid in which the club's patrons were photographed, resulted in a successful class-action lawsuit by the ACLU. The police raided Carol's one weekend night. "They turned up the lights, shut the bar down, and they made everybody lie down on the floor, and they took everybody's ID and didn't release people for hours. Without a warrant. With no provocation. It was partly this multi-government agency drug enforcement thing called MEG and partly Chicago cops from that district. That district's commander at that time had an anti-gay reputation," Bert Thompson told the authors. It led to a big protest from the community. The owners of Carol's filed a $15 million lawsuit against the MEG.

In June 1991, Carol's Speakeasy changed its name to just Carol's, then closed in October 1991, shortly after it was revealed that serial killer Jeffrey Dahmer picked up many of his victims at the bar.

Before it was Carol's Speakeasy, this was the site of Den One and Our Den.

Carousel/White Spider
Oak St. and Dearborn St.
Circa: 1940s

The Carousel was a "swanky joint." It was sometimes called the White Spider. The bar was gay downstairs, mixed upstairs, and managed by a Jewish couple, Ann and Sol, who ran several other gay bars in the city.

FW recalled, "Lucrezia, who was Chicago's answer to Mabel Mercer, played piano and sang. Her theme song was 'It's a Big Wide Wonderful World We Live In.' This was a more elegant bar than the others, and you had some feeling of class when you went in there. It was two stories with only a bar and check room on the first floor, and a bar and a good-sized room with tables and the piano set up on the second floor."

Charles B. remembered, "I knew Lucrezia very well. Lucrezia could have been on top of the world, but she wouldn't listen to anybody. There was a club with class, it was mixed, and it was on Oak and Dearborn, Ann and Sol ran it, and downstairs was gay, upstairs was sort of mixed, and Lucrezia worked there for a long time ... I'll tell you who tried to help Lucrezia a lot was Victor Borge. They were very close friends. She was a singer, she was a chanteuse. She played the piano, and she sang."

Carr's Halsted Street Cabaret
3320 N. Halsted St.
Circa: 1993-1994

Carr's Halsted Street Cabaret originally opened as Bugle Boy but had to change its name after being sued by the clothing company. It was owned by Tim Carr and featured nightclub acts by local actors and the occasional comic drag performer. Among those booked were David Dillon (playwright/director) and cast members of the hit play *Party*, Jane Blass with Chuck Larkin, Rus Rainear as Carol Channing, Honey West with Paige Turner, Joe Kregor, Sue Conway, David Hamilton, Laura Wells, and Suzi Petri.

Touring companies of Broadway and local shows stopped in and performed on "dark" nights. Among those were the cast of *Joseph and the Amazing Technicolor Dreamcoat*, and *Cats*.

This was also the location of G-Spot, Niteline, Bushes, Rocks, Bugle Boy, Gentry on Halsted, and Scarlet.

Casa Puertorriqueña!
1237 N. California Ave.
Circa: 2002-2005

Featured performances by drag king Andres de Los Santos y Juicy, including, in January 2005, "Dias de Los Reyes, Noche de Las Reinas" presented by Amigas Latina, with music by DJ Wanda.

Casino Club
4834 N. Winthrop Ave.
Circa: 1930s

Located in a basement, one visitor described it as, "A dingy place where they served beer. The queens were groping each other and dancing together and acting very sissified."

C Club
Fullerton Ave., west of Milwaukee Ave.
Circa: 1950s

William Rydwels told the authors, "There was a lesbian bar up on Fullerton, west of Milwaukee Ave. ... where I don't know, but I think it was called the C Club, it had a big letter C. What is strange, is all these stories of how tough the dykes were, but we had a group of dykes that we used to go around with, and they were very receptive to being with the gay boys. I left Chicago in 1962 for New York, so that had to be in the '50s."

CC's Lounge
644 N. State St.
Circa: 1970s

This was later the location of the 644 Club.

Celebrity Club
1017 N. Rush St.
Circa: 1975

The club opened in June 1975 as a gay bar and changed its focus to a straight crowd in October.

Celebrity Club
6465 N. Mannheim Rd., Rosemont
Circa: 1982-1983

This club opened on March 26, 1982. In *Gay Chicago Magazine*, Nancy Reiff and Ralph Paul wrote, "Stop out at the new Celebrity Club in the Grand Plaza Hotel on Mannheim Road not far from the Rosemont Horizon. We received quite a warm welcome opening night last week from Roger Franz, the hotel's promotion director. He showed us some of the spacious rooms that will be available at reduced rates to guests of the club. The Olympic size swimming pool could prove to be a real winner with bar and food service at poolside this summer."

March 1983 saw the grand opening of its "New and Very Private Room for Men Only." Events at the Celebrity Club included Orlando Del Sol's "Guys Will Be Dolls" show starring Diana McKay, Isadora Sei, Tamara Lee, and Monica Monet. That same month there was also a magic show with Walter King Jr., with the talented and exotic belly-dancing of Marianna.

Cellar
State St. and Van Buren St.
Circa: 1950s-1960s

Ken, a Black customer at the Cellar, told the authors, "The Cellar was a mixed bar; when I say mixed, I mean it was a gay bar with all races. You could meet people there and either go home with them or go to a hotel. The bars got raided a lot, especially during election time. The Cellar would get raided on a Friday night one week, then a Saturday the next. Sometimes they would raid it twice in one weekend. The jail was down the street. Dope has always been around, and you got these people who would get out of jail, and they heard you could come there and pick somebody up and make some money. So, they started hustling and robbing people, and that brought the police out more than was usual. It was the same thing with Zack's."

Cell Block
3702 N. Halsted St.
Circa: 1995-present

Cell Block held its grand opening on May 12, 1995. David Boyer was the manager, and the owner was Roger Hickey. It has a back room and a small dance floor featuring DJs such as TL Noble and Jim Otey. It attracts a leather crowd, although it has also hosted a party for the Windy City Gay Naturists as well as welcoming Thomas Smith, Mr. International Rubber 1999, the Pantheon of Leather, the Grabby's (adult video) Awards, and ONYX/Chicago, a leather club for men of color and their friends. Other events at Cell Block include Comedy Night hosted by Mark Peurye and an appearance in December 2003 by the band Super 8 Cumshot

The Sisters of Perpetual Indulgence at the Cell Block

In December 2011, Cell Block sponsored a winter coat drive, run by longtime bartender, Mark Bowden. All men's items were donated to HIV-positive clients of GroceryLand, the food-providing arm of Vital Bridges Center on Chronic Care, while women and children's items went to the Cornerstone Community Center in Uptown.

In 2020 the manager was Matthew Scott Dontje and the owner, Rob Noha. Dontje was also a bartender at Bucks.

This address was previously home to the Aloha Bikini Lounge, Loading Dock, and Vista Hermosa.

Center Stage
3730 N. Clark St.
Circa: 1977-1979

Charles "Chuck" Renslow owned Center Stage. It was managed by Gary Chichester. The grand opening was on October 21, 1977. *Gay Chicago News* wrote, "The new entertainment complex housed in the North Side Auditorium Building at 3730 N. Clark St. will contain Center Stage disco and a Cabaret Nightclub. ... Completely redecorated in peach-colored walls accented by gold leaf trim, the second-floor disco will provide a first-rate light show. The system, according to Chuck Renslow, is a combination of three types, the laser, a multiple projection slide show, and the standard system including strobes and chasers. A complimentary sound system places base speaker cabinets on the dance floor level, mid-range speakers on the balcony and the high range speakers suspended from the ceiling."

Many stars performed at Center Stage, including Grace Jones, Karen Mason, Denise McCann, Sylvester, and Two Tons of Fun. Comedienne Pudgy performed in the cabaret room, which became Smart Bar. A popular DJ was Peter Lewicki.

Center Stage closed on January 20, 1979.

This was also the location of Stages, Smart Bar, and Metro.

Century
2810 N. Clark St.
Circa: 1965

Female impersonator Viki St. John told the authors, "There was a bar on the first floor in the Century Theater, which is now a mall. They had a guy playing the organ up behind the bar. It was mostly older guys."

Century Disco
2828 N. Clark St.
Circa: 1975

A show in September 1980 featured Rachel with Vicki Rodriguez and Roxie Tiu.

This was also the location of Allegro International and Siegelman's Allegro.

Cesar's
674 W. Diversey Pkwy.
Circa: 1993

This was also the location of Dickies, Piggen's Pub, and Cocktails & Dreams.

C'est La Vie
Calumet City
Circa: 1950

William Rydwels remembered, "C'est La Vie had upholstered seats along the wall. I did not go up to the bar. I was underage and they didn't approach me. Other than that, it just seemed dark and that's all I remember of that."

C'est La Vie
2045 W. Lawrence Ave.
Circa: 1970

In the *Mattachine Midwest Newsletter* it's noted that, "The C'est La Vie ... has a brand-new look and a brand-new show called Le Girls."

Chain
7860 S. Cottage Grove Ave.
Circa: 1974-1976

Attracted a young, gay, Black crowd.

Chakiris Club
5820 N. Clark St.
Circa: 1977

This Latin bar opened October 28-31, 1977, with a four-day Halloween party.

Chalmers
1502 W. Jarvis Ave.
Circa: 1928-1970

Chalmers was an illegal speakeasy in the 1920s. It was opened in 1928 by a woman called Pauline and her husband – he is said to have died young. Pauline ran the bar up into the 1960s. She was very strict. Men were required to keep their hands placed on the top of the bar at all times, and there was no touching allowed among the customers, not even shaking hands. The art deco décor featured carvings by sculptor Paul Manship, best known for his sculpture of Prometheus in the fountain at the Rockefeller Center in New York City.

"That's an incredible place. They used to bootleg out of there ... it was a bootlegging place. There's supposedly a tunnel running underneath the bar over to Greenview, I think, the street past the overpass, and they would smuggle in the bootleg liquor when it was a Speakeasy," Chandelle told the authors.

This was also the location of Pepper's and Charmers.

Chariot Lounge
Rand Plaza on Rand Road (Route 12), Palatine
Circa: 1977

This gay men's bar opened in May 1977.

Charlie's
405 W. Ontario St.
Circa: 1992-1994

In January 1993, John King opened the Chicago location of the Charlie's chain of bars. The bar's slogan was, "That Lil Ole Pissant Country Place." The bar was doomed from the start, as it was too big, difficult to get to, and completely removed from other gay bars. The She-Devils, drag stars from Chi-Town Squares (a gay square-dance group), were regulars at Charlie's.

In February 1994, American singer-songwriter and line dance entertainer Scooter Lee performed at the bar.

Charlie's
3726 N. Broadway
Circa: 1994-present

Charlie's relocated to Broadway, to the space formerly occupied by Augie & CKs and opened in February 1994 as a Country & Western bar, but later became a late-night dance bar. It hosted many events for the Illinois Gay Rodeo Association and held a monthly Mr. Charlie's contest – judged by how much money a contestant could raise for charity in the bar. Another popular event was the weekly riotous It's Just Bingo Bitch! with Lauren Jacobs and Frida Lay. Another regular drag queen at the bar was Minerva Rex (born Jeff Geiger), who died from a heart attack in July 2012.

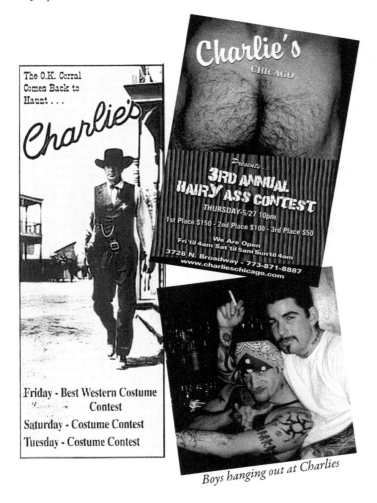

Boys hanging out at Charlies

Two-steppin' and line dancing lessons were given free by Crystal Kimmey and Stina. Charlie's also hosted benefits for community organizations such as Open Hand Chicago, Children's Place, and AIDS Walk Chicago.

In the last ten years, Charlie's became less "country" and more of a young gay man's dance bar. February 2009 saw the grand opening of Resurrection Sundays with DJ Lulu bringing yesterday's club hits back to life.

Augie & CK's and Darché's were also at this location.

Charlie's Angels
8710 Golf Rd., Des Plaines
Circa: 1978-1986, then 1988-1992

Charlie's Angels opened November 4, 1978, with an appearance by Cher Delight and a clown. A beef and chicken buffet was served. The bar was in a strip mall on Golf Road, and except for those at the bar, the mall was abandoned at night. It was a neighborhood-style bar with a devoted group of regulars. There was a small dance floor and occasionally entertainment, like disco dancing with DJ Al Siewert.

The bar was owned by Raul and Evelyn Esparza, who closed the bar in October 1986. It was replaced by Club Bolero, then reverted back to Charlie's Angels in January 1988.

Steven August Papa told the authors, "You had people there in the suburbs who weren't really openly gay. ...There was heavy cruising. And then you had truckers, people from the surrounding suburbs, even farmers in there looking to pick up guys. It had this no-nonsense sexual trip to it. The bartenders were nice guys, but they were really savvy, of course, and they knew everything that was going on. Because I was a baby back then they would always look out for me. If someone came in, they would say, 'No, honey, don't go there, that's trouble.'"

Charlie's Angels closed in May 1992.

Charmers
1502 W. Jarvis Ave.
Circa: 1989-2005

Prior to being called Charmers, this location was Chalmers. Charmers was owned by John Ellis. The bar held a grand opening party on August 25, 1989.

Galen Davis was a bartender there in 1994.

In June 1996, the new Charmers owners, "Ana" and Sharon Haines, took over. Haines was previously a bartender at Augie & CK's.

Charmers closed in 2005, and shortly afterward, reopened as a coffeeshop.

This was the location of Pepper's.

Chat Chat Lounge
4526 N. Sheridan Rd.
Circa: 1963-1965

The Chat Chat Lounge was owned/managed by Nathan Zuckerman, a shady character who also ran the Front Page. Dee LoBue told the authors, "Pudgy Roberts came in from Minnesota, a talented man, made his dresses, his own wigs, his make-up and designed everything for the stage. So here we are at the Chat Chat Lounge, and Pudgy Roberts said, 'You know, anybody can go up there and sing a song.' So, we would do production numbers. We did *Gypsy*, we did *West Side Story*,

Nab Women in Raid
Fifteen women, who police said were male impersonaters, were arrested early yesterday in a vice raid on the Chit-chat lounge, 4526 Sheridan rd. All

you know ... 'Two ladies in the shade of a banana tree.' We would do all these production numbers with costumes and props. At the time, the dressing room was in the basement – everything was in the basement – the dressing room was on the street side of the club, and there were small windows. The syndicate was having fights with each other over territory. We're on stage, and they threw two bombs through the window of the dressing room. The only thing that saved our asses was all those goddamn gowns. There were so many gowns they took the impact of the explosion."

Chatterbox
744 N. Clark St.
Circa: 1977-1982

The grand opening of Chatterbox was June 10-12, 1977. The bar was closed by liquor officials on July 30, 1982. In July 1979, a gay newspaper reported, "Breaking away from the usual gay bar entertainment, Bobo the Clown appears at the Chatterbox."

This was also the location of George's Lounge.

(Paul's) Checkmate
2546 N. Clark St.
Circa: 1965-1976

Checkmate was a neighborhood bar. It was known as Paul's Checkmate in 1965 and from 1966 on, just as Checkmate.

Don, a regular, told the authors, "It was a neighborhood bar, and if you went in there, you probably knew 75 percent of the people. It was very nice, very friendly, good bartenders, and Paul did pay off the cops. You'd be sitting there drinking, and this big burly cop would walk in. There wouldn't be a sound ... all the glasses were on the bar ... he would go in the back, go in Paul's office, they'd be in there maybe 10, 15 minutes, then the cop would walk back out ... and all the glasses would start clinking again. You'd see it two or three times a year, maybe more than that, so it wasn't a strange happening, but every time it happened, there was this sudden silence."

This was also the location of Checkmate II, Inner Circle, and Virgo Out.

Checkmate II
2546 N. Clark St.
Circa: 1980–1982

This gay men's bar held its grand opening on February 24, 1980. It was owned by Wes and Bob Middleton. One gay newspaper wrote, "The Checkmate II offers a Victorian atmosphere with lots of dark wood, flags flying above the bar, and a warm feeling. The kind of place a real gentleman would enjoy. Johnny from the Blue Pub bartends, and Jim Hardy plays piano."

Also playing piano at Checkmate II was Sam Hill and Eve. In his column, the Polish Princess (born Ron Helizon) wrote, "Saturday nights ... spend time sitting around the piano singing along with Eve at the Checkmate II. Eve has been playing the piano for over 30 years (but doesn't look like it) to such fans as Billie Holiday and Liza Minnelli, and she can tell the stories too."

In December 1980, Beverley "Tom" Woolard, a bartender at Checkmate II was found dead on the sidewalk. He had severe facial and cranial injuries. Police wondered whether it was a fall from a second-floor window or if Woolard was beaten to death. Woolard had been working the afternoon shift 4-7 p.m. on weekdays and 1-7 on weekends for about five months and was very popular with the cocktail crowd. Yet months later, the crime was still unsolved.

This was also the location of (Paul's) Checkmate, Inner Circle, and Virgo Out.

Cheeks
2730 N. Clark St.
Circa: 1975–1990s

Cheeks was a popular late-night bar (it had a 4 a.m. license), owned by Steve Strauss and Bobby Belcher, and being on the way home for men who had been in the Clark and Hubbard area bars, it was the last chance to pick up a trick. It also had some of the most popular bartenders in the city, Alan "Baby Cheeks" Boyd, Feathers, and Steve Allman. Cheeks opened on December 19, 1975 – *GayLife* wrote, "Chicago opens its cheeks. Now open, wide open."

Cheeks occasionally held faux beauty contests, although it was not known as a drag bar. In September 1979, Larry "Molly" Berlandi of the Nutbush City Limits bar was the emcee for the first Miss Piggy Contest at the bar, a benefit for the Gay Athletic Association. On January 9, 1989, Ginger Grant and Cesar Vera hosted the Miss Chubby Cheeks 1989-1990 contest.

Steve Allman remembered, "After they sold the bar to Jim Barr [in 1987] it became a hustler bar. A drag queen and hustler bar."

There were many accounts of serial killer John Wayne Gacy hanging out at Cheeks. Mike Morreale told the authors, "I saw him lurking in there once or twice. I remember him because he looked creepy just hanging in the shadows near the go-go boys."

Cherry Tree Lounge
3714 N. Clark St.
Circa: 1974

This was also the location of the F-Beat.

Chesterfield
2829/2831 N. Clark St.
Circa: 1964–1967

This drag bar was owned by Nick Dallesandro – who also owned the Annex. It offered shows by female impersonators Roby Landers, Terri Paige – the Pantomime Rage, and Tilly the Dirty Old Lady. It also featured visiting headliners such as Skip Arnold from the Jewel Box Review.

Tillie the Dirty Old Lady worked at the Chesterfield from 1962 to 1966. Tillie told the authors, "I heard that the Chesterfield was having an amateur day on Sunday afternoons, and I went down, and I saw this crowd of young kids, and I thought, 'Oh, they're not going to like this.' So I went up and did my Sophie Tucker number, and they loved it, honey! Roby Landers added the Dirty Old Lady to my name because when I was at the Chesterfield all these young boys used to hang around me and buy me drinks like crazy. It was one big, long, U-shaped bar, and we dressed behind a curtain. There were back-up boys who were gay. We had three shows nightly."

Jim Henritze was the manager. He told the authors, "I was never in a raid. I did get busted once at the Chesterfield, when I started. That was because Nick hadn't paid off. I was working a split shift from 4-8 and from 10-4, and I came in early and was setting up the bar, and these two kids came in and ordered a beer. I served them a beer and all of a sudden two cops came in and went right over to them and checked their IDs. They were, supposedly, underage. The cops closed the bar and took me to the Town Hall. My statement was already written for me before I ever got there, because in those days you had to pay off. Nick had a bad habit of saying, 'I'll catch you tomorrow,' or he was going out the back door and they were coming in the front. He never wanted to pay his bills. He just stalled for long enough and he owed so much money that the only way to get him to pay was to bust him. Of course, it was all thrown out. It was just a setup deal.

"In fact, one time, I was just starting work, and a big black Cadillac pulled up outside, and four or five guys from the outfit came in, and they all walked back to the office. They emptied all the registers. The only thing they left was coins. Then they all left. Nick hadn't been paying off his partners. That's how they got their money."

Chesterfield Club
1800 W. Pershing St.
Circa: 2006-2008

The Chesterfield was a Latin club in the McKinley Park neighborhood on the southwest side, owned by Jose Antonio Casco. Aurora Pineda, a longtime community activist, told *Windy City Times,* "Jose was always willing to lend a helping hand to those in need, including providing a location for HIV testing when he owned Chesterfield's."

Casco later owned Antronio's. He died April 3, 2016.

Chez Ron
4210 N. Lincoln Ave.
Circa: 1970-1972

The following is from St Sukie de la Croix's *Chicago After Stonewall: Gay Lib to Gay Life,* "One notable example was the closing of Chez Ron, a mafia-controlled lesbian bar. The bar had a troubled history with the gay community. In November 1970, an ad for Chez Ron appeared in the *Mattachine Midwest Newsletter*: "THE GAY PLACE TO GO. WITH AD 1 DRINK FREE.""

In the following issue, an apology read, "We regret to learn that customers have been refused admission to Chez Ron, 4210 N. Lincoln Ave. That was altogether contrary to our understanding when accepting their ad. We apologize on our behalf as well as theirs."

An obituary for Chez Ron appeared in *Lavender Woman,* reprinted in the 1985 book *Are We There Yet? A Continuing History of Lavender Woman, a Chicago Lesbian Newspaper 1971-1976,* edited by Michal Brody:

"Chez Ron Obitz

"What can you say about a 18 month old lesbian bar that died?

"That it was Mafia run. And male dominated. That it loved bad bands, no windows, cheap drinks, and not 'us.'

"Where was the love? And why did 'we' go?

"It can be said that this bar rated lowest in almost every area on the now infamous CLL [Chicago Lesbian Liberation] Bar Survey: that the pictures of 1930 chorus girl types passed off as gay women should have been hung around necks instead of on walls: that – thanks be to lesbian power – the bar was forced 'under' by the addition of new and better social gathering spots; and that it is no longer."

Chicago Cabaret
4726 N. Western Ave.
Circa: 1983-1985

Chicago Cabaret held its grand opening in July 1983. One gay newspaper described the club as, "An elegant, private club for gentlemen." By March 1985, this was a lesbian bar. It was above a funeral parlor and openly run by the mob. One woman told the authors, there were "big bruiser guys on the door."

Chicago Eagle
5015 N. Clark St.
Circa: 1993–2006

Opened by Charles "Chuck" Renslow in June 1993 in the space that formerly housed Bistro Too and was at times part of the Man's Country bathhouse. On the opening night, Ron Ehemann, Paul Gleason, and Jaime Krohn were among those in attendance. Entry to the bar was through an old semi-trailer wedged into a walkway.

As with most leather bars, the Chicago Eagle held theme nights and hosted many events, including "Meet the Titleholder's" the night before the International Mr. Leather contest, and IML's post-contest infamous "Black and Blue Ball." Among the popular bartenders were Jim Stephens, Robert Harvey, Jim Stivers, Harry Shattuck, and Beau Lee James. In February 2000, Jim Stephens was the manager.

The bar regularly featured male dancers and provided a meeting space for a variety of leather clubs and organizations including, S.L.U.T.S., the Society of Leatherwomen United Towards Sado-Masochism. This was also the location of Bistro Too.

Chicago Mining Co.
5006 N. Clark St.
Circa: 1990

The bar was open from August to October 1990, then the corporation filed for bankruptcy. During the few months it was open, Viola Wills performed. The owner was Sam Gibson, the manager was Greg Myster. Bar staff included Terry Chapmound, Jean Leigh, and Todd Ballard.

This was also the location of Rage.

China Club
616 W. Fulton St.
Circa: 1992

This was a mixed gay/straight club. On August 1, 1992, the Village People performed there. Popular DJ Psycho Bitch told the authors, "It was a very large space and hosted many live acts there. There was a VIP room, Dragon Room (rock music), and a dance club room. Fridays were more clubby, and Saturdays were more B96."

Chloe's
800 W. Belmont Ave.
Circa: 2014

In June 2014, the Windy City Empire's Pride ceremony honored Charles "Chuck" Renslow, the Leather Daddy of All Leatherdaddies at Chloe's.

Cho Cho San
Surf St. and Broadway
Circa: 1964-1965

Cho Cho San was a neighborhood piano bar. Terry (Theresa) owned the bar. Franco, who was Cuban, played piano – he was a classical pianist. Terry sang. On Sunday afternoons, they had operettas.

Don told the authors, "It covered two rooms, and the front part was the bar and the back part had the grand piano and people would just come in there and sit and drink and listen to the piano. Again, that lasted about two years. They didn't get that big of a clientele. It came and went in a hurry, and it didn't have a lot of notoriety, but it was jammed to the rafters on weekends."

Viki St John told the authors, "A lot of the theatrical people went after the shows were over... The owner's husband tended bar, but she would bring the show people back into the lounge area where the piano was. She would say, 'You have to sing, you have to sing, and everybody would clap, and they'd sing until two in the morning. But the owner's husband ran away, and she didn't know how to run the place and so they closed it."

Christopher Street
3458 N. Halsted St.
Circa: 1982-1990

Jeff Tessler was a real estate investor who bought a building that had a shuttered bar. Jeff got his brother-in-law, Steve Brahill, and his husband, Pat Kasaras, to front the bar. Christopher Street held its grand opening in December 1982. Unlike most gay bars at the time, rather than blacking out the windows, they left them clear. It was a different approach, not hiding behind darkened glass. There was a large bar in the front, and they later expanded to make a dance area in the neighboring storefront.

It was known for its handsome bartenders. Among them, Ron Riskey and Tommie O'Connell. Entertainment varied from drag queens to lesbian singers to tarot card readers to comic Judy Tenuta. In 1989, the Canadian post-disco duo, Lime, performed.

Not long after Brahill died from AIDS-related illnesses in 1988, Tessler and Kasaras closed Christopher Street. They opened a larger club called Vortex. On the day Christopher Street closed in October 1990, a coffin was carried from the bar down the street to Vortex.

This location later became Manhole and Hydrate.

Christie's on Clark
3474 N. Clark St.
Circa: 1987-1988

A small neighborhood bar that offered entertainment, such as Stardust, a female trio noted for their rendition of 1940s songs.

In November 1987, Christy's on Clark hosted a benefit for Strike Against AIDS. Bartenders and waiters that night included John Selvey, Greg Holzwart and Tony Faifer. The event took place in many gay bars around the city. It was sponsored by Anheuser-Busch who donated $27,000 to cover the expenses of the fundraiser.

This was also the location of Party Party, Studio 69, the Factory, and Zo-ran.

Chromium Nightclub
817 W. Lake St.
Circa: 2004-2005

In March 2004, this mixed straight/gay club was listed in *Nightspots* as, "Femme la Femme. Sandy and Edith present brand-new hotspot for the gay community. Hot Salsa Nights with DJ Sandy." Among other events, in March 2005, Chromium hosted Femisty, a woman-only night presented by B. Blyss! House hip hop, salsa, pop, reggaeton, and dance mixes spun by DJ Chosen One.

Circle Lounge
616 N. Rush, St., Croydon Hotel
Circa: 1930s-1984

On April 28, 1985, Steve Kerch in the *Chicago Tribune* described the Croydon Hotel thus, "For years the Croydon Hotel was the gathering place for aging vaudeville performers who mingled with cocktail waitresses and assorted hangers-on in the golden days of Rush Street. "Pianist Oscar Peterson and bandleader Harry James used to play for nothing after hours at the hotel's Circle Lounge. James is said to have proposed to Betty Grable as she sat on a barstool there."

One gay man recalled, "It was a small bar, and I remember they had a piano player – it was Lil Armstrong. Lil was the first wife of Louis Armstrong. She'd take requests. Songs like ... Oh my man don't love me, he treats me oh so mean, wears high drape pants, stripes all red and yellow. Old, old Blues things. You always wore a shirt and tie – you have to remember this was the '30s, early '40s."

Circuit/Rehab
3641 N. Halsted St.
Circa: 1997-2015

Originally opened by Mike Macharello as the Halsted Street Cafe (1995-1997). When it got a liquor license in March 1997, it was relaunched as Circuit. The front lounge was known as Rehab. Circuit, the back bar, which was much larger and didn't open until later in the evening. A large warehouse-type space. It was a difficult undertaking to get open, according to Macharello, "It took two years to go through the liquor licensing process ... By then I was completely broke but managed to survive until Qwest, the west side Latin club closed, and I acquired their business. Things got better and came to a peak when Vortex – Fusion at the time – closed, and I acquired their business as well. By then, I had achieved getting a 4 a.m. (5 a.m. on Saturdays) license, and things were great until the Dakota – a condominium complex – was built, and it started a seven-year public battle with a small group of neighbors."

Circuit was home to Chicago's longest-running Latin night, featuring Miss Ketty. It also featured regularly scheduled women's events such as the Chix Mix "Black Bra Party" with DJ Dani B. Club personalities included Miss Foozie, Sal-E, Eddie Couture, Mz. Ruff 'n' Stuff and DJs Fast Freddy, Rock-o-Mix, Stoney, Lulu, Carlos Valderamma, Hugo, Julio, and Paolo. Guests included major recording artists and personalities such as Lady Bunny and RuPaul.

This was also the location of Fantasy Night Club and M7.

Circus
901 W. Weed St.
Circa: 2003

At the 2003 grand opening, Fresh and Fruity presented Pistachio Fridays with DJs Chris Eterno and Oskar.

City Nights
1680 Dolton Rd., Calumet City
Circa: 1991-1993/4

City Nights was a dance bar for men with DJs Frank Lipomi, Fred Hands, and Ed Wanders. Vincent G. Giff was the bartender, and City Nights' assistant manager was Julian Stryczek. On April 26, 1992, City Nights presented, "A Celebration of Life" in memory of Sherman Heinrich (head of ad sales at *Gay Chicago Magazine*) to benefit the Dan Di Leo PWA fund. There were appearances by Nan Mason, Alexandra Billings, and the City Nights Revue and special raffle prizes, autographed Oprah Winfrey shirt, autographed Liza Minnelli scarf, autographed Jane Byrne book.

The bar burned down in 1993 or 1994.

CK's
1425 W. Diversey Pkwy.
Circa: 1974-1978

In 1975, Loretta Mears and two other Black women were turned away from CK's lesbian bar, after Lee, the bouncer, asked them for five IDs. While they were standing at the door, several White women entered the bar without a five ID check. On March 10, the Illinois Liquor Control Commission issued a citation charging CK's with "inconsistent ID checking standards." In April the citation was dismissed after Carol Kappa (CK) entered into an agreement with lesbian lawyer Rene Hanover who represented the complainants.

Trish Koch told the authors, "It was relatively tough. A lot of pool playing going on. They used to serve food in the back. It was rough. It was rough and tumble. It was almost like a biker bar, except it was all women. Everybody was pretty cool, but it was really a 'rules defined' kind of bar, you had your big dykes, and you had your femmes in there. Lots of butch women playing pool, and lots of femmes sitting at the bar drinking."

CK's
2417 N. Milwaukee Ave.
Circa: 1979-1980

This was the second incarnation of CK's.

Clark's On Clark
5001 N. Clark St.
Circa: 1988

Clark's on Clark was a popular neighborhood bar owned by Larry Balgro, Scott Van der Weele, and Scott Wurley. In 1991, the bartenders were George Tanuta, Joey T, and Sam Olin. In 1988, Tuesdays were leather night. After the bar was sold to new owners, it developed a reputation for drug dealing. On March 10, 1995, it was raided, and five people were arrested for possession of controlled substances. It closed down in 2007.

Clark Street Station
3216 N. Clark St.
Circa: 1977-1978

Owned by Esther and Jack Barnes, Bobby Kessler was the manager. The grand opening was on November 4, 1977. In December 1977, Lan Puesser in his "Barflying" column in *GayLife* wrote, "As you walk in the small, quiet, front bar, you're greeted by Esther. She's a doll and makes you feel at home, something a lot of owners couldn't be bothered with."

On Sundays, Esther cooked and served a hot buffet.

In January 1978, the owners decided to go for a straight clientele, but the gay patrons refused to stop going there, and the bar remained gay.

Cleo's
South Side
Circa: 1982

A lesbian bar.

Closet
3325 N. Broadway
Circa: 1974-present

JUMP BACK BOOGIE DOWN DISCO NIGHTS and one more round

The Closet is celebrating 1978 . . . because it was a good year. Drinks were cheaper and the music discoed.

So, stop in July 1 thru July 7th. Relive the past. If you'd rather not, we'll help you forget it.

3325 n. broadway chicago

The Closet

The Closet opened in May 1974 and was owned by "Andy." In the 1970s, when 4 a.m. licenses were rare, the Closet was famous as a "last chance" bar, and there would be lines out the door waiting to get in from 2-4 a.m. In August 1974, the *Chicago Gay Crusader* described the bar as a mixed bar, "There's almost an equal number of gay men and lesbians. It's nice to have a place where we can all get together sometimes." In 1976, *Gay Chicago Magazine* described the Closet as a "popular late-night north side lounge with a friendly, neighborly atmosphere. A place where both men and women are made to feel welcome."

Judy and Rose Pohl later bought the bar. Popular bartenders were Linda Leslie, Linda Rogers, and Trish worked the door. Later, Paté, from the Swan Club was a bartender as well.

Trish Koch told the authors, "The first place I went to was the Closet, and that was when Andy still owned it, and it was way back before Rose and Judy. It was the same kind of thing, but the windows were closed in, and it was a little hole in the wall, and it was always packed on Friday nights. There was no live

entertainment, just the jukebox ... and it was mostly men, a lot of guys in black jeans and leather jackets, but everybody was really friendly there."

In October 1975, the Closet held a pumpkin carving contest, a tradition that continues to this day.

Clouds
147th St.
Circa: 1950s

Bob Egan told the authors, "It was like a storefront, a strip mall type place. It was a block away from the state trooper's station. I can remember the only way you knew it was there was a little blue light in the window."

Club
706 State Line Ave., Calumet City
Circa: 1965-1966

Appears in the *Bob Damron Guide* in 1965-1966.

This was also home to Our Way II (Gallagher's), and Bells.

Club 50
5400 N. Sheridan Rd.
Circa: 1940s-1960s

Female impersonator, Lynzi Kay, told the authors, "Club 50 was a big club that was built in the 1940s. Danny Kaye played there, Mae West ... a lot of big names. At night when the lights were low, it looked lovely, like the Aragon, but if you turned up the lights it needed to be cleaned and burned immediately. There was an inch of dust on the balcony. When I worked there, I worked with the John Conrad Trio and John's still around, playing at some piano bar at some restaurant."

Kay also performed at the Orange Cockatoo and much later was a coat-check person at Touché.

Club 77
7740 S. Stoney Island Blvd.
Circa: 1980

In September 1980, Bertha Butt performed at Club 77 in a show put on by Mr. Aretha Franklin.

This was also the location of Burning Spear and High Chaparrel.

Club 950 (Lucky Number)
950 W. Wrightwood Ave.
Circa: 1980-2000

A gritty, distinctly urban feel, with a dance floor, lounge area, and a room with pool tables. The music included: new wave, ska, rockabilly, punk, gothic, industrial, reggae, underground, rave, trance, techno, progressive, electronic, pop, and, of course, alternative. Paté was a popular bartender. She told the authors, "Club 950 Lucky Number was one of the oldest and longest-running punk venues in Chicago. In the early days of the Chicago scene, 950 had a lot of shows but tapered away from that as the 1980s went on. Later on, they were well known for their Thursday '80s night."

Club 2506
2506 N. Clybourn Ave.
Circa: 2008–2010

Club 2828
2828 N. Broadway
Circa: 1990

A calendar listing in the gay press in February 1990, read, "Every Thursday Memory Lane hosts an open mic at Club 2828."

Club 7301
7301 W. Roosevelt Rd., Forest Park
Circa: 1998–2001

Wayne Giese opened Club 7301 in October 1998. There was a large bar on the main floor and a second-floor dance area with another bar. In March 1999, the bar held a cabaret night with Rudy de la Mor. David Hamilton also performed there.

In October 1999, there was a Battle of the DJs contest with DJs Corky, Duane, Blake, Aaron B, Brian, Queenie, Spane-E, Ken-e, and Bert-Bert.

This was also the location of Hideaway II and, for a short time, Ultimate Oz, before reverting back to Hideaway II.

Club Bolero
8710 Golf Rd., Des Plaines
Circa: 1986–1988

Charlie's Angels was also at this location.

Club DeLisa
5522 S. State St.
Circa: 1933–1958

Club DeLisa was a Black nightclub and music venue. It was owned by the four DeLisa brothers, Louis, John, Jimmy, and Mike.

Jim Wickliff told the authors, "That was a very famous Black and tan, and it was mainly straight, but an awful lot of dykes

and faggots went there. You could make out there too, I heard. It was probably the most popular club in Chicago for Blacks at that time. That was in the '50s. I got there after the golden era was gone and apparently during the war and just afterwards it was really going, and a lot of Whites went down there. They had name Black people entertaining then and floor shows. I understand the Club DeLiza had a long bar, besides the tables. A lot of White guys went there because it was safe to meet Black guys. And Black guys would go there to meet White guys. It was all very discreet. It wasn't real open, but I'm surprised it didn't raise more eyebrows."

Club Escape
1530 E. 75th St.
Circa: 1997–present

In November 1998, Club Escape hosted the South Side Coalition Task Force on AIDS Prevention "Celebrating Our Community." The honorees include *Blacklines* magazine. Popular DJs were Tyrone Mixx and Sherron.

Club Evergreen
1322 N. Clybourn Ave.
Circa: 1952–1960

Description from St Sukie de la Croix's book, *Chicago Whispers*, "Another lesbian bar was Club Evergreen ... a Black jazz club with female exotic dancers. The proprietor of the club was Corwin "Pokie Dott" Marbly with Minnie Drewitt as manager. In August 1952, entertainment at Club Evergreen included blues singer Lil "Upstairs" Mason, the Jack Cooley Band, and the exotic dancer Eleanor King. Other dancers were Big "House Rockin'" Bertha, Modernistic Shake Dancer Verda Gibson, Little "Miss Korea," Laverne Satis, and Sheila Collazo. From October through December 1952, Buster "Leap Frog" Bennett played the club, his bass player was William Lee, father of filmmaker Spike Lee. In March 1953, Club Evergreen held its first "Parade of the Lilies Bathing Beauty Contest." The winner was crowned "Miss Evergreen of 1953." The club stayed open until the end of 1960, and one of the last shows was a Jazz Jamboree starring King Kolax and Danny Overbea with Foxie the stripper and Allen Young the ventriloquist."

Club Fantasy
2520 N. Lincoln Ave.
Circa: 1978

Club Flamingo
440 N. Halsted St.
Circa: 1988

Thursday and Saturday were gay nights at Club Flamingo.

This was also the location of Rialto, Red No 5, Jokes on U, Clubhouse, and the second incarnation of Redoubt.

Club Foot
1824 W. Augusta Blvd.
Circa: 1995-2014

A neighborhood "old man bar" that became a popular dive bar in Wicker Park until rising rents forced its closure.

Clubhouse
3127 N. Clark St.
Circa: 1989-1990

Clubhouse opened on December 21, 1989. The club was owned by Samuel F. Davis, who also owned Pangea and Deeks. Clubhouse tried to recreate the essence of the popular Warehouse – birthplace of house music – in the gay Lakeview neighborhood. After less than two years, it moved down to the warehouse district and a larger space.

This was also the location of Thumbs Up and Windy City Bar & Grill.

Clubhouse
440 N. Halsted St.
Circa: 1990-1994

Marcello Castro was the manager. Clubhouse featured DJs Freddie Bain, Yolanda, Frankie Knuckles, and Ron Trent, and brought in such performers as Jennifer Holliday, the Outhere Brothers and Martha Wash.

In October 1991, Thomas Productions presented the first Miss Ebony Illinois contest, hosted by Taisha Thomas.

This was also the location of Redoubt, Rialto, Red No 5, Jokes on U, and Club Flamingo.

Clubhouse at Convent
1529 W. Armitage Ave.
Circa: 1998

Mixed gay/straight crowd. In July 1998, there was a drag contest with DJs Mike Ezebukwu and Ron Carroll.

This was also the location of Communion.

Clubhouse Players
13126 S. Western Ave., Blue Island.
Circa: 1990-1998

In June 1992, Clubhouse Players hosted a benefit for the MCC South Suburban Fellowship Church. Those performing in the drag extravaganza were Cha Cha, Patty Pauper, China Doll, Chandelier, Leslie Gay, and Tracy Trash.

This space was also home to the 131 Club, Club Krave, and the Edge.

Club Illusions
1620 Plainfield Rd., Joliet
Circa: 1983-1987

In 1983, Club Illusions co-owner was "Dwayne," while John Zielinski bartended, and the DJ was Roger Wolfe.

This was also the site of the A-Frame and Continental Club West.

Club Inta
308 W. Erie St.
Circa: 1998

An ad in a gay publication touted, "the women's place to meet and greet – cuz girls just wanna have fun!! Music by Chicago's hottest DJs, a lavish buffet, private rooms available for rent, drink specials, and valet parking."

This was also the location of Buzz and Cuvee.

Club Krave
13126 S. Western Ave., Blue Island
Circa: 2007-present

Club Krave is the South Side's LGBT center. It features monthly drag shows, male strippers, weekend entertainment, and hosts numerous community benefits and fundraisers. It also features gambling machines.

In December 2012, Club Krave's 5th Anniversary show featured Lindsey Devereaux, Serina DeVine, Lindsay Bryant, Theresa Dawn, Brandi Wyne, Katie Gaga, Butter Scotch, Crystal, and Jay Franze. In August 2011, Club Krave hosted a male impersonation show with $12 oversized mixed drink pitchers, $4 Long Island (and Blue Island) iced teas.

This was also the location of Edge, Clubhouse Players, and the 131 Club.

Clubland
3145 N. Sheffield Ave. (in the Vic Theater)
Circa: 1986-1989

Steve Jarvis and Thad Gentry opened Clubland, a video club when the new trend for music videos was played over large monitors. The space often hosted theatrical productions and concerts (Karen Mason) earlier in the evening, then would reopen as the dance club. However, a production of *Hair* had many of the theater's patrons staying for the club night and it changed the atmosphere of the club. It closed shortly after the play's run. The theater was eventually bought by Jam Productions, which uses it as a live music venue.

In December 1987, Chicago Molly (born Larry Berlandi) was an MC at a benefit for Strike Against AIDS.

Club La Ray
3150 N. Halsted St.
Circa: 1986–1989

Club LaRay was frequented mostly by Black gay men. One patron describes the club, "The place was absolutely huge. You would walk in, and there was a huge dance floor off to the right corner, a big circular bar, and then level after level walking back off different rooms. There was a room off to the left when you first walked in, little tables and stuff, and if you went back a little farther, there was a pool table room, but I don't remember anyone ever playing pool. You walked back even farther, and I think there was another bar back there. There were a lot of dark corners where people had sex."

Frankie and Ronny after partying at Club LaRay

The bar's manager was Quintin Kelly.

The bar, owned by Ray Doyle and Ray Hill, faced a lot of police harassment. In March 1988, the club was raided, and four men were arrested on drug charges after five packets of cocaine were found in the bar's office. In August 1989, more than 100 people – mostly White – protested the club's closing. Demonstrators accused city officials and 44th Ward Alderman Bernard Hansen of racism.

This was also the location of Trianon.

Club Lower Links
954 W. Newport Ave.
Circa: 1990–1992

On May 30, 1990, Lucy and Ricky's Traveling Review column in *Nightlines*, describes Club Lower Links, in the basement of the Links Building, "Dark walls with deep red curtains draped around the ceiling border, and red material covers the lamps that sit on tables waiting for Dangerous Pleasures. Performances of *All My Partners: A Safe Sex Opera* by the Women's Caucus of ACT UP; *Girls, Girls, Girls* by Catherine Evans and Paula Killen, and *4 Or 5 Or 6 Times*, a performance by Marcia Wilkie."

Gurlene and Gurlette, gender-bending performers, made numerous appearances at the club.

Also at this location were Crawlspace and Houndstooth.

Club Midnight Blue
301 E. North Water St.
Circa: 2002

In October 2002, Club Midnight Blue hosted Howard Brown's Health Center's annual gala with MC Bruce Vilanch and entertainment by Donna Blakely, Linda Clifford, Gina Coconato, Lynn Jordan, Suzanne Palmer, Madam X, Honey West, the Gay Men's Chorus, and Jeff Thomas Band.

Club Reunion
811 W. Lake St.
Circa: 2008

In September 2004, Club Reunion hosted Chicago's only lesbian comedy act, Hysterical Women, and in January 2003, Windy City Black Pride.

This was also the location of Rooster Blues.

Club Sappho
5153 N. Broadway
Circa: 1996

Described in the gay press as "a new ladies bar with dancers and two dance floors. Open 4 nights a week, salsa, and old-school house from the Pitch Control."

Club Victoria
3153 N. Broadway
Circa: 1983–1986

Club Victoria, owned by Jennifer Hammersmith, held its grand opening on March 26-28, 1983, with a champagne buffet and music by DJ Mickey. It was a drag show bar, with Brian Winston as the headliner. It is best known for the debut of drag performer Shanté, who later transitioned and went on to international stardom as actress Alexandra Billings, appearing on television series, films, and playing Madame Morrible in *Wicked* on Broadway. The club also occasionally hosted theater companies' shows.

This was formerly the location of Crystal's Blinkers, and the Other Side.

Club Voyage
738 W. Randolph St.
Circa: 1998

Featuring DJs Lego, Dave Britton, and Earl Pleasure. Hosts Mike D and Jayson Versace.

This was also the location of the Warehouse.

Club Yo-Yo
3909 N. Ashland Ave.
Circa: 1971-1975

An ad in the gay press at the time read, "Where Gentlemen Meet."

Club X
77 S. Stolp St., Aurora
Circa: 1991-1992

In 1991, Eric Schardt and Randy Skeens owned Club X. Sandy Davis was listed as the club's owner in 1992. Holiday parties and theme nights such as "Dance Your Ass Off" with Chris Pappas, "Miss Thang contest," and "Wild & Wooly Western Night" were popular. In July 1991, staff caused trouble when they visited other suburban bars and handed out flyers trying to lure people away to Club X.

In July 1991, Friday nights were '50s rock 'n' roll nights. Customers were encouraged to wear "a white t-shirt and jeans, a poodle skirt, and a scarf around the neck – dress in '50s outfit and get in free."

Cocktail
3359 N. Halsted St.
Circa: 1996-2012

In March 1996, Cocktail was opened by Geno Zahakaris, Chris Bukrey, Elizabeth Walker, and David Breckinridge. It was a small sidewalk bar with large windows facing onto Halsted St. An early ad in the gay press quoted Noel Coward, "For gin, in cruel, sober truth, supplies the fuel, for flaming youth."

In May 2010, Cocktail hosted the Grabby's, in a meet & greet with Chi Chi La Rue and porn stars, such as Craig Reynolds, Kyle King, Steven Daigle, Diesel Washington, Cameron

Teri Yaki at Cocktail

Cocktail bartender, Robert

Marshall, Scott Tanner, Paul Wagner, Chad Manning, Ryan Raz, Wolf Hudson, Ricky Sinz, Jason Sparks, Lucky Daniels, and Rob Romani.

Many drag queens performed at Cocktail, such as Monique Green, Vanity Fair, Teri Yaki, Paula Sinclaire, Miss Foozie, and Lady Ashley.

Cocktail was notable for hosting a community discussion with Barack Obama in 2003, when he was running for senator. In 2009, they served brunch on Sundays. It was closed for a short time in 2012 for non-payment of taxes, then reopened for a short time before closing permanently.

This was also the location of Men's Room, Loading Zone, and Progress.

Cocktails & Dreams
674 W. Diversey Pkwy.
Circa: 1991

This was also the location of Dickies, Cesar's, and Piggen's Pub.

Something New Up North? You Bet!

Cocktails At **Coconuts**
Daily 4:00 to 8:00 p.m.
FEATURING:
Reduced Drink Rates
($1.00 Most Drinks)
Hors D'oervres/
and
Bambi As Your Bartender
Join Us For Cocktails & Snacks
or
Stay For Dinner & Dancing
(Dining Room Opens At 6:00 p.m.)
5320 N. Sheridan   275-2222

Coconuts
5320 N. Sheridan Rd.
Circa: late 1979–1983

A restaurant with a dance floor that converted to a gay club at night. It was run by Weil Enterprises (The owners of Coconuts were Steve Weil, Al Freeman, and Eddie Dugan) with Michael Anderson (former doorman at Bistro) as the manager when the club opened. Later on, Rick McDonough was the manager along with Diane Carey, and Michael O'Callahan.

The primary DJ was Frank Lipomi. The Bearded Lady performed there.

Go-go boys danced on cubes that lined the dance floor. Patrons often got up and danced on the cubes as well. James, one of the club's dancers, told the authors, "That got pretty wild...I came out wearing only a raw sirloin steak and I stitched it up with the turkey stitcher on the side with the string. I had a lot of fun trying to keep it up. There was a photographer there from the Art Institute and he did a series on it, where I'm flying through the air wearing only meat."

The Club closed when the building was sold to a real estate developer, a high-rise apartment building occupies the space now.

Coconuts
5246 N. Broadway
Circa: 1980s–1990s

Opened by Weil Enterprises after the original Coconuts closed. Armando was one of the DJs and Frankie Knuckles made guest appearances.

This was previously the location of Normandy.

Columns
1347 S. Michigan Ave.
Circa: 1981

Private membership club with music by Kenny Newber every Saturday at midnight.

Communion
1529 W. Armitage Ave.
Circa: 1998

This was also the location of Clubhouse at Convent.

Company
2683 N. Halsted St.
Circa: 1983–1994

Christmas is coming, and so is
COMPANY
Ron 'POLISH PRINCESS' Helizon your host
2683 N. HALSTED STREET 348-9800

Neighborhood tavern with a devoted following. The bar was owned by Ron "The Polish Princess" Helizon and his lover, Gordon Burrows. It sported posters from Broadway shows and occasionally hosted productions by theater companies, including the premiere of *One* by Jeff Hagedorn on Sunday, August 14, 1983, the first play about AIDS ever produced. Carl Forsberg - who played the hero - walked out onto the small stage and said, "I have acquired a disease that means I am going to die. This does not make me exceptional or special ... just a fact."

Company was first and foremost a saloon, with Mardi Gras, St. Patrick's Day, and Halloween parties. It also hosted benefits for local charities. In the late '80s, they hosted meetings of the Girth & Mirth group for large men and their admirers. The bar gained a reputation as a "chubby chaser" bar.

Helizon told the authors, "Pepe, who owned the building, did not want another gay bar there. He had gotten burned by

Harlequin's and by El Dorado, and he said he didn't want to rent it to any more gay people. I guess back taxes and stuff like that. But we were dressed up in suits, we were business people, we showed him our portfolio, we showed him the money we had, and we told him we were going to renovate the whole place, which we did. We gutted and renovated the whole first floor. ... That was about the time that Christopher Street opened, and it always hurts me to say this, but I wasn't accepted by that crowd. They looked down on me because of the people I had in my bar. The old Dandy's was across the street, and a lot of those people would come in and snick~~ at my people. ... We started getting the Girth and Mirth crowd in there, and people would come up to me and say, 'Why do you allow these people in here?'

Ron Helizon, the "Polish Princess," bartender at Bobby Love's and the former owner of the bar, Company, with Tillie, the Dirty Old Lady

"We closed because the business was going North. The landlord became greedy, he raised the rent, that whole area is now Yuppie-ville. Everyone loved the bar, but the bottom line is that you have to make money, and if you don't have a lot of street traffic coming in, then you don't make any money."

This was also the location of Harlequin's and El Dorado.

Compound
808 W. Waveland Ave.
Circa: 1992

The grand opening was on June 26, 1992. The ad reads, "Join us in leather pride."

Condo Club
1931 N. Milwaukee Ave.
Circa: 1998–1999

This Latin gay men's bar specialized in salsa, merengue, pop rock Espanol, and cumbia. At the bar's 1st annual Drag-A-Thon, the stars included Puerto Rican diva Alex Soto and stripper El Pirata de la Salsa. There was also a "girl's night" for lesbians.

Continental Club East
118 E. Jefferson St., Joliet
Circa: 1977–1981

This is currently the location of Maneuvers.

Continental Club West
1620 Plainfield Rd., Joliet
Circa: 1981

This was also the location of A-Frame and Club Illusions.

Cookie & Shirley's
22nd St. and Washtenaw Ave.
Circa: 1970s

Nancy Reiff told the authors, "I went to Cookie and Shirley's all the time. It was owned by a woman by the name of Cookie. The bar was women-only. It was your typical neighborhood saloon, a corner bar type of atmosphere, with a very small area for dancing. It wasn't called a dance floor, it was just an empty little space, and there was a pool table in the back. You could dance together but if anyone came in you had to stop. Then Cookie and Shirley's became Jo-Jo's and that was also a women's bar."

Coq d'Or
Drake Hotel, Lake Shore Drive near Michigan Ave.
Circa: 1933-1970s

Coq d'Or was the second bar in Chicago to obtain a liquor license after prohibition. Like all large hotel bars in Chicago, this was a popular meeting place for gay men from the 1930s until the 1970s.

Cornelia's
750 W. Cornelia Ave.
Circa 1989-2005

Although primarily a restaurant, near the end of its run, Cornelia's marketed itself as a supper club with a variety of cabaret performers, such as Jeff Roscoe, Ginger Tam, Kathryn Payne, Paul Marinaro, Justin Hayford, and Buddy Charles.

This was also the location of Taverna 750.

Corrado's Club
440 N. Orleans St.
Circa: 1971

Cotton Club
1710 S. Michigan Ave.
Circa: 1998-2005

Gay nights at the Cotton Club were Tuesdays and Sundays. Among the events it hosted were a "Gay Pride Steppin' Contest and Jam" with judges CC Carter, Kinyatta Buford, live jazz performances, and a BBQ buffet. In 2005, an ad in a gay newspaper read, "No caps, gym shoes, jerseys."

Crawlspace
954 W. Newport Ave.
Circa: 1994

A non-alcohol club featuring punk and new wave bands on Thursday, Fridays, and Saturday nights.

Club Lower Links and Houndstooth were also at this location.

Crazee Babee Lounge
1240 E. 47th St.
Circa: 1960s

A Black club where gay celebrity Wilbur "Hi-Fi" White performed.

Crew
4804 N. Broadway
Circa: 2004-2017

Steven Milford and Brian Wells were the owners/managers of the bar/restaurant that opened July 19, 2004, in a building left from Chicago's "Roaring '20s." It was a sports bar hangout on weekends and during the day. At night they played contemporary and alternative music with DJ John Gorske. Other diverse events included in October 2012, a *Rocky Horror Picture Show* sing-along, a regular Hot Jock contest hosted by Sofia Saffire, and a pub quiz night with Sister Mary Monistat.

Marc Felion told the authors, "I was taken into the basement of Crew to see the old giant urinals that served a park that was once nearby. I think an adult film was made down there too. It must have been a fun place to cruise at one time."

In 2017, it was announced that the bar would be moving to a new location, as soon as one could be found. The bar closed just four days shy of its 13th anniversary.

Crimson Closet
3136 N. Narragansett Ave.
Circa: 1980

The Crimson Closet opened as a "private membership club" in September 1980 to great fanfare in the gay press, with an ad that read, "Enjoy cocktails and exotic drinks while relaxing in a romantic atmosphere. Walnut tables and upholstered crimson armchairs line the balcony and add to the dimly lit intimacy of the room. Membership is $25 a year." A later ad offered a special introductory membership of $2. The Polish Princess wrote in his column: "Popular bartender Paul (Flo) Dobson, of Blinkers and Charlie's Angels, is now serving your favorite beverage Fridays and Saturdays at the Crimson Closet." The owner was Russ Moryl. Fred Marr was a bartender.

By the following month, there were no more ads and the club closed.

Crobar/GLEE Club
1543 N. Kingsbury St.
Circa: 1994–2010

Mary Jane Suarez, Tony Lopez, Roderick Nollovca, and Miguel Pepsin party at GLEE Club. *Photo by Terry Gaskins*

GLEE Club was gay night at Crobar. The original owners were Kenny Smith and Cal Fortis. Frankie Knuckles was a DJ when the bar first opened. Other DJs included Earl Pleasure, Freddie Bain, Jim Belanger, Tom E and Teri Bristol.

Performers included Taylor Dayne, Bronski Beat, Suzanne Palmer, Pussy Tourette, and Judy Tenuta.

In November 1996, Crobar hosted "Night of a Thousand Chakas," an evening of performance hosted by Joan Jett Blakk with Charlene Unger and the Ungertones, Osaka Hernandez, Gurlene Hussey, a Real Read Ensemble, Fausto "Chaka King Khan" Fernos, Shannon Suddoth, Avery Young, Somillia Smith, and a host of Funky DIVAS.

In November 1996, a gay newspaper reported that, "Crobar is trying to make Sunday nights (GLEE) more gay after one of the GLEE club managers was called faggot for bumping into a straight man. They now say you have to prove you're gay at the door."

In February 1994, it was rumored that Daisy Mae was suspended from the ceiling at Crobar.

In January 1999, Circuit Mom, Joseph Lopresti, and Paolo presented Dream Tea, a celebration of those that have dreams.

Byrd Bardot guarded the door.

Crocodile Lounge
221 W. Van Buren St.
Circa: 2005

I-Candy hosted "Twist," a gay and lesbian party.

Crosscurrents
3206 N Wilton Ave.
Circa: 1980–1987

The make-up of the audience for this bar/theater complex often reflected whatever show was playing, either theatrical productions or concerts. Originally owned by Thom Goodman. Near the end of its run, the business had become a not-for-profit arts company.

Crystal's Blinkers
3153 N. Broadway
Circa: 1977–1980

Fronted by Robbie Crystal, the four-level bar began with an entry-level, then split into a lower-level lounge, upper-level disco, with beveled mirror walls and an underlit dance floor. A side stairwell led to a rooftop deck – the Sunstar Plastic Palace – with a small interior lounge area.

In addition to being a dance club, it also held community events – the Gay Atheist League and Illinois Gay Rights Task Force met there – and exhibited local artists such as Pat Haney and Michael Frank.

This bar was purchased by Elly Cook and Robbie Crystal in July of 1977, on the edge of what is now known as Boystown. Crystal lived in a loft upstairs. Earl Reid, who was an alternate for Lou DiVito at Dugan's Bistro, became the club's first DJ in July 1977, spinning Monday through Thursday.

It's time to partee, says Robie Crystal who's always in a party mood whether behind the bar at Blinkers, at the door, or just mingling with the party-goers there.

Crystal's Blinkers was a sight to see, with a huge, angled, rectangle of mirrors across the front façade. Inside, the dancefloor lit up like the one in *Saturday Night Fever*. In the summer, patrons looked out over Broadway from a rooftop bar and sun deck. "We could hang out, and we'd hang off the edge," Danny Goss recalls. It was eventually revealed that Chicago serial killer John Wayne Gacy picked up a young victim outside the club in October 1977.

One patron told the authors, "I moved to Chicago in 1978, and there was really very few gay establishments on Halsted, they

tended to be on Broadway. There was Broadway Limited, Crystal's Blinkers, Eddie Dugan opened Paradise after the Bistro closed. Crystal's Blinkers catered to the younger crowd, it had a dancefloor that was raised a little, and it was made out of Plexiglass or some kind of hard substance that you could dance on, and the lights were underneath the floors, hence the blinkers ... the lights were flashing and the strobe lights. They played disco music of the late '70s and early '80s."

This was also the location of Club Victoria and Other Side.

Cullen's Green Parrot
3478 N. Broadway
Circa: 1940s

Cullen's was Kitty Sheon's first bar. It may or may not have been gay. Her subsequent bars all were.

Cuvee
308 W. Erie St.
Circa: 2010-2121

Primarily a Black bar. There were claims of homophobia made against the staff, and there were multiple shootings in the parking lot. It had its liquor license revoked.

This was also the location of Buzz and Club Inta.

Cyrano's Tavern
8 E. Division St.
Circa: 1951

On July 8, 1951, the *Chicago Sun-Times* noted that this Near North area was a "cesspool of wickedness." This "cesspool" included a neighborhood of gay bars around N. Dearborn and W. Division Sts., or "Queerborn and Perversion" as it was known. On December 31, 1951, police raided Cyrano's Tavern, "a reputed hangout for homosexuals." Fifty-eight were arrested and charged with being inmates of a disorderly house, and the owner, Howard Blencoe, and two bartenders, with serving liquor to intoxicated persons.

D

Dago Rose's Hideaway (see 905)

Dairy
1936 W. Augusta Blvd.
Circa: 1983

This gay/straight bar/supper club featured entertainment such as Stardust, a female vocal trio specializing in music from the 1930s, '40s, and '50s. Stardust also performed at the Factory, Christy's on Clark, Kitty Sheons, Trianon, Dandy's, and at the grand opening of Stars.

Daisy Patch
Broadway near Granville Ave.
Circa: 1969

This was a teen drop-in center during the week, but on Friday and Saturday nights, it featured rock bands and became predominantly gay. It was owned and operated by Marsha Smulevitz Emanuel, whose son Rahm later became mayor of Chicago.

Dancers
5244 N. Sheridan Rd.
Circa: 1980-1985

Dancers was advertised as, "Edgewater's Bar for Men to Meet Men." One patron told the authors, "It was a piano bar, and there was a long narrow bar, and you walked in and there was a bar at the front that curved around. At one point, there was a piano player in there doing sing-along stuff. Again, that was one that either wasn't there very long, or I discovered it just before it closed."

It later tried to reinvent itself with male dancers and showing music videos. Carmen Rodriguez was a bartender there.

This was also the location of Mr. T's.

Dandy's
2632 N. Halsted St.
Circa: 1981-1988

Dandy's, "a gentlemen's piano bar," opened in June 1981. Alan Putz was a bartender. This upscale bar was co-owned by Bobby Schroeder, Rudy Cistaro, and Henry Clarke. Tony Simes was a regular performer there – Simes played piano at Kitty Sheons in the 1950s. Among the other performers at Dandy's were Mary Lynn Morrison and Bill Muzzillo, Stardust doing 1940s tunes, and opera with Cecelia Razo, Elizabeth Hale, William Diana, and Stan Clark, and a special appearance by comic actress and singer Martha Raye.

In July 1982, Dandy's held a Hot Daddies Mr. Dandy's Senior Contest. Winners were George Myers, then 1st runner-up Jim Miler, and 2nd runner-up Don Jefferson.

However, Dandy's was best known as a sing-along piano bar and one of the first bars in Chicago to host karaoke.

Dandy's
3729 N. Halsted St.
Circa: 1992-1999

Dandy's second location opened November 1992 by Rudy Cistaro, and Henry Clarke, of the original Dandy's, and was a

Ken Eckstrom was crowned Mr. Dandy's last week. With him, from left, are Henry Clarke; Richard Zarnicki, second place; Rudy Cistaro, and Craig Clauston, third place. Clarke and Cistaro are co-owners of Dandy's.
Photo by Sherman Heinrich

similar piano bar format. David Hamilton, Michael Scott Brooks, and Honey West were among the performers.

In June 1996. Dandy's new owner was Wayne Dekens.

Also at this location were Big Red's, Bobby Love's, In Between, Norma's, and Augie's.

Danny's Tavern
1931 W. Dickens St.
Circa: 2008–2020

A straight, but LGBT-friendly, neighborhood bar popular with millennials.

Dan's on Clark
6341 N. Clark St.
Circa 1981–1984

This cruisy men's bar was advertised with the slogan, "If the crowd isn't becoming to you, you should be coming to us." In October 1983, the bar hosted a Prairie State Democratic Club, in conjunction with America for Mondale-Ferraro, fundraiser to help defeat Reagan. A $10 donation was collected at the door.

This was also the location of Badlands, Parlour, and Pelican

Darché's
3726 N. Broadway
Circa: 1979

Darché's opened in February 1979 and closed in June 1979. The bar was owned by Lance Darché and Paul Domico. One gay newspaper described the bar as being, "a comfortable 'good old days' atmosphere. A dance floor in the middle of the room, and everyone sat around the fringes at tables with funky dim candles and real tablecloths."

Steve Richardson was a waiter. Jeff O'Hern worked behind the bar.

Other bars at this location include Augie & CK's and Charlie's Chicago.

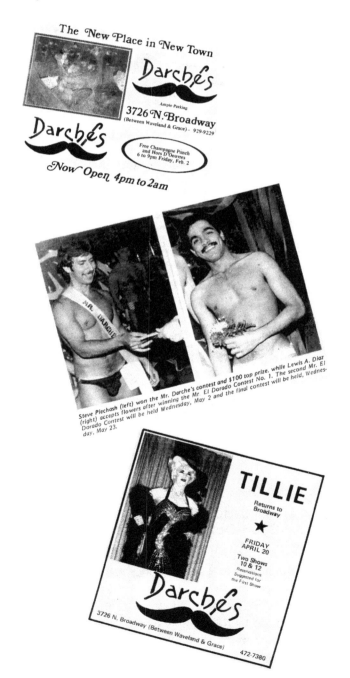

Davenport's Piano Bar & Cabaret
1383 N. Milwaukee Ave.
Circa: 1999-present

Originally fronted by Bill Davenport, Sue Berry, and Donna Kirchman, the bar is now solely owned by the women. It has a piano bar in the front and a cabaret room in the back which

books local and nationally recognized talent such as Broadway and NYC cabaret star, Karen Mason, Alma Mendoza, Tommy Femia as Judy Garland, Ruth Bonnet, and Stephen Rader singing the songs of Dolly Parton. In March 1999, Davenport's hosted a benefit for Season of Concern and Broadway Cares/ Equity Fights AIDS with the cast of *Ragtime*. The clientele is mixed, LGBT and straight, men and women.

David's Place
5332 N. Sheridan Rd.
Circa: 1972-1975

David's Place opened on November 10, 1972 and was described in *Michael's Thing* as "a cocktail lounge and restaurant extraordinaire. Chicago's most unique entertainment." It was laid out like a nightclub, rather than a bar. There were two rooms: one was a showroom with a proscenium arch stage. The owners were John Gast, James Earl Botrager, and Marvin Cyron. David's Place was a drag bar and featured female impersonators such as Artesia Welles, Ebony Carr, and Wanda Lust. One patron told the authors, "There

was a drag queen who went by the name of Jackie Knight. She was stunning. She was beautiful. Jackie ... she had the change, the operation, and she hooked up with some young gangster who looked like something out of a 1940s B movie. She would come in there swathed in furs and jewels and everything else, and as time passed ... here she was, a full female now. She's with this guy and everything on the surface seems rather glamorous. Well, the next I heard about her, she was a lesbian. She was gorgeous. But that was David's on Sheridan Road."

On January 24, 1973, David's Place offered a space as a coffeehouse for the Loyola University Campus gay group.

Michael Bergeron, writing a piece called, "*Reader's* Guide to the Gay Scene" described the bar, "... seems to have invested more in lights and equipment than Mr. Kelly's. The dazzling drags and handsome male entertainers often boggle the minds of straight observers. A common exclamation is, 'I can't believe that's a guy!'"

Debonair Social Club
1575 N. Milwaukee Ave.
Circa: 2007-2020

A mixed straight/gay/hipster club.

Deeks
Entrance on 3401 N. Sheffield Ave.
Circa: 1991-1994

Deeks was owned by Samuel F. Davis and Paul Deeter. Davis founded and co-owned Clubhouse and Pangea. Deeks had its

grand opening on November 15, 1991. Bartenders that night were Phil Aronian, Chuck Klinger, Paul Malkowski.

Deeks was a leather dance bar, where designer clothing and cologne were banned – they sniffed you at the door. Some of the events were a full moon party, a "Mommie Dearest" dance party, an erotic banana-eating contest, and the Rodeo Riders' "Rodeo XVII." The bar also hosted fundraisers for the Reimer Foundation, a charity run by Del Barrett that handed out free condoms in bars.

In December 1994, the police closed Deeks for sexual activity taking place in the bar. It reopened in March 1995 as a private club.

This was also the location of El Palacio and Normandy.

Déjà Vu
2559 N. Southport Ave.
Circa: 1980

The grand opening of the lesbian bar, Déjà Vu, took place in March 1980. The bar was advertised in a gay newspaper as, "The newest gathering place for women." They offered, "A relaxed friendly atmosphere. With a new dance floor and lighting. The latest records, and golden oldies, too. A separate conversation area. The best in electronic games."

This was also the location of Petunia's.

Déjà Vu Lounge
3010 N. Mannheim Rd., Franklin Park
Circa: 1982-1983

The bar, owned by Salvador Barrutia, was in the Kings Plaza Hotel – it later became a Super 8. It featured male dancers and occasional drag performers, such as Tamara Lee.

Delores and Eddie's
3700 N. Broadway
Circa: 1986

Delores and Eddie's opened June 1986 as an "art bar" with a benefit exhibition for Chicago House, with works by Gabor, Marya Veeck, Tom Steward, Liz Krause Wolf, and other Chicago artists. In October 1986, Madam Pompadour, a lesbian drag queen, performed. They also had go-go girls.

Del Prado Hotel Bar
5307 N. Hyde Park Blvd.
Circa: 1972

Another hotel bar frequented by gay men.

Den
3200 N. Halsted St.
Circa: 2014-2016

After a short-lived attempt at making this a straight bar named Chloe's/Whiskey Trust, the second incarnation of Manhole was located in the basement of the Den.

This was previously the location of Foxy's, Spin, Eons, Manhole, and VII.

Den One
1355 N. Wells St.
Circa: 1974-1978

Den One advertised itself as "The Gay Disco of the Future" and as "100% gay-owned and operated." The owners were Fred Kramer and David Myers. The manager was Leo Baker.

"We partied at Den One. Oh wow! When we were doing the Bus Stop, it was a sight! To see that entire floor doing the Bus Stop. It was predominantly a men's bar, but they were friendly." Sheree Anne Slaughter told the authors.

Donna Rose remembered, "They would have a $6 or a $3 cover and they'd have an open bar from 8 'til 10, and honey, the children would be lining up, 'Give me six vodka gimlets.'"

Jim said, "The restaurant used to be out on the dance floor before it was a dance floor. There was an octagon bar, then under the DJ booth was a small bar. Shortly after they started being a dance bar, they closed the restaurant. It went from Our Den, to Den One, and the owners were definitely not straight."

This was also the location of Our Den and Carol's Speakeasy.

Deromas Riversedge
3548 River Rd., Franklin Park.
Circa: 1986–1991

Photo by Jack Sitar
Patrick DeRoma, owner of DeRoma's Grand Ritz, the city's newest bar, with Adrien.

Riversedge, at its opening July 23, 1986, was owned by Pat Belmonte (or Patrick DeRoma) and billed itself as a "cabaret and dance bar for men." By 1987, it rebranded itself as River Edge Cabaret, "a suburban meeting place for women." It held an annual prom for at least three years, with a buffet, dancing, and a crowning of a king and queen. The bar featured female strippers. It billed itself as "a gay suburban entertainment complex," featuring the Riversedge Revue starring female impersonators Lisa Eaton, Genice Grant, Erica, and Diana McKay. By March 1991, the new owners were Michael Caliendo and John Campise.

Devil's Den
168 Burton Pl.
Circa: 1973

Described in *Chicago Gay Crusader* as "a cozy little spot has become a welcome addition to Old Town's nightlife. Besides dancing, the Devil's Den offers dining. With delicious pizzas as the order of the day." There's also an ad that read, "GO GO BOYS! FOOD!

This was also the location of Burton Place.

Diamond Lil's
909 N. Rush St.
Circa: 1928

Diamond Lil's opened on October 15, 1928. The club offered "Real Southern Cooking" and same-sex dancing later in the evening. It was owned by Roy Spencer Bartlett, known as "Diamond Lil," after a Mae West play. On Saturday nights, by 2 a.m., the place was packed. It was the height of prohibition, so the liquor consumed was brought in by the patrons, and the management denied responsibility. The clientele were mostly gay men, but some women went there.

One visitor wrote, "The point this place has in common with the dance hall is that it is a place of meeting. Everyone turns to look at newcomers. Everyone stares quite boldly at everyone else, and if you want to talk to a person across the room or at the next table, you simply walk over and begin talking. Many of these men appear to wear cosmetics. A lot of them wear slave bracelets and other jewelry. Frequently they call each other by pet names. Lil wears a red tie with a huge imitation diamond stick pin. He makes no attempt to conceal what sort of a place it is. In fact, by the use of such a name, he advertises it."

Diane's
49th St. and Damen Ave.
Circa: Unknown

Dickies
674 W. Diversey Pkwy.
Circa: 1981-1982

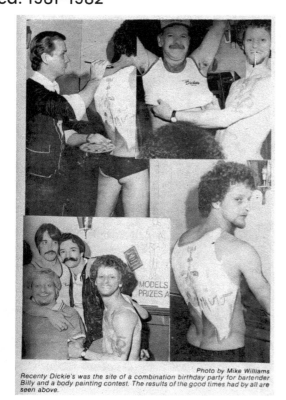

Photo by Mike Williams

Recenty Dickie's was the site of a combination birthday party for bartender Billy and a body painting contest. The results of the good times had by all are seen above.

Dickie's grand opening was on April 3, 1981, with Bob Farthing at the piano. In June 1981, the bar held a Mr. Dickie's contest. By January 1982, the bar was closed.

This was also the location of Piggen's Pub, Cocktails & Dreams, and Cesar's.

Dick's R U Crazee
48 154th Pl., Calumet City
Circa: 1992-2007

Different Strokes
4923 N. Clark St.
Circa: 1984-2002

The grand opening of Different Strokes was on June 8, 1984. It was a neighborhood bar with a beer garden, advertised as, "the perfect place for those without both oars in the water." It was owned by Robert E. Leahy who died from cancer on October 15, 1987. It was later owned by Dem Hopkins and "Gary." And finally, Larry Linton.

Bartenders included Feathers, Dakota, and Jeanetta Matters. Different Strokes played host to many community groups, including the Gay and Lesbian Town Meeting, which held its monthly planning sessions there.

Frankie Da Kat and Gina hosted a drag show featuring Da Chicago Kats Goils and go-go-boys. The Goils included Vera

Storm, Skye Chandeler, Rhodesia, Mina Howard, Darchavia, Michelle Fyre, Arianna de Costa, Gina Foxx, and Helen Blazes.

In September 1988, a makeshift Molotov cocktail was tossed into the beer garden. Customers chased two youths, capturing one and holding him until the police arrived – the second was arrested later at his home. They were upset with the bar because "the fags were taking all the parking spaces in the neighborhood."

In November 1994, the bar was raided and two people were arrested on drug-related charges.

This later became the location of SoFo Tap.

Are you thinking of a new place to relax, have fun, and meet new guys?

Think of...
different strokes

4923 North Clark Street
Chicago
312-989-1958

Open Sun - Fri - 12 Noon - 2am
(Saturdays until 3am)

(Top) Gina, (bottom) Frankie the Kat

Digger's Pub
2503 N. Clark St.
Circa: 1978-1983

Diggers was a piano bar and was owned by "a well-known mortician," according to one press report. The bar was open from 7 a.m. – 4 a.m. The host was Alexopoulos and Mike Lescher played piano.

Dil Pickle Club
10 Tooker Alley
Circa: 1917-1935

A speakeasy, cabaret, theater, and hangout for bohemian, progressive thinkers of the day. Tooker Alley was a tiny pathway between State and Dearborn Streets. The Dil Pickle was a rambunctious forum where hobos, poets, artists, rebellious academics, college kids, opera stars, scientists, prostitutes, psychoanalysts, revolutionaries, and con men debated, argued, performed plays, and lectured to a chorus of hecklers. The

speakers included suffragists, Druids, single-taxers, free-love advocates, speakers who claimed the Earth was flat, and one eloquent soapboxer delighted the crowds by waxing lyrical on the joys of oral sex. One popular subject was homosexuality, referred to as "third sex" or "sex variants."

In 1931, Magnus Hirschfeld, founder of the German Scientific Humanitarian Committee in 1897, the first gay rights organization in the world, lectured at the Dil Pickle.

Dingbats
247 E. Ontario St.
Circa: 1976-1983

Dingbats was primarily a dance club but hosted theatrical productions, such as Fred Silver's *In Gay Company*, starring Ben Rudolph, Raymond Ruggeri, Dennis Kinsella, and Thomas Kelly, produced by the Echo Theater Company.

In May 1977, Dingbats responded to rumors they were going straight with an ad in *GayLife* that read, "Is Dingbats gay? YES OR NO. Dingbats is for everyone."

Troy "Allen" Spitzer was assistant manager of Dingbats, a bartender/assistant manager at Carol's Speakeasy, and later bartended at North End. David Thedans was one of the DJs.

This was also the location of Tenement Square.

Dirty Dan's Saloon
2446 N. Lincoln Ave.
Circa: 1980

Dixon's
1600 W. 16th St., Oakbrook
Circa: 2003

Dixon's, a gay restaurant bar, celebrated its grand opening in August 2003. It was the first openly gay restaurant/bar in DuPage County.

It closed in 2004.

Doll House Cuna
1113 W. Belmont Ave.
Circa: 2013

Mixed gay/straight with a gay night.

Dolly's Place
4153 W 26th St.
Circa: 1960s

Also at this location were La Cueva and Stargazer.

Dome Room
10 S. Wabash St., Sherman Hotel
Circa: 1930s-1980

Affectionately known as the "Do Me" Room. Marlene told the authors, "I was working at the Dome in the late '60s. It was businessmen, better class. I played piano. Every hotel piano bar in the city of Chicago at that time was undercover gay. If you knew what you were looking for, you could find it, let's put it that way."

The Dome had two entrances, one from the street and another from the lobby. On each door stood a "house officer" to control the crowds and keep out the riff-raff. In the 1950s, it was famous for its female piano players: in 1951, it was Virginia Torcom, alternating nights with Barbara Sims, a retired college professor who taught music theory at the University of Indiana. The following year it was Patti Goodman and Avis Kent, and then in 1953, it was Peggy Gay and Jacqui O'Shea. In St Sukie de la Croix's book *Chicago Whispers,* O'Shea remembered the gay crowd, "I always say that at the Dome I wasn't a pianist, I was a social secretary. One would come in and

say, 'If Joe comes in, tell him to meet me at Kitty Sheon's but if Jim comes in, tell him you haven't seen me tonight.'

"The owners of the Dome knew the bar was gay, but O'Shea didn't, 'I remember when I started there, I thought, 'Oh my goodness, this is Utopia, maybe I'll get a husband.' And one of the girls said, 'Forget it kid, they're all gay.' And I said, 'Well, I don't understand what that means.' I was really stupid, you know.

"The guys used to give me jewelry for birthdays and Christmas, and then on Halloween, they would borrow it all back. All my evening bags went out on Halloween, but they always brought me pictures of themselves in drag, and it was wonderful.

"Homosexuals were not allowed to touch each other back then; some bars insisted customers keep their hands on top the bar at all times. House officers patrolled the Dome looking for indiscretions. 'I used to laugh,' said O'Shea, 'because the piano bar was set up so there was four inches between the piano and the bar and you could see through there, and you would see a little bit of hand-holding now and again, and I'd go, 'Uh uh uh. Watch it.'"

The Sherman Hotel was demolished in 1980.

Donaway's owner, Mark Donaway, is surrounded by beauties, Dane Chase and Honey West, during Easter Sunday brunch at the popular Halsted Street spot.   *photo by Terry Gaskins*

Donaway's
3255 N. Halsted St.
Circa: 1993-1994

This was a restaurant – an American Café – owned by Mark Donaway. Honey West presented her Banana Fanna Fro Frunch Brunch with a flashback to the 1960s.

Double RR Lounge
200 State St., Calumet City
Circa: 1987-1989

The Double RR Lounge opened in June 1987. The owner was Ron Johnson. The manager was Jeff Lowery. The bar had a beer garden bar and privacy fences. Rick Plantenga was DJ/VJ. The bar featured male dance troupes such as Men, Inc., Atlanta, Georgia's Burkhart Boys, and Rockets male dancers.

This was also the location of the Bank Vault, Ms. Behavin, and the Kismet Club.

The staff of the Double RR Lounge in Calumet City during the bar's grand opening.

Downtown Bar & Lounge
440 N. State St.
Circa: 2010-2015

This was a gay men's upscale three-room bar – two on the upper level, one in the basement – opened in November 2010 with $5 Ja¨ger and Jack shots.

Formerly the location of Gentry on State.

Dragon Room
809 W. Evergreen Ave.
Circa: 2003

The Dragon Room was a Black club. In June 2003, I-Candy Productions presented Unite in Pride Rodeo Style with go-go dancers and a wet t-shirt contest.

This was also the location of Tunnel Chicago.

Dreamerz
1516 N. Milwaukee Ave.
Circa: 1986-1993

This was a mixed gay/straight bar. Dreamerz' manager was Mary Joe Parks.

This was also the location of the Artful Dodger.

Drew's on Halsted
3201 N. Halsted St.
Circa: 1996-present

A restaurant/cabaret attracting a mixed gay/straight crowd.

Drink
702 W. Fulton St.
Circa: 2001

On February 18, 2001, Drink hosted Chicago's first lesbian circuit party, Chix Mix Productions' "Black Bra Party."

Druids
112 W. Hubbard St.
Circa: 1980

Druids opened August 1, 1980.

This was also the location of Oz Again, Ozone, Ranch, IC Station, and the White Elephant Bath Lounge.

DS Tequila Co.
3352 N. Halsted St.
Circa: 2010-present

DS Tequila is primarily a restaurant, but after dinner service, tables are cleared, and it becomes a bar. In March 2015, WCPT OutChicago radio stars, Scott Duff and Ellen Miller, brought their show live to DS Tequila Co. with special guests, all-American boy Steve Grand, Sami Grisafe, and comedian Peter Kim.

Dude Ranch
State St.
Circa: 1950s

Dugan's
2875 N. Clark
Circa: 1979-1980

Dugan's was located in the basement of an apartment building across the street from Shari's. It burned down in 1980.

Dunes
Division St. and State St.
Circa: 1953

Don told the authors, "Dunes was on the north side of Division, east of State Parkway. The building still stands, and there's a bar or restaurant there now. I'm guessing it got its name because when they all came back from the beach in the summertime, they'd all stop in there. Division Street beach was a very, very, very gay beach at the time. It was a small bar, and it was always packed."

E

Eagle's Nest
1138 W. Granville Ave.
Circa: 1987-1989

The bar's owner was Larry Janclura, the bartender was Brian Bells. It closed in May 1989.

Photo by Sherman Heinrich
From left, bartender Brian Bells, owner Larry Janclura and customer Dave Millhiser at the Eagle's Nest on W. Granville.

East End
53rd St. and Hyde Park Blvd.
Circa: 1972-1974

East of the Ryan
914 E. 79th St.
Circa: 2000

East of the Ryan was a predominantly Black bar with performances by female impersonators, Indigo Blue, Amailia Black, Tajhee Iman, and Tiara Russell.

Edge
13126 S. Western Ave., Blue Island
Circa: 1998-2007

Guys at the Edge

Having fun at the Edge (photo courtesy of Kirk Williamson)

The Edge opened in May 1998 with a blues band, a drag show, and a back porch cookout. The owners were Mike Dailey and Martin Dunn. This neighborhood bar attracted both lesbians and gay men. Drag shows featured Miss Ketty, Regina Upright, Tajma Hall, Tina Stefano, Eileen Dover, and Sassy Trade. The bar also had go-go boys. Sometimes the bar was referred to as the Edge, other times as Edge Island.

The same location housed Clubhouse Players, the 131 Club, and Club Krave.

Edge
3548 N. River Road, Franklin Park
Circa: 1991–1994

Edna & Regina's House of Fun
837 E.79th St.
Circa: 1977

Edna and Regina were mother and daughter who also had something to do with Foster's on the north side. Donna Rose told the authors, "One of the best bars for me on the South Side was a little hole in the wall called Edna and Regina's House of Fun on E. 79th St. It was a community bar, but except like Tuesday nights and maybe a Thursday night they were lesbian nights. The thing about it ... they didn't want us slow-dancing. Now we could disco all we wanted, but no slow dancing. ... But oh man, Edna and Regina's House of Fun, sometimes if the party got really good, they would just lock the door, so the outside patrons ... the neighborhood folks couldn't come in, because that would be too much. It would be jam-packed with women, they were so hungry to find someplace, and so on a Tuesday night you got maybe 250 women squeezed up in ... and in the summer, there was no air-conditioning, she would open that door. She would have to, because it would be stifling."

An ad in 1982 touted, "Blues and jazz + "After Hours Breakdown" every Tuesday where a BBQ and other dishes are served. Edna bartends."

Lola told the authors, "It had a long bar, and you would dance in the aisle. You couldn't touch each other. You could dance together, but you couldn't touch each other ... house rules."

Edye Room
6403 S. Martin Luther King Dr.
Circa: 1987–1989

This was also the location of Sculpture Room.

El Baron Rojo
4957 S. Ashland Ave.
Circa: 1984

A Latin club.

El Cabana
45th St. and Kedzie Ave.
Circa: 1966–1969

A Latin club.

El Dorado
2683 N. Halsted St.
Circa: 1976–1980

In 1976, the El Dorado reopened under new management. The grand opening was May 2. The bar was a Latin club owned by Guy Betton. The manager was Angelo Rios. The bar featured

go-go boys and held an annual Mr. El Dorado contest. In May 1977, Mario Garcia was Mr. El Dorado, and in 1979, it was Jose Cabero.

PR John (Juanita), a dancer at El Dorado, told the authors, "The bar was mostly Spanish people; they played a lot of salsa and merengue. There was a mix of people there, but late at night most of the drag queens came in. But in the daytime, it was just gay guys hanging around. That was around '77. When you were dancing, you couldn't show everything, I danced there for a couple of months and that was it. They didn't pay you much, just drinks and tips. I used to do it just for the kicks."

This was also the location of Harlequin's and Company.

El Gato Negro
1461 W. Irving Park Rd.
Circa: 1980s-2000s

El Gato Negro was a Latin bar with a drag show.

El Infierno
2756 N. Sacramento Ave.
Circa: 1984

A Latin bar.

Elixir Lounge
3452 N. Halsted St.
Circa: 2011-present

A tiny storefront where mixologists produce craft cocktails.

Elixir Andersonville
1509 W. Balmoral Ave.
Circa: 2015-present

The second location of the popular cocktail lounge is known for craft cocktails by mixologists. The Andersonville location is a bit larger and, thanks to its kitchen space, can offer a larger array of signature cocktails by mixologist Vlad Novikov.

El Mirador
4300 W. North Ave.
Circa: 1976

The grand opening of El Mirador was June 24, 1976. A listing in a gay newspaper reads, "Boogie-on-down at the new El Mirador. Las Vegas type Disco Bar and Lounge."

El Morro Lounge
4247 W. Armitage Ave.
Circa: 2012-2014

In October 2012, El Morro Lounge hosted a "Trans Benefit" with donations going to the Human Rights Campaign and the transgender community. Performing in the drag show were Nicole Starr, Monica Beverly Hill, Gia Gunn, and birthday girl Jade Sotomayor. The DJ was Ark Angel. The party featured male and female go-go dancers.

El Palacio
Entrance on 3400 N. Sheffield Ave.
Circa: 1982

The grand opening of this Latin bar was held in October 1982. When it first opened it was called the Palace, but the name was soon changed to El Palacio.

This location was later the Normandy, then Deeks.

Elsewhere
3170 N. Clark St.
Circa: 1979–1980

Formerly known as Jamie's Elsewhere, with an opening on August 16, 1979, it reopened on April 27, 1980, under new management and featured live rock bands. Opening weekend, Painter Band, a Chicago new wave group, performed.

El Tunnel
5553 W. Belmont Ave.
Circa: 1996

In December 1996, an ad in a gay newspaper, read, "El Tunnel … proudly invites you to their 1st Posada X-Mas Latino Party."

Emerald City
26029 W. Rt. 173, Antioch
Circa: 1997–2021

In 1998, the owner was Paul Brown.

Empty Bottle
1035 N. Western Ave.
Circa: 1992–2004

Primarily a straight bar and music venue, but many LGBT acts have performed there, including Ellen Rosner, Patty Elvis, and the Lickity Split Cheerleaders. In February 2003, the Chicago Kings – a group of male impersonators – performed at the Empty Bottle with Vic Ferrar, Bill Gemini, Sebastian Cock, Maxx Hollywood, Georgie Orgy, Rosebud, Mr. Izzie Big, Chip Starlight, Jack Pretty Boy Black, Harley Poker and Pussy Galore.

En El Tropic Zone
5220 N. Sheridan Rd.
Circa: 1984–1986

On June 20, 1984, this Latin bar hosted the Miss Gay Latina Contest.

Eons
3200 N. Halsted St.
Circa: 1992

This short-lived bar held its grand opening in May 1992. The owner was Tom Gorsuch. By August, problems came to a head when there was a mass exodus of management staff over

Drinking, Dining, Dancing

3200 N. Halsted • Chicago, Illinois 60657 • (312) 327-1222

disagreements with the non-gay ownership about how to work with the gay community. The bar's manager, Paul Wiseman, says the bar's owner "is a taker, not a giver. He doesn't belong on the strip."

Eons closed in November 1992.

This was also the location of Foxy's, Spin, Den, the second incarnation of Manhole, Whiskey Trust, and finally VII.

Episode
77th St. and Cottage Grove Ave.
Circa: 1973–1977

A bar for Black gay men.

Erotica
4400 N. Clark St.
Circa: 1993–1994

This was also the location of Lolita's.

Escapades
6301 S. Harlem Ave.
Circa: 1990–2007

A martini bar in the shadow of Midway airport with a nautical theme, seashells, parrots, etc. The grand opening in August 1990 showcased DJ/VJ Big Mike and bartenders Rae and John-John. Conrad Barth and Tony Martelli were the owners – on March 31, 1993, Martelli died in a car accident.

This was also the location of the Inn Between and Scorpie's.

ESCAPADES presents...

Back to the Beach
Friday, July 30th

Prizes for Best 50's Beachwear

Twist, Swim & Limbo Contests

50¢ Miller Lite Drafts

$1.00 off all mixed drinks

So be here for the best music from the 50's with DJ Blake spinning off at midnight!

6301 S. HARLEM AVE. CHICAGO
773-229-0886

Espial Bistro
948 W. Armitage Ave.
Circa: 1993

Esquire
211 N. Chicago St., Joliet
Circa: 1965–1973

The back part of the bar was gay.

Estelle's
2013 W. North Ave.
Circa: 1994

Estelle's is a gay/straight bar that has hosted LGBT events.

Europia
2838 N. Lincoln Ave.
Circa: 1991

Excalibur Nightclub
632 N. Dearborn St.
Circa: 1989–2012

This gay/straight bar hosted many LGBT events. This was a sister-bar to Vision Nightclub at the same address at the same time. In May 2002, the Hearts Foundation hosted Hot Tea 2, an officially sanctioned IML event, with DJ Mark Anthony. The dance benefited the Hearts Foundation and the Leather Archives and Museum. In March 2011, the hottest Chicago designers and merchandisers, such as House of Cleon, Vex Clothing, and Neysa's Peaces, with the sexiest genderqueer models STRUT the runway for a benefit fundraiser for the Women's AIDS Project. This location was also Limelight and Sanctuary.

Exit
1653 N. Wells St.
Circa: 1982–present

This is a mixed gay/straight club.

F

Faces
940 N. Rush St.
Circa: 1975–1979

Although primarily straight, near the end of its run, when business was fading, it made a push for gay clientele. In August 1979, Monica Monet & RM Productions presented the 5th annual Miss Gay USA, Illinois Pageant at the club.

Faces
1517 N. Ashland. Ave.
Circa: 2000–2001

In December 2000, Faces, a primarily gay Latino club, reopened under new management with Miss Ketty & Her Latin Revue. It closed after a fire raged through the properties at 1511-1517 N. Ashland in October 2001.

Factory
3474 N. Clark St.
Circa: 1984–1986

The bar was owned by Peter Zagrofas and Bob Randall. In 1987, Asians and Friends met there.

This was also the location of Christy's on Clark, Party Party, Studio 69, and Zo Ran.

Factory Disco
1665 W. Fullerton Ave.
Circa: 1978–1983

The Factory Disco was owned by Bob Randall and Peter Zografos. They were lovers and operated a few restaurants

Photo by Ralph Paul
The inside of the Factory Pub may look a little different, but luckily some things never change. Like the owners Bob Randall and Peter Zagrafos. We're sure, like most people, we are all happy to see these two at it again.

before getting into the bar business. They later owned Zo-ran, a short-lived piano bar.

The Factory Disco opened in June 1978, reopened on August 15, 1981, and closed for remodeling in 1983. An ad in *Gay Chicago Magazine* read, "Grand reopening party Sunday, March 5, 1983. Free buffet served. Come and see the Factory's new look, new lights, new sound, new DJ Jimmy Del."

One popular bartender was Jimmy Evans, who once worked at the Glory Hole, and Crystal's Blinkers.

This space was also home to Music Factory, Liar's Club, and Risqué.

Famous Door
Location unknown
Circa: 1969-1976

Dion (AKA Diana McKay) told the authors, "It was a drag bar. That made me decide that I wanted to be Diana McKay because I saw these white queens up there, and they didn't even know the words to anything. And I thought, 'I could do better than that.' It was a small bar, from what I remember. I think they just came out from a side door and performed on the floor, and there was a circular bar in the middle of it."

Fantasy Night Club
3641 N. Halsted St.
Circa: 2016-present

Mike Macharello opened Fantasy Night Club.

Also at this location were Halsted Street Café, M7, and Circuit/Rehab.

Farragut's on Clark
5240 N. Clark St.
Circa: 1990s-present

A mixed straight/LGBT neighborhood bar serving reasonably priced drinks.

F-Beat
3714 N. Broadway
Circa: 1981

A July 1981 ad in a gay newspaper reads, "... sick of disco, get into the F-Beat, 3714 N. Broadway. Chicago's only Gay Rock 'n' Roll Club."

This was also the location of Broadway Lady.

Felt
3341 N. Halsted St.
Circa: 2001-2004

Having fun at Felt

Felt opened in October 2001.

This was also the location of Minibar Ultra Lounge and Café..

Fiesta
43rd St. near Wabash Ave.
Circa: 1950s-1960s

This was a mixed gay/straight bar.

Fill Up Station
4325 W. Fullerton Ave.
Circa: 1993-1994

In 1993, a regular women's night was produced by Woman 2 Woman productions at the bar.

Final Approach
1090 S. Milwaukee Ave., Wheeling
Circa: 1984

Gay Chicago Magazine reported in July 1984, "Drag has moved to the suburbs. Patti Kakes' 'Fabulous Fakes Revue' starring Ginger Grant, Diana McKay, Ginger Spice, Shante, and Monica Monet will be performing Tuesday through Saturday at the Final Approach, a dinner/cabaret complex at 1090 S. Milwaukee Road in Wheeling." Now the site of a Ramada Inn.

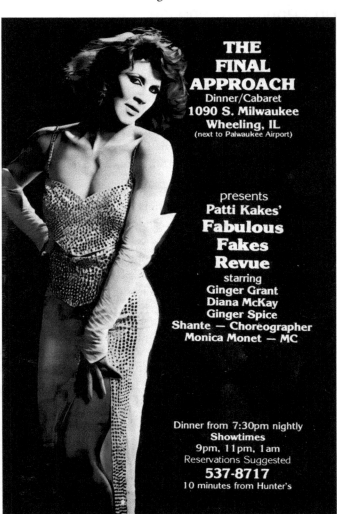

Finochio's Lounge
2835 N. Broadway
Circa: 1964-1974

Finochio's Lounge was the first Chicago bar to advertise in a gay publication. An ad appeared in the December 1965 *Mattachine Midwest Newsletter.* It read, "Finochio's Show Lounge ... Chicago's Foremost Female Impersonators & Pantomimes. Shows – 10 p.m. - Midnight – 2 a.m. Extra show Sat. Nite 3:45 a.m. Closed Mondays. No cover! No minimum! Popular prices! Featuring alluring and seductive Mitzi Monet. The Vivacious Personality of Jamie Jan's. Chicago's Queen of Comedy Jerry North."

Ira Jones, one of the founders of Mattachine Midwest, was the manager of Finochio's. Jim Henritze told the authors, "It was kind of gay. Gay/straight. In fact, it was very hard to do a drag show in a gay bar. You've got the same clientele night after night, and so it's got to be fresh all the time."

Finochio's Lounge
1400 N. Wells St.
Circa: 1974-1976

This was the second incarnation of Finochio's Lounge.

Fin's Dance Warehouse
5200 W. 159th St., Oak Forest
Circa: 1996

Fire Island
1177 N. Elston Ave.
Circa: 1986

The bar's grand opening was on May 8, 1986. The bar's main attraction was that it was on the Chicago River, and it had a dock with a boat that took customers out for a quick joy ride.

Chuck Renslow told the authors, "It was a very short-lived bar. It was located at Elston and Division, right on the corner. What happened was, they had a barge, and they put people on it and went up the river with it. But the coastguard came along and said, 'You have to have a captain on this thing, and you must have a life preserver for everybody.' Well, I can understand that; if a speed boat comes through and hits it, and you sink a barge with 500 screaming faggots on it. It lasted one summer, but it was nice."

One patron recalled, "I think it was one Saturday night, we decided to go to Fire Island ... I don't really remember what the bar looked like, except it was large inside and done up fairly nicely. You know, mirrors, lots of chrome, very 1980's!"

This was also the location of Scooters, and Bridge.

Fireside Bowl
2646 W. Fullerton Ave.
Circa: 1994-2004

A former bowling alley that was converted to a live music venue, it booked many LGBT acts, including Pansy Division, the Butchies, and Kelli Hogan. It was converted to an upscale bowling alley in 2004.

Forest View Lounge
4519 S. Harlem Ave., Forest View
Circa: 2012-2018.

In August 2018, the lesbian-owned Forest View Lounge hosted Drag Queen Bingo to raise money for Holy Covenant MCC in Brookfield.

Foster's
7 E. Chestnut St.
Circa: 1980-1982

This was also the location of Punchinello's.

Foster's Little Club
868 N. State St.
Circa: 1977-1979

This was also the location of the Yellow Unicorn.

Foster's North End Social Club
850 N. Clark St.
Circa: 1978

In May 1978, the Powder Puff Revue from St. Louis arrived in Chicago for shows at Foster's North End Social Club. Shirelle and Regina Wells were among the female impersonators in this traveling show that also boasted a male dancer.

Fosters On Broadway
4086 N. Broadway
Circa: 1982–1985

This was also the location of Jacquelyn's.

Foxy Ladies Studio 31 Disco
3739 W. Fullerton Ave.
Circa: 1983–1985

The grand opening was held on June 24, 1983.

Foxy's
3200 N. Halsted St.
Circa: 1992–1994

Foxy's opened in November 1992, but the grand opening was held in January 1993. The owners were Blue, Foxy, and Tom. Foxy's roots were in the underground, an alternative to the other bars on Halsted Street. Foxy's featured many popular DJs such as Freddie Bain, Ralphi Rosario, Earl Pleasure, Wess Kidd, Daniel Wang, Steve LaFreniere, and Spencer Kincy. Foxy was the host, Blue was the manager, and Tom was in charge of promotions and events. In *Gay Chicago Magazine*, Alyn Toler wrote, "It is not uncommon to see Foxy sitting at the front door wearing a green plastic mac and seven-inch platforms." In November 1993, Sundays were Raunch O Rama, a night of grunge and rock and disco. Mondays were Cult-O-Rama, a night of cult films like Ken Russell's *Tommy,* or 1974's *Phantom of the Paradise.*

Among those who performed at Foxy's were Aqua Netta and London Broil, Pussy "French Bitch" Tourette, and "la grande mee-maw du Wigstock," Lady Bunny.

Foxy's also held benefits for the Pink Angels, Open Hand, ACT UP, and the March on Washington.

The bar closed on July 3, 1994.

This is also the location for Spin, Eons, the Den, the second incarnation of Manhole, Whiskey Trust, and VII.

Freddy's
1064 W. Lawrence Ave.
Circa: 1966–1968

This was a semi-private membership gay men's club.

Friends Pub
3432 W. Irving Park Rd.
Circa: 1996–1998

Don Slater was the owner of Friends Pub. In December 1997, the Illinois Gay Rodeo Association Christmas Show was hosted by Minerva Rex with the Friend's Femme Fatales, Taffy Pull, Virginia Slim, and Summer Clearance, to benefit Children's Place.

This was also the location of Vision.

Frog Pond
2917 N. Sheffield Ave.
Circa: 1977–1981

The Frog Pond was owned by Jimmy Asta. It opened in December 1977. At the time, Asta told a gay newspaper that he was "excited about his new club that will feature a fantastic beer garden with frogs and princesses." And frogs there were. Hundreds of them.

Their ads in *GayLife* read, "Things are really jumping at the Frog Pond." In 1980, they offered a "comfortable back yard atmosphere with chaise lounge chairs for sunning, and umbrella tables." Popular bartenders at the Frog Pond included, Danniel Lambert (the Dragon Lady), Dago Rose, Rico, Scotty, Ginger, and Kay.

The Cabaret Players often performed there.

This was also the location of Baskets and Backstreet.

Front Page (Why Not Club)
530 N. Rush St.
Circa: 1950s–1960s

POLICE SEIZE 40 IN RAID AT RUSH ST. INN
Witness Men Kissing and Move In

The Front Page had several spats with the law. *The Chicago Tribune* headline on March 27, 1962, read, "Witness Two Men Kissing and Move In." The article read, "Thirty-nine men and women were arrested last night in a police raid at the Front Page Lounge ... Detectives Arthur Tyrrell and Edward Kalaich said they found two men kissing each other at the bar and saw several other men dancing with each other. They then announced the raid. Six squadrols were called to take 40 to the East Chicago Ave. station."

The Front Page was a straight bar on the first floor, a gay bar in the basement. It was owned/operated by Nathan "Nate" Zuckerman, John Coleman was the manager, and the bar was allegedly syndicate. "Nate Zuckerman, interesting guy," recalls Rose to the authors, "Brilliant when it came to liquor and managing bars. He was the first one to start buffets on Sunday. He said, 'Why don't we have sandwiches and a buffet on Sunday. Let's see if we can get people in on a Sunday afternoon.' It was syndicate beer from Cicero. We called it the Green Piss. It was the world's worst. Of course, everything you bought in the bar you had to buy through the syndicate."

Dee LoBue told the authors, "They had to have a doorman because at that time we weren't allowed to touch, we weren't allowed to send drinks to anybody, we couldn't move our drinks and go and walk over to the other person. They were

pretty strict, but then they started to loosen up. We could do line dancing, but we couldn't dance together."

Shortly before it closed, they sometimes locked the front doors so the patrons could dance.

Funky Buddha Lounge
728 W. Grand Ave.
Circa: 2007–2015

A mixed gay/straight club that hosted many gay-related events like "Art & Soul: The Brown Sugar Festival"with CC Carter. After two high-profile shootings, the bar's liquor license was revoked.

Funny Firm
318 W. Grand Ave.
Circa: 1994

This was also the location of Karma.

Fusion
3631 N. Halsted St.
Circa: 1996–1999

Huge multi-level dance bar featuring DJs Julian March, Mark Hultmark, Orlando, Michael Serrafini, and Matt Nelson. In February 1997, Scott Thompson of *Kids in the Hall* made an appearance. Other stars who performed at Fusion included, Viola Wells, Jody Watley, Deborah Cox, Ru Paul, Deborah Harry, and Thelma Huston. Tony Marchese was the manager.

This was also the location of Vortex and Rhumba Room.

Galaxy
604 N. Clark St.
Circa: 1979

In February 1979, there was a Hotter Than Hell dance party. This lesbian bar was torn down in 1983 to build the Rock 'n' Roll McDonald's.

Galaxy
1415 E. New York St., Aurora
Circa: 1983

The grand opening of Galaxy was on May 14, 1983. A ribbon-cutting ceremony was performed by Regina, the Morning Train Girl.

This was also the location of Odyssey.

Galick's Hut
5219 W. Diversey Pkwy.
Circa: 1958–1959

Joe Galick was the owner. His life was shrouded in mystery. He was almost certainly murdered by his young lover in the 1960s, but the gay aspect of the murder was covered-up. Galick, Catholic and Polish, was rumored to have some connection to the police, and was possibly married, though he didn't live with his wife. He lived in the back of the bar.

Garfinkel's
2918 N. Clark St.
Circa: 1983

The clientele at Garfinkel's depended on who was performing. Ginni Clemmens sang there in June 1983. Clemmens also performed at Opal Station and His 'n' Hers.

Garland's
3510 N. Broadway
Circa: 1976

The bar opened in June 1976 and was named after "Judy" – of course. At the time, *Gay Chicago Magazine* wrote, "Featuring the city's largest beer garden, this fairly new establishment has a popular jukebox and medium-sized dance floor. Special cocktail prices daily and occasional buffet served in the beer garden. New rooms to open shortly and special features and additions in the planning stages."

Other bars at this location include Broadway Kunfusion and Carol in Exile.

Gate
650 N. Dearborn St.
Circa: 1972–1977

This bar was located on the lower level.

Gateway Bar & Grill
7545 N. Clark St.
Circa: 2001

Gazebo
188 N. Wacker Dr.
Circa: 1980–1982

Gazebo was a dance bar. It opened in December 1980 and closed in September 1982.

Generator
306 N. Halsted St.
Circa: 1993–2007

Generator was a mostly Black gay dance club. Sundays were Boys Night Out with Otis Mack, known as "Chicago's Heavy Diva." In March 1995, the Greater Chicago Committee's Bayard Rustin Award for Club of the Year went to Generator and the DJ of the Year was Tyrone Mixx. Events at the club included, in September 1994, the Advisory Council on Gay

and Lesbian Issues held a fundraising event in support of the 1994 Gay and Lesbian Hall of Fame, and the Mod Squad (Men of Diversity) Hip! Hot! Safer Sex Dancers!, and the Gong Show with Flame Monroe.

Pickles, a bartender at Generator, told *Windy City Times*, "The customers were great. That was the first boy bar I ever worked in. I was at CK's for ten years, but I love the boys, they tip well, they're friendly, they're out every night ... I miss my customers ... the only problem that they had was management. It's the usual story; you have the two white male heterosexuals making money off Black gay boys."

Gentry
712 N. Rush St.
Circa: 1983–1997

In March 1983, Gentry was opened by Alden Jones in an old Greystone three-story townhouse. The main floor held a bar and a cabaret room dominated by a baby grand piano. The basement housed a casual bar with a dance floor. The second floor housed several unsuccessful restaurants and was leased for private events and group meetings, such as a bridge club. The upper floors contained office space and were not open to the public. In January 1989, Robert Russell and Dave Edwards announced sole management of Gentry.

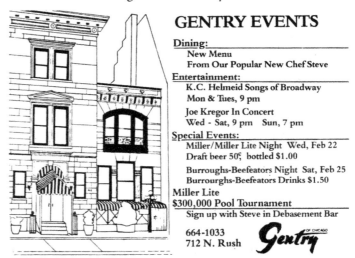

The piano bar booked local favorites such as Joe Kregor, Faron Evans, K.C. Helmeid and Denise Tomasello, Debbie Matt, Evelyn Price, Alexandra Billings, Valerie Lewis, Honey West, Tommi & Nanette, and Beckie Menzie, as well as nationally known performers such as Romanovsky and Phillips, Lynn Lavner, Khris Francis, Rudy de La Mor, Irene Soderberg, and Ann Hampton Calloway. Sunday night's open mic, led by Beckie Menzie, was popular with local stage and cabaret performers and became a must-stop for Broadway roadshows and visiting celebrities, such as Michael Feinstein.

Gentry on Halsted
3320 N. Halsted St.
Circa: 1995–2006

Gentry on Halsted opened as Chicago's gay bar scene shifted from downtown to the Halsted strip. The grand opening was held on February 14, 1995, with Khris Francis and Honey West. Gentry Jr., as it was sometimes called, featured many of the same performers as Gentry on Rush and Gentry on State. New performers included Alma Mendoza, Lauren Jacobs and Frida Lay's Name That Tune, Rus Rainer as Carol Channing, and Catherine Smitko and Lex McCauley.

This space has also housed Carr's Halsted Street Cabaret, G-Spot, Bugle Boy, Rocks, Niteline, Bushes, and Scarlet.

Gentry on State
440 N. State St.
Circa: 1997–2008

Dave Edwards owned this bar, also Gentry on Rush, and Gentry on Halsted. The public relations and special events manager was Eric McCool.

Gentry on State opened in December 1997 with a performance by Beverly "Pudgy!" Wines, the Queen of Tease. The three-room bar (two on the upper level, one in the basement) looked very much like a bar in an airport hotel. A cabaret room featured the same roster of performers as Gentry on Rush, also Ruby and Vicky Boofont, Jeremy Rill, Kerry Kincanon,

Kathryn Payne, Job Christenson, Michael McAssey, Mark Farris, and Jeff Roscoe. Gentry on State also continued the tradition of Sunday night open mics.

Owner Dave Edwards died February 27, 2005, of lung cancer. He left both the State St. and Halsted bar to an employee, but it never gained as much of a following. After this location closed, Downtown opened in the same space.

George's
744 N. Clark St.
Circa: 1984-1986

George's advertised in the gay press as a "men's bar."

This was also the location of Chatterbox.

George's
230 W. Kinzie St.
Circa: 1980s

An upscale supper club with cabaret performers, owned by restaurateur George Badonsky (he owned Tango and Le Bastille). How gay it was depended on who was performing. Some of the acts particularly popular with the gay crowd included: Phyllis Hyman, "An Evening with John Waters" in 1988, Charles Pierce in April 1986, Barbara Cook in 1987, and Judy Tenuta. Other featured performers included Betty Buckley, Bruce Vilanch, and Sandra Bernhard.

Gerry's Club (see Gold Coast)

Giovanni's
3724 N. Clark St.
Circa: 1977-1978

Giovanni's opened as a disco on November 30, 1977, and offered the "Latin Experience." Mike Morell and Giovanni Caloretti were the owners, the manager was Cesar Vera.

The bar had a mural, and sculptured wall art, depicting "Faces and Hands of Lost Souls Where Heaven and Hell Meet" – it became the bar's motto.

On February 25, 1978, Giovanni's had a raffle where the first prize was a free trip to Acapulco. In June 1978, the Nicole

Williams Revue performed sophisticated jazz with MC and hostess Carla Edwards, dancer Kim Spaulding, and music by Soto Sound Studio.

The bar remained open for less than a year.

By October 1978, this location housed the short-lived Macho/Chicago, a gay men's leather bar.

Girlbar
2625 N. Halsted St.
Circa: 1996-2002

Lynn Malec and Jennifer Murphy were the owners of this lesbian bar. Murphy later went on to open Parlour on Clark. Girlbar regularly hosted entertainment such as the Hysterical Women comedy troupe, Jen Porter, Kerri Grant, Sean Wiggins, Cathy Richardson, ½ Mad Poet, Erin Tedesco, Kimi Hayes, Paula Marr, the Chicago Kings, and the band Heather's Damage. Tim Cleary and Tom E were DJs/VJs. There was a weekly boy's night.

On December 11, 1997, Col. Margarethe Cammermeyer, who was running for Congress in Washington State, made a personal appearance at Girlbar.

The bar closed for "a facelift" in October 2002. Then closed permanently in June 2003.

82

Girlbar Burbs
20 E. Irving Park Rd., Bensenville
Circa: 1997

A short-lived lesbian bar in the suburbs.

Having a good time at Girlbar (Photo by St Sukie de la Croix)

GLEE Club (See Crobar)

Glenwood
6962 N. Glenwood Ave.
Circa: 2008-present

An intimate straight-friendly gay bar originally owned by Renee Labrana and Colm Treacy – Treacy owned T's, Sidecar (with Tom Hoang) and Sofo Tap. In April 2013, Labrana and Treacy had an acrimonious split. Treacy continued to run Glenwood, while Labrana went on to open R Public House. Popular events included Mikey Harniker's open mic for musicians, singer/songwriters, poets, storytellers, theatre-makers, dancers, male and female impersonators, ranters/ravers, live editorials, and comedians. Also, Marla Depew's comedy night – in April 2014, the performers included Aaron Ellsworth, Laura Hugg, Anna Lucero, Alicia Molina, Samuel Priest, Kristin Ryan, and Dave Stinton.

Gloria's Café
E. 35th St.
Circa: 1930

Black female impersonator, the Sepia Gloria Swanson (born Walter Winston), opened Gloria's Café in February 1930. It was opposite the Sunset Cafe at 315-17 E. 35th St.

Glory Hole
1343 N. Wells St.
Circa: 1972-1987

A neighborhood bar with go-go boys and a reputation for raunchy behavior. Robert Jobst was the co-owner with "Richard." It had a backyard patio with an above-ground swimming pool and offered BBQs every Sunday. It was raided numerous times, most famously in June of 1984, when vice officers and a television camera crew burst into the bar. Six men were arrested, the State's Attorney decided not to proceed with the charges, as the case couldn't be proved. One dancer, however, received a sentence of 30 days court supervision for exposing his genitals. In another raid in June 1985, Tactical officer Terry Pekara claimed that Robert Link, a dancer, used his snake, Shleena, in an obscene manner.

George Nichols was a bartender at the Glory Hole – he later served at North End.

The bar changed its name to GH shortly before it closed.

Don Creech reported to the authors, "It was a neighborhood bar with a long narrow bar, that had cheesy little go-go boys on top of unstable tabletops. I remember a couple of times I was there, they almost fell off."

Gold Coast
1130 N. Clark St. (or 1138 N. Clark St.)
Circa: 1958-1962

In 1958, Charles "Chuck" Renslow became manager of the Gold Coast bar at 1130 N. Clark St. (or 1138), turning it into a gay leather/Levi bar. At the time, the local gay leather scene consisted of five or six men hanging out at another bar, Omar's at 10 N. Clark St., where they were kicked out because they scared the customers. After trying several other straight bars, they moved to the Gold Coast, where after a few months, the owner died, and his son asked Renslow if he wanted to manage the bar. He did and bought it on March 16, 1960.

Gold Coast
1110 N. Clark St.
Circa: 1962–1965

This was the second incarnation of the Gold Coast.

This was also the location of New Jamie's.

Gold Coast (AKA Gerry's Club or GC)
2265 N. Lincoln Ave.
Circa: 1965–1967

This was the 3rd incarnation of Charles "Chuck" Renslow's Gold Coast. In *Leatherman: The Legend of Chuck Renslow* by Tracy Baim and Owen Keehnen, the authors wrote, "The Gold Coast location at 2265 North Lincoln was one long-wall bar with a back room that had tables and chairs. It sounded like a step up, but there were several problems. The first was that, because of the raids from years ago, Renslow could not get a liquor license in his name. Instead, at this location, friend and employee Gerry Probuski had the license in his name. As a result, even though it was called Gold Coast in all the advertising and on the sign, in all legal matters it was really

'GC,' which Renslow and other core people called Gerry's Club."

Gold Coast
501 N. Clark St.
Circa: 1967–1984

This incarnation of the Gold Coast featured murals by Renslow's lover, the erotic artist Etienne (born Dom Orejudos). In October 1980, the manager was Phil Spence; in November 1981, R.J. Chaffin was the manager; David Morgan was the assistant manager. Other managers included Pat Jordan and Jim Dohr. Dohr told *Windy City Times,* "Back in '81, Chuck fired his manager at the Gold Coast, and the bartenders were all asking, 'Who's the manager, what's going on?' I kept telling them I didn't know, so eventually, I walked into Chuck's office one day, and I said, 'Chuck, things are starting to get out of hand at the Gold Coast; we need a manager down there. Have we interviewed anybody? Do we have a new manager?' He just looked at me said, 'Yes, you are.' That's how I became the manager of the Gold Coast."

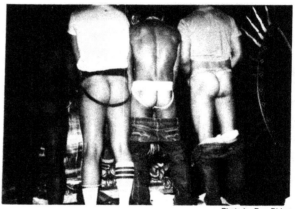

Photo by Dan Di Leo
Judges were supposed to only consider buns in the Glory Hole's Buns Contest. These were the top four contestants. Which one was Number 1? Give up? The one on the left.

In 1971, a lower-level "back room" known as the Pit opened, along with the Leather Cell, selling adult toys.

One popular event at the Gold Coast was the Sunday afternoon movie. The movies were rented from the Public Library and shown on a 16 mm projector. Movies like *Hush,*

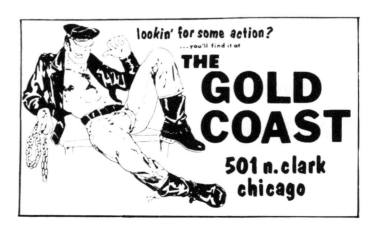

Gold Coast ad in the Chicago Gay Alliance Newsletter, June 1972

Hush, Sweet Charlotte, and *Jesus Christ Superstar.* When they showed *Jaws,* an ad appeared in *GayLife* that read, *"Jaws,* starring the biggest fucking fish we've ever seen."

The Gold Coast and the Chicago Health Department jointly sponsored a VD bus that traveled to various bars testing patrons. The bus first rolled out on September 23-29, 1975. It was hosted by drag queen Wanda Lust. During the first week, 1,000 persons were tested. The anonymous numbered results of the tests were published in *GayLife* on October 15.

A highlight of the year was the selection of Mr. Gold Coast, who represented the bar in the International Mr. Leather contest – founded by Renslow.

Among the groups holding functions at the bar were the Chicago Knights Motorcycle Club and Windy City Rainbow Society of the Deaf.

The bar closed in 1984, because Renslow's lease was up, and he felt it was time for a change. He decided to move it to a property he owned in Chicago's Andersonville neighborhood, then an up-and-coming area for the LGBT community. He later admitted in *Leatherman: The Legend of Chuck Renslow,* that it was the worst decision he ever made, "I think if I moved the Gold Coast up to Halsted, just up the street from Little Jim's, it'd still be here today."

Gold Coast
5025 N Clark St.
Circa: 1984-1988

The grand opening of the 5th location of the Gold Coast was held in September 1984. Renslow owned *GayLife* newspaper at that time. *GayLife* was in trouble when Renslow offered to be an investor in the newspaper. Frank Kellas traded his share in the newspaper for ownership of the Gold Coast. However, Renslow still owned the property and received rent from Kellas. The bar did not do well.

According to Renslow, "When I sold him [Kellas] the bar, it was making about $4,000 a month, so I charged him $1,000 a month in rent and 10% of any profits over $4,000. Kellas didn't know how to run a bar; he fired all the bartenders and worked the bar himself. ... The bar just dropped, dropped, dropped until finally, he didn't have any business at all. The city ended up revoking his license."

Another factor was that this was at the height of the AIDS crisis. The bar closed in 1988.

This later became the location of T's and Meeting House Tavern.

Three people who held the title "Mr. Gold Coast" were among those who attended the bar's final night. From left, Jack Hagen (1987), Harry Shattuck (1986), Gold Coast Frank Kellas and Larry Burke (1985).

Photo by Jack Sitar

THE GOLD COAST STAFF & THE G.C. 8 PRESENT

CRUISING 101

CRUISING 101 is an introductory course in the fine art of meeting someone in a bar and taking them home for ? ? ? ? This course will be offered in six parts.

FREE ! ! ! From THE GOLD COAST

LESSON 1: PREPARE YOURSELF

The first step in cruising starts at home. Choose an outfit that is appropriate for the bar you are going to. For the **GOLD COAST,** we recommend Leather or Levi.

Be sure your understand what signals you are sending ! Know where to put your keys and hankies.*

*Left is dominant, right is passive.

Next go to your favorite bar (hopefully **THE GOLD COAST** and buy yourself a drink. At the same time, look around the bar to see who is there that you may want to take home.

Next week . . .

LESSON 2: POSTURE & EYE CONTACT

THE GOLD COAST 5025 N. CLARK ST.
MON – FRI 8pm - 4am
SAT 8pm - 5am
SUN 2pm - 4am

Golden Horseshoe
1232 S. Halsted St., Chicago Heights
Circa: 1971

Listed as a gay bar in the *Bob Damron Guide.*

Golden Shutters Lounge
1810 N. Sedgewick Ave.
Circa: 1966

the Golden Shutters

● Cocktails
● Dancing

Completely Remodeled
NOW OPEN EVERY NITE
6 PM to 2 AM
Sat. 3 AM

Your Host, BOB THOMPSON

Specialties- Sunday 3 to 6 PM
HANGOVER HOUR - One Half Off on All Drinks
Tuesday 9 to 12 Midnight - TWENTY-FIVE CENT
NITE - All Beer and Bar Drinks

THE GOLDEN SHUTTERS LOUNGE
1810 SEDGEWICK STREET - IN OLDTOWN＊CHICAGO
TELEPHONE 944-8565

Listed as a gay bar in the Bob Damron Guide.

Good Times Tavern
3237 W. Armitage Ave
Circa: 1981–1984

A Latin disco run by brothers, Ramon and Rich Rosado. It opened in January 1981.

Gordon's
Location unknown
Circa: 1930s

A bar for gay men.

Gotham
444 N. Des Plaines St.
Circa: 1994

Gran Caribe Lounge
2234 N. Clark
Circa: 1994

Grant's Tavern
2138 N. Halsted
Circa: 1986

Granville Anvil
1137 W. Granville Ave.
Circa: 1988-present

The Granville Anvil, also known as the Anvil, opened in late-1988. Early ads in *Gay Chicago Magazine* were printed upside down with one line reading the correct way, "Turn your days upside down with Tommy 7:00 a.m." Another ad read, "69 steps from the El Stop." In July 1993, yet another ad read, "The best little no bullshit bar in the city ... for your no bullshit encounters."

Feathers – Bartender
"Ivan the Terrible. He was a real tit man."

Grape Street & Vine
226 E. Ontario St.
Circa: 2002

A piano bar.

Grapevine
E.75th St., near Langley Ave.
Circa: 1960s

One male patron told the authors, "It was run by two lesbians. We're talking '60s. One of the owners was called Janet, and I think the other was Claudia. It was a Black bar, and it was men and women. That was my first gay bar, and that was about '67 or '68, maybe a little bit earlier than that."

Grapevine
2548 N. Halsted St.
Circa: 1976-1977

In 1976, *Gay Chicago Magazine* described the Grapevine as, "Art and decor with Palmer House influence make this newer edition to the Halsted Street area attractive as a social gathering spot. A large comfortable 'island' bar is highlighted by friendly service of established gay Chicago area personalities."

It was destroyed by fire in May 1977. This was also the location of Julie's, Mother's Other, and Redford's..

The Granville Anvil invited college kids from nearby Loyola University, with promotions offering reduced drink prices for those wearing college gear.

A popular bartender there was William "Feathers" Gary.

In 1993 new management took over, but there were no noticeable changes made.

This location was also the Hi-Ho Terrace and Mike's Terrace Lounge.

GRAPEVINE
GRAPEVINE
GRAPEVINE
WHERE THE BEAUTIFUL BUNCH GET-TO-GETHER NOON TIL 2 AM
2548 N. HALSTED CHICAGO

Chicago for young people, mainly because it was located near Loyola and Northwestern universities. When the bar opened, the ads boasted "a pool table, soccer, a video, tennis and bowling machines, and a medium-sized dance floor." The bar's slogan was, "There are no strangers here, only friends you haven't met yet."

It featured performers such as Carol Ann Kyrias and Matt Ward, Marc Allan and Maria Jones, Jimmy Walker Blues Band, Lynda Elimon, Ellen Rosner, Tricia Alexander, Linda Mitchell, and Star Kissed: A Tuna Band.

COME HAVE FUN AT THE FRIENDLIEST GAY BAR ...!

In 1978, the bar was attacked by a gay basher. Charles Lucker, 17, pleaded guilty to charges of aggravated assault. Lucker had been arrested and charged with assaulting Chuck Hadley, co-owner of the bar, with a tire iron. Lucker, according to Hadley, entered the bar and threatened the patrons. When Hadley approached the youth, he was hit by the tire iron. Cook County Circuit Court Judge Ben Edelstein placed Lucker under one year's court supervision and ordered him to pay, within nine months, a total of $500 restitution for damages.

In 1979, the bar got a 4 a.m. license and celebrated by hiring go-go boys. In January 1980, it changed its name to Oz for two months, then closed.

Green Dolphin Street
2200 N. Ashland Ave.
Circa: 2007-2009

It was a straight bar/restaurant that tried to develop a gay following on "slow" nights. In October 1996, the Green Dolphin Street hosted the 5th annual Pumpkinhead with music by DJs Ralphi Rosario and Tom E with "door witch" Byrd Bardot. In November 2009, Grammy-winning DJ Frankie Knuckles appeared there for "The Power and the Music," a pre-Thanksgiving celebration.

Green Lantern Club
714 N. Clark St.
Circa: 1940s

Licensed to Helen Benedict.

Greenleaf
1770 W. Greenleaf Ave.
Circa: 1976-1980

The bar opened in September 1976 and was managed, operated, and co-owned by Dick Nielson, who had once been a bartender at Lost & Found when the popular lesbian bar was located at 2959 W. Irving Park Rd. In November 1977, ownership was taken over by Dem Hopkins who managed the bar with Chuck Hadley as a silent partner. During its four years in existence, the Greenleaf became an integral part of gay life in

Green Mask Tearoom
8/10 E. Grand Ave.
Circa: 1920s

The Green Mask Tearoom was in an English basement under a Greek syndicate-owned brothel. The tearoom was owned by Agnes "Bunny" Weiner and her lover Beryl Boughton. Wiener had been a burlesque queen, chorus girl, and snake charmer, and Boughton, a silent movie actress. They were friends of the anarchist Emma Goldman.

The beat poet, Kenneth Rexroth, put money into the tea rooms. Rexroth described the Green Mask, "Around the walls were blue nudes with silver fauns under crimson trees and

35 "Bohemians" Seized in Raid on "Green Mask"

The "Green Mask," a resort of Bohemians at 10 East Grand avenue, was raided again this morning. Twelve women and twenty-three men were loaded into the patrol wagons. The police entered the place after standing outside for some time listening to what they say was the reading of indecent poetry by George Lexington. Agnes ("Bunny") Weiner, owner of the cafe, was booked as keeper of a disorderly house.

shelves with books of free verse and books about the sexual revolution, and all the current little magazines. ... After the shows, the place filled up with headliners from the Follies and the Orpheum circuit as well as people from the burlesque shows. The girls had a friend, Gertrude, who was a concert pianist devoted to modern music, and she brought in serious musicians who came to the city – composers and performers." Regular visitors to the Green Mask were female impersonators Bert Savoy, Julian Eltinge, and Carole Normand, 'The Creole Fashion Plate.'

In the summer of 1922, the police raided the Green Mask, and Weiner was charged with keeping a disorderly house. Another raid followed in January 1923 when twelve women and twenty-three men were carted off in paddy wagons.

16 WOMEN AND MEN TAKEN IN GREEN MASK RAID

Chicago avenue policemen early this morning raided the Green Mask, newest of the near-north side's bohemian cafés, at 8 East Grand avenue and arrested sixteen men and women—artists and young society folk.

A charge of keeping a disorderly place will be lodged against the proprietor, Agnes Weiner, according to Patrolmen Ralph Weaver and Frank Schultz, who made the arrests.

Numerous complaints of neighbors that the bohemian atmosphere was too noisy for sleeping in the vicinity caused the raids.

G-Spot
3320 N. Halsted St.
Circa: 1990–1992

A short-lived bar, this was also the location of Bugle Boy, Carrs Halsted Street Cabaret, Rocks, Niteline, Bushes, Gentry on Halsted, and Scarlet.

Guzzlers
3209 N. Halsted St.
Circa 1982–1984

An ad in a gay publication in December 1982 read, "Merry Christmas from the staff at Guzzler's." The bar was owned by Chris Langford.

This was also the location of Happy-Hours, Pangea, and Stars.

Haig Lounge
800 N. Dearborn St.
Circa: 1940s–1982

The Haig opened sometime in the 1940s. Situated directly across the street from the Lawson YMCA, it was a hard-drinking bar and was known by the late 1970s as a "wrinkle room," catering to older gay men. It changed over the years. Phil told the authors, "In the summer of 1955 ... a friend of mine mentioned that there's a bar where the homosexuals go, the term gay wasn't used then, which was on the corner of Dearborn and Chicago. The name of it was the Haig. I went over, had a beer, and the feeling was pleasant. At that time, the gays dressed to the hilt. Dark suits, white shirts, and ties. Everyone was dressed."

Another patron said, "The bar was always fairly busy with local characters and was considered pretty rough at the time, which was the 1970s. It was frequented by some rough trade from the YMCA, drag queens, and some hustlers from Bug House Square. ... I remember the night Miss Tina, a very large drag queen who was a bartender at the Haig, threw a straight guy through a closed bar door. He landed on his head in a pile of glass and almost got hit by a car. This 'straight' punk came in and started yelling about how he hated 'fags.' So, Tina tells him to get out, and he won't go. So, she comes out around the bar, picks the trash up off his barstool, and throws him out the door, which happened to be closed! Tina was a real doll, and we all really miss her."

Old Marlene said, "Then we had Betty Grable and Dan Dailey in the Haig, because she was doing her *Hello Dolly* at the time,

and they called me on the phone, 'You'll never believe who's in here singing, and whose dancing.' It was Betty Grable and Dan Dailey. They were best friends, no romance or anything. Dan Dailey was gay, and Betty Grable was straight. I didn't believe it. So I went, and it sure as hell was, they both were."

On April 26, 1981, Aron Przanowski, the 74-year-old co-owner, suffered a fatal heart attack while running from an explosion and fire at the rear of the bar. Arson was suspected. The bar opened again soon afterward but closed permanently in October 1982.

The HAIG
800 N. Dearborn
Chicago's oldest
existing gay bar
free chili every Wednesday night
holding court:
• Timmy (formerly of King's Ransom)
• our own Tina
• & Howard serving on weekends

Halsted's
3700 N. Halsted St.
Circa: 1985-1986

Halsted's was owned by Steve Rempas. Manager, Bob Lombard, told the authors, "It was an alternative to the Loading Dock, more cocktail club atmosphere, neighborhood-style bar that featured a small restaurant in the back portion of the bar. The then famous Cesar [Vera] was my assistant manager there. However, after much time and work, the bar never really caught on and was sold to Norm [Janus], from the Saugatuck Lodge in Saugatuck, MI, and he opened it as ... basically a hustler-oriented bar."

This was also the location of Kit Kat Club and LA Connection.

Halsted's Bar & Grill
3441 N. Halsted St.
Circa: 2007-2014

Owned by Mark Liberson, Halsted's Bar & Grill was primarily a restaurant. It was popular for brunch on weekends and known for its luxurious back garden area.

In December 2014, Halsted's Bar & Grill hosted the New Year's Eve 2014 Celebration, with love from the Black Ensemble Theater with live jazz music from Zole Moser and the Ali Wyatt Sextet Band. In December 2015, it hosted the 5th annual Black and White New Year's Eve Party: Masquerade 2016 with live burlesque DJs All the Way K and Kirby.

This was also the location of the Lark Lounge, Madam B, and Voltaire.

Halsted Street Café
3641 N. Halsted St.
Circa: 1995-1997

Mike Macharello operated this space, a rather crudely converted warehouse, as Halsted Street Cafe until his liquor license came through. He then converted it to Circuit Nightclub. The space hosted an "Open & Out" gay poetry night, shows by Miss Ketty, Gong Show Croak-EE with Memory Lane, and "A Commitment to Love" in 1996, the third annual production of the world's first LGBT wedding expo.

Hamburger Mary's/Mary's Attic
5400 N. Clark St.
Circa: 2005-2020

Originally opened as a Hamburger Mary's franchise by twin brothers Brandon and Ashley Wright. It became so successful that the duo soon bought out the entire franchise operation. The main dining room expanded a brewery room into the neighboring storefront. A large studio on the second floor was opened as Mary's Attic, with a large bar and performance space. For many years the room was home to many theatrical ventures, most notably Hell in a Handbag Productions, known for

Mary's Attic - Photos by Kirk Williamson

campy sendups of old Hollywood, such as *L'imitation of Life* and the musical version of *The Poseidon Adventure*. It also featured drag shows such as the Paper Dolls Revue with Vanity Fair, and Velicity Metropolis hosting the Gong Show.

Happy Hours
3209 N. Halsted St.
Circa: 1978

Happy Hours was a Latin bar.

This was also the location of other short-lived ventures, including Guzzlers, Pangea, and Stars.

Hard Wood
7414 W. Madison St., Forest Park
Circa: 2017-2018

This was also the location of Blue Max.

Harlequin's
2683 N. Halsted St.
Circa: 1980–1982

The grand opening was in August 1980, with local celebrities, Chicago Molly and Sophie, in attendance. The bar was owned by Harold Meyer, who also owned the Knight Out. The bar featured drag shows starring Lady B, Jan Howard, Lady Angelique, and Andrea. It also hosted a benefit for the Gay and Lesbian History Project on September 19, 1980 – it featured slideshows by local historians Marie Kuda and Gregory Sprague. A $1 door charge was collected at the door. Another benefit was held on October 23 for Gay Horizons.

This was also the location of El Dorado, and Company.

Harlow's
27 E. Ohio St.
Circa: 1976–1978

Harlow's opened on December 17, 1976. The new owners wanted to make Harlow's "the classiest establishment in town." The first level was an intimate lounge, the second floor featured live entertainment, and the third floor was a disco. On December 24, 1976, they promised "an old-fashioned but decadent Christmas Party with hot rum toddy, featuring real pieces of toddy, and entertainment from 'singing sensation, Mila Inés." New Year's Eve 1976 was "Saturnalia Celebration, Roman-style! Fountains of imported, fermented bubbly, a glorious buffet feast, and outrageous doings. $25 per person (reservations required)."

In February 1977, "Midnight at Harlow's," Chicago's first gay radio show, began broadcasting from the bar five nights a week from 10 pm to midnight on WVVX 103.1 FM. Hosted by Bob Sandman, the show aired live with interviews and music.

This was also the location of the Trip.

Hayride (Wagon Wheel)
1001 N. Clark St.
Circa: 1973

In 1973, US Attorney James R. Thompson (later Governor of Illinois) investigated police shakedowns of Chicago bars. The Hayride was one of them. Norbert Springer, a bartender, told the court that the bar paid the police $100 a month.

Headquarters
4139 S. Harlem Ave., Stickney
Circa: 1973

Helen's
75th St. and Maryland Ave.
Circa: 1973–1979

Donna Rose described Helen's, "It was like a butch/femme big daddy/little mama kind of bar. It was rough. You would go in the front part, and it was the regular neighborhood bar, but

then you go past the curtain, and honey … it was happening up in there! Invariably, somebody got stabbed, there was a fight. I witnessed some knock-down-drag-outs, and people just stepped over the people fighting and just kept on partying. There were no men back there. It was all Black. Well, maybe there were a couple of Latina women that would come every once in a while.

"I was going there in '73-'74, and I think after the last shooting, that was about it, because … someone gets shot. I mean, it's hard; everyone is piling out the door, trying to get out before the police come. But I think Helen's stayed on 'til maybe '77 or '79 and then just changed. People got tired of that scene and then there was a lot of pressure from the cops, because they were getting raided, and all that kind of thing."

Hell
1117 N. North Branch St.
Circa: 2000

In February 2000, this new nightclub featured Thunderpuss 2000, the guys behind dance hits by Whitney Houston, Pet Shop Boys, and Donna Summer.

Heroes
2347 S. Michigan Ave.
Circa: 1989–1990

A gay/straight restaurant with female impersonation shows.

Hev'in
54 E. Walton St.
Circa: 1988–1990

Hev'in was an upscale piano bar and lounge. In June 1989, John Ortiz was the manager. Among the featured performers were Charlene Unger (born Peter Mohawk), Beckie Menzie, and Kenned & Carl. Pianists included Evelyn Price, Sally Richards, Chuck Masny, and Anne Pringle.

Hev'in closed in August 1990.

Hideaway
154th St., Calumet City
Circa: late 1960s

One patron told the authors, "It was named Tocci's – The Hideaway, but after enough people kept coming in and trying to order tacos, they decided to change the name. It was open to the public, so there were always problems with patrons of the male persuasion. Carol Chesser was a bartender there, and there were many stories about events at the Hideaway. There were fights there often enough that the two women involved would be sent to a coat room, which later became known as 'the blue room' for its blue lightbulb. There, they would be encouraged to duke it out and be done with it."

"Since the Hideaway was open to the public, there was a group of bikers who came in, and each night they left, the last gentleman would always drop his pants and moon the entire clientele. One night, Tocci had had enough. There were three steps outside the front door, and as the person performed the usual act on his way out, Tocci assisted his departure. When he got his pants around his ankles, Tocci kicked his sorry ass right down those stairs and out onto the sidewalk. I don't know if he ever returned."

Hideaway
6322 W. 111th St.
Circa: 1973-1974

Listed in the *Damron Guide* as a dance club.

Hideaway II
7301 W. Roosevelt Rd., Forest Park
Circa: 1973-1997, 2002-2014

In December 1979, the owner of Hideaway II was Arthur Sim. There was a dining room on the first floor and a discotheque on the second floor. The dining room closed in October 1974 and was converted into a cocktail piano lounge. The upstairs remained a disco, complete with DJ. The first floor had stone walls and exposed wood accented by stained glass windows in front. A spiral staircase led to the upstairs discotheque. The manager was Bob Anderson. Bar staff included Jim Dougan, Ed Walsh, Pat Hogan, Bill Houlihan, Tim Hoyt, Jim Nixon, and Mike McVoy.

In May 1978, Jim Dunken played piano in the lower bar.

There were also drag shows including one in May 1992 with Fifi DePraved (The 'V' is silent) and Daisy Mae. In July 2003,

Photo by Sherman Heinrich
Arthur Sim, owner of the Hideaway II in Forest Park, with Steve Boice, Mr. Hideaway II.

another show featured Regina Upright, Tajma Hall, Lulu D'Luv, Raven Cole, Kely Siland, and Dee Dee Divine.

In May 1993, the Hideaway got rid of its spiral staircase. By April 1994, Craig (Precious) and Brad Ogilvie were the co-owners of Hideaway, and male strippers such as the Men of Adonis and Men of Unicorn performed.

The Hideaway II in Forest Park held a "Kinky Fetish Fantasy" contest where the winner in the Chicago Policeman's uniform was Mr. Flash. And with Girl Master Angie Ferrentino are Slave Boy 2 Tom Kuczynski and Slave Boy 1 John Miko.
Photo by Terry Gaskins

The bar also served as a meeting place for such groups as REVIEW, a bi-gay married men's support group, and CARGO, Chicago Area Republican Gay Organization.

This was also the location of Club 7301 and Ultimate Oz.

Guys and Dolls at Hideaway II

Hideout
1354 W. Wabansia Ave.
Circa: 1934-present

This is a mixed gay/straight bar and has been called the Hideout since it opened (legally) in 1934 but became a hipster hangout in 1999. The Hideout is a small prohibition-era bar that hosts music, poetry, and art shows, many of which cater to the LGBT community. Its motto is, "It's not for everyone, but for every one!"

Among the LGBT artists who have performed there are lesbian singer/songwriter Anne Marie Akin, Lavender Country, Ellen Rosner, and Jinx Titanic and the LadyKillers.

High Chaparral
7740 S. Stoney Island Blvd.
Circa: 1973-1976

This was also the location of Burning Spear and Club 77.

Hi Ho
3010 Broadway
Circa: 1965-1966

Hi-Ho Terrace
1137 W. Granville Ave.
Circa: 1973-1974

Joanne, the owner of the Hi-Ho Terrace, told the authors, "I didn't know anything about gay people, and I didn't know we had gay people coming in here, so I had a couple of people tell me, 'Joanne, why don't you turn the bar gay?' I was, 'What do you mean?' ... 'You would be surprised how many gay people you have coming in here.' So, I said, 'Well, I don't know anything about that.' So, they took me around to some of the gay bars, and I'm telling you, it's what they call a 'Gay Tax.' They were subjected to dirty business and high prices. So, I talked to ... I don't think I should say his name ... Deputy Superintendent ------. He used to come in here. His son was gay. I said, 'I've been approached to turn the bar gay, and he said, 'Go ahead.' I asked him if I was going to have trouble with their men, and he said, 'No, if you run it like you run it now, you won't have any problems, no minors, no dope, no hustling, the only thing you've got to do is watch the washrooms.' And I said, 'How do I turn the bar gay?' And he said, 'I suggest you close for three weeks, get your people used to going elsewhere, and then let them know what it's going to be when you open up again.' And so that's what we did. We never had a problem. I turned the bar gay in September of 1973."

This became Mike's Terrace and later the Granville Anvil.

Michelle Faithe performed at His 'n' Hers

In 1986, Marge Summit, with then Gold Coast owner, Frank Kellas, started the Gay $ campaign.

Frank Kellas and Marge Summit were named Organizers of The Year from Gay Chicago for their tireless

Food Served til 1 am Nightly

His n' Hers

His n' Hers

Play With Us

Pool, Bridge, Chess Backgammon, Cribbage, etc.

Open Mike Every Sunday
Starting at 9:30 p.m.
Good Food Every Night

935-1210   944 W. Addison, Chicago

Women's Erotica Film Festival

3 sizzling videos

COME SEE THE VIDEOS

Saturday
August 24
10pm & midnight

**His 'n Hers
944 W. Addison**

$4 for women

DEANNA DAVIES
AND
TRISH KOCH

HIS 'n HERS

FRIDAY, AUG. 25th
944 W. ADDISON

$2 AT DOOR

His 'n' Hers
2316 N. Lincoln Ave.
Circa: 1975-76

This was the first location of Marge Summit's legendary His 'n' Hers bar. The bar closed when the property was bought by Children's Memorial Hospital and turned into a parking lot.

His 'n' Hers
944 W. Addison Ave.
Circa: 1976-1987

Marge Summit's legendary bar was tucked under the el tracks, just steps from Wrigley Field. It was a single storefront that served a limited menu from a small kitchen (the burgers and chili were popular). A small stage featured a variety of performers ranging from lesbian folk singers such as Ginni Clemmens, Kristen Lems, Diana Dewey, Paul Walowitz, Michelle Faithe and Diana Straight As An Arrow to Sister Blues, the Blue Suede Dyke Band and Starkissed: A Tuna Band. It also featured a gay gospel choir, gay activist/songwriter Charles Murphy and popular duo Trish and Lori.

Trish Alexander told the authors, "One of the things that made it such a magical place was that it had the feeling of being a neighborhood bar, or like a pub, and there was this really amazing sense of community there. There were gay people, there were lesbians, there were straight people. His 'n' Hers became one of 'the' places to do concerts in the city in the early '80s. Lori Noelle was someone I partnered with in the music scene, also performers like Big Ed; he was a comedian, he was a huge piano-playing comedic guy, he was just hysterical."

Richard T reported to the authors, "I remember a vocal trio called Wacker Drive, consisting of Skip Hartstirn, John Salewski, and Vivian Leigh Davis. Skip also played piano and made their dizzyingly complex vocal arrangements; he was one of the most gifted and accomplished musicians I've ever known. Eventually, the group went to New York and put together an evening of Sondheim tunes that had a successful off-Broadway run."

In 1986, Summit, with then Gold Coast owner, Frank Kellas, started the Gay $ campaign as a protest against the city of Chicago's refusal to pass an LGBT rights ordinance. In an attempt to show how much money (and clout) the community wielded, the duo had rubber stamps made that read "Gay $." They sold the stamps at cost and urged the community to stamp their money. It created such a furor that US Attorney Anton Valukas sent letters to Kellas and Summit warning them to 'cease and desist' because the campaign violated federal law against defacing currency.

The ordinance passed a little more than a year later.

His 'n' Hers
5820 N. Broadway
Circa: 1987-1992

The grand opening of the third incarnation of His 'n' Hers was in May 1987. This cozy bar had many events, such as a Pajama Party in November 1991, a Dress as Your Favorite Politician or Their Spouse in October 1988, and in August 1989, a Laugh Lines open mic comedy night.

In October 1992, the bar was the victim of an aggravated arson attack and closed down for good.

Hitching Post
13101 S. Cicero Ave., Crestwood
Circa: 1974-1979

This was also the location of Ranch.

Holiday Club
4000 N. Sheridan Rd.
Circa: 2000s-present

A mixed straight/gay hipster club serving food and featuring alternative music. The self-described "Swinger's Mecca" originally opened in Wicker Park in 1993 but moved north in the mid-2000s.

Hollywood Bowl
1300 N. Clark St.
Circa: 1940s-1952

Anna Lauda held the license for the Hollywood Bowl. The bar was raided on July 20, 1949, after two policemen claimed they saw acts of perversion by two men sitting at the bar. Capt. Michael Ahern of the Hudson Ave. police station described the bar as "a hangout for perverts, homosexuals and degenerates." However, when the case got to court, the cops changed their story and were suspended.

The license was finally revoked in 1952 as part of a crackdown on bars in the area.

Hoots
2350 N. Clark St.
Circa: 1977-1979

The grand opening of Hoots was November 23-24, 1977. The bar was owned by Jim Bergman and JP – JP was also the manager.

This was also the location of Neo.

Hothouse
31 E. Balbo Dr.
Circa: 1998-2005

A mixed gay/straight venue hosting many LGBT events, such as the Radical Faeries "Feast of Fools," a "Dyke Night Extravaganza" in June 1998, and in October 1998, an ethnically and genderistically all-inclusive "Queer Beat Science

Party" with resident DJs Bathsheba and Gigglybyte with special guest Daniel Givens. Silky Jumbo also performed there.

Houndstooth
954 W. Newport Ave.
Circa: 1993-1994

Primarily a straight venue, but gay bands played the club from time to time.

Also at this location were Crawlspace and Club Lower Links.

House of Blues Chicago
329 N. Dearborn St.
Circa: 1996-present

While primarily a straight music venue, it has also hosted such LGBT events as Wigstock, Fireball Hearts Weekend, IML Black & Blue party, Chuck Renslow's White Party, and the Gay Games VII party with Frankie Knuckles.

House of Ivy
557 E. Jackson St., Joliet
Circa: 1965-1969

House of Landers
936 W. Diversey Pkwy.
Circa: 1973-1975

PROFILE

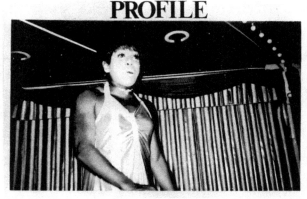

TERRI PAGE has been in the business for a long time. Currently starring at THE HOUSE OF LANDERS, Terri started his female impersonations at the old "FRONT PAGE". Where he picked up his professional name, "PAGE". He's played practically all bars in and around Chicago. Having been with THE HOUSE OF LANDERS since they opened last August, Terri would like to try his hand at singing and dancing "LIVE" again.

TERRI PAGE

roby landers

BILLY, at THE HOUSE OF LANDERS, has good style for a night bartender.

The House of Landers was a drag bar. Some of the performers, in addition to Roby Landers, included Wanda Lust, Ebony Carr, Terri Paige – the Pantomime Rage, Tillie the Dirty Old Lady, Verushka, Artesia Welles, and Diana McKay.

This was also the location of Zolar.

936 West Diversey Chicago

BOAU ERICSON

NUMBER ONE MALE LEAD IN CHICAGO

HOUSE OF LANDERS

House of Night
233 W. Chicago Ave.
Circa: 1992

Indulgence Sunday was gay night with DJ Freddie Bain.

House of Tiki
1632 E. 53rd St.
Circa: 1973

In late-1973, the House of Tiki requested, through attorneys, that they be removed from Chicago's Gay Directory. However, it was a gay bar.

House of Tut
1211 W. Lawrence Ave.
Circa: 1994-1995

Hoxie's
1801 W. Lawrence Ave.
Circa: 1998-1999

Hoxie's was a lesbian-owned restaurant that hosted a party for underage LGBT youth in the basement every Wednesday.

Hugo's
1840 N. Wells St.
Circa: 1965

This was also the location of the Place.

Hunger/K-Dron
3336 N. Milwaukee
Circa: 1992-1998

A mixed gay/straight Latin club that hosted weekly LGBT events. In September 1992, Miss Ketty (born Ketty Teanga) and DJ Mike Zuaz hosted a hot pants contest. In September 1998, Comité Organizador de Chicago invited all lesbian, gay, bisexual, and transgender Latinx and friends to "Nuestro Encuentro Kick-off Party for El to Encuentro."

Hunter's
1932 E. Higgins Rd., Elk Grove Village
Circa: 1982-2012

Congratulations! MARK HUNTER ON 15 YEARS OUT AND PROUD IN THE SUBURBS Thanks from the staff at Hunter's

A large complex in a building that once housed a branch of a steakhouse chain, it was a gathering spot for north suburban gays and travelers on layovers from nearby O'Hare airport. The grand opening was November 13, 1982.

The bar, owned by Mark and Marion Hunter, often featured its own troupe of male dancers, Hunter's Hunks, and drag shows featuring such performers as Pepper MaShay as well as national recording artists such as Kristine W. *Gay Chicago Magazine*'s Garden Walk of Beer Gardens in July 1989, includes Hunter's, 'This large patio looks like a small town main street. If it were utilized fully, it'd be like a gay version of Disneyland's Main Street."

Photo by Sherman Heinrich
Hunter's owners Marion and Mark are flanked by the winners of the 1985 Mr. Hunter's Contest. From left are Ross Kalb, 2nd runner-up; Alan Schwartz, Mr. Hunters 1985, and Jeff Rutter, first runner-up.

In 1985, Tom Parks and Roy Coffey were the DJs. Other DJs over the years included Michael Graber, Donnie Warner, and Jim Lewis.

This was also the location of Phoenix before the city of Elk Grove bought the property and tore it down in 2020.

Hydrate Nightclub
3458 N. Halsted St.
Circa: 2003–present

Hydrate is a popular dance club in the heart of the Halsted strip. The multi-room bar features events such as "Retro Flashback Dance Party," "Martinis, Manicures, and Tarot Readings," and an amateur strip contest hosted by Summer Clearance. Drag performers include DiDa Ritz, Naysha Lopez, Sorraya Dash, Cyon Flare, and Erica Andrews. For 11 years, Tajma Hall hosted the Hydrate Hy-Drag Revue.

DJs included Laura B., Paolo, Greg Drescher, Ralphi Rosario, Tony Moran, Brett Locasio, Steve K, Tracy Young, and Frankie Knuckles.

Amy Armstrong and Freddy Allen regularly performed at the bar.

The space formerly housed Christopher Street and Manhole.

I

Icon
710 N. Clark St.
Circa: 1996

Icon was a dance bar for women, but "boy-friendly." It opened in February 1996. Popular events were salsa nights with DJ Jungle Jorge Suarez and High Energy dance weekends. One gay newspaper noted in March 1996, "Icon installs a new light and sound system guaranteed to blow your skirt up." In May 1996, the Official Women of IML Leather, Lace, and Latex Ball was held at Icon.

IC Station
114 W. Hubbard St.
Circa: 1981

A neighborhood bar for gay men.

This was also the location of Druids, Ozone, Oz Again, IC Station, and White Elephant Bath Lounge.

Ifs, Ands, or Burt's
5 W. Superior St.
Circa: 1968

In 1973, US Attorney James R. Thompson – later Governor of Illinois – investigated police shakedowns of Chicago bars. Ifs, Ands, or Burt's was one of them. Bartender Norbert Springer (also a bartender at the Hayride, AKA Wagon Wheel) told the court that the bar paid the police $150-$300 a month. In the mainstream press coverage, the *Chicago Tribune* amusingly misspelled the bar's name as Ifs, Ands and *Butts*.

Illuminati
2354 N. Clybourn Ave.
Circa: 2011

This straight bar held a gay night called Plan B.

In Between
3729 N. Halsted St.
Circa: 1970-1973

The November 9, 1972, edition of *Michael's Thing* reads, "Our congratulations to Pat of the Inbetween (sic) for a great job of bringing boys and girls together." Two women owned this bar.

Although Little Jim's is often cited as the first gay bar on the Halsted strip, the In Between opened five years earlier, so the area known as Boystown actually started out as Girlstown.

This was also the location of Augie's, Big Red's, Bobby Love's, Dandy's, and Norma's.

Inca
2149 S. Halsted St.
Circa: 1996

Gay/straight Latin bar.

Industry
640 W. Hubbard St.
Circa: 1990

Industry was a mixed gay/straight club that held a variety of gay events and had a gay night.

Inn Between
6301 S. Harlem Ave.
Circa: 1981–1990

The bar's grand opening party was on March 25, 1981. The bar was owned by John Santoro. A gay press listing from August 1981 notes, "Tony and His Boys, an all-male dance revue at the Inn Between."

This was also the location of Scorpie's and Escapades.

Inner Circle
1842 N. Wells St.
Circa: 1967–68

Claudia Murphy owned this bar wedged between Clark and Wells Sts., on the edge of Lincoln Park. Steve Clark told the authors, "My favorite bar in 1967-'68 was a place called the Inner Circle; it was on Clark approximately where Hemingway House is today. The crowd was pretty much college-age and young professionals. Rumor had it that it was mob-owned because they always seemed to know when vice was going to pay a visit. You might walk in, and the manager or bartender would ask whether or not you had your ID with you, because the cops were expected sometime during the evening. Sure enough, at some point during the night, vice would come in,

and everyone would have to produce their ID to prove they were of legal age to be in a bar. I remember during the Democratic Convention in '68 that there were some young folks camped out across the street in Lincoln Park. The police made a sweep of the park, and things got a little hot because all-of-a-sudden a group of "hippie-types" came running into the bar in an attempt to dodge the cops."

Buddy King recalled, "I was a bartender there. It was the year of the political riots in Chicago, 1968, because I was bartending when the tanks were in the park. The bar was owned by a woman named Claudia, and she wasn't a mafia person, which was kind of difficult, but her bar wasn't with all the other gay bars, and I don't know who she managed to pay off, so they weren't raided. I remember Allen Ginsberg came in during the riots, and we talked, and he got drunk."

In 1973, US Attorney James R. Thompson – later Governor of Illinois – investigated police shakedowns of Chicago bars. The Inner Circle was one of them. In St Sukie de la Croix's *Chicago After Stonewall*, it reads, "Myron Minuskin, a former Chicago assistant corporation counsel, admitted he acted as lawyer and payoff conduit for Claudia Murphy, owner of the Inner Circle. He also admitted charging Murphy fees for making the shakedown payments and failing to report the money on his tax returns."

Inner Circle
344 W. Armitage Ave.
Circa: 1969–1971

This was the second incarnation of the Inner Circle at 1842 N. Wells St.

Inner Circle
233 E. Erie St.
Circa: 1975

This bar had no connection to previous Inner circle bars. The Inner Circle was a gay show bar that opened in February of 1975 and closed three months later after a devastating fire. The bar included a small disco dance floor and was open for lunch and supper. Shows were featured twice nightly from Tuesday through Sunday, and there was a private dining room with catering available for parties.

The grand opening was on February 14, 1975. An article from the June 1975 *Chicago Gay Crusader* reads, "The Inner Circle, a recently opened gay show bar at 233 E. Erie, was gutted by fire May 10 in what investigators suspect was arson. Impressionist Craig Russell had just begun an engagement at the bar, and a long list of other well-known entertainers on the gay circuit had been lined up for future engagements, including Gotham, Michael Greer, Daphne Davis, Liz Torres, and others. Fire officials reported that they found a safe open and empty and that four 5-gallon plastic bags filled with gasoline were discovered. However, the *Chicago Tribune* quoted employee Bradley Carlsen as saying that the bar had a cashbox, not a safe, and that he and the manager saved it with the previous night's receipts."

Nancy Reiff told the authors, "I worked at the Inner Circle ... I can't remember who owned it, but he also owned a jewelry store on Rush St. ... Billy something ... Billy and two attorneys. Then the place burned down, and all the records burned too. The bar was wonderful, a huge bar, huge stage area, and dance floor area, and tiered seating with booths and tables all around."

Inner Circle
2546 N. Clark St.
Circa: 1986-1989

In November 1981, Ben Allen and Bobby Lee (born Robert LeMoyne Smith) opened Inner Circle. It was not affiliated with the previous Inner Circle bars of the 1960s and 1970s. Seven months later, the patio opened. On November 30, 1982, Inner Circle held a benefit for the Action AIDS project of the Howard Brown Memorial Clinic. This was possibly the first Chicago fundraiser in a bar for AIDS. And in 1986, the bar hosted "Meet Jim Flint, candidate for Cook Co. Commissioner." However, the Inner Circle was best known for having male dancers.

This was also the location of (Paul's) Checkmate, Checkmate II, and Virgo Out.

Inner Circle
3169 N. Halsted St.
Circa: 1989

Ben Allen moved his bar from 2546 N. Clark St. to Halsted St. before re-christening it Lucky Horseshoe Lounge.

This location was also home to Irene's Diamonds.

Inn Exile
5758 W. 65th St.
Circa: 1987-present

The grand opening of Inn Exile was July 1987. The owners were Ruben Nieves and Kelly Fitzgerald. Located close to Midway Airport, Inn Exile is a neighborhood bar serving the South Side. In July 1989, *Gay Chicago Magazine*'s Garden Walk of Beer Gardens described Inn Exile, "Picnic tables, latticework, and shade trees make this a home away from home for Southsiders."

Drag shows have featured Regina Upright, Angelique Munro, Tajma Hall, Kelly Siland, Sassy Trade, and Raven Cole. Popular VJ/DJs include Kasey Crabtree, Dianne De Ville, and Brad Erickson. Popular bartenders include Terry Brown, Dave Grant, and Terry Tidwell.

The Lambda Antique Car Club met at the bar.

Photo by Kevin O'Brien
InnExile owners Ruben Nieves and Kelly Fitzgerald enjoy the bar's grand opening party.

CRUISE THE NILE '96
Sunday, August 11
After Market Days
Rain or Shine
6p.m.-10p.m.

Lake Michigan Cruise Ship "Jamaica"
Boat Docked on Lower Wacker at Wells
• Open Bar Including Call • Music • Dancing • Buffet

After the Woods Sunday . . .
B.B.Q. & Karaoke with Jeff & Tony

Near Midway Airport Open 6p.m. Daily

InnExile
CHICAGO
A VIDEO NIGHTCLUB

Now $60 on Boat / 1st Come 1st Served

In the Mood
601 Collins St., Joliet
Circa: 1980

Intrigue
582 Stateline Rd., Calumet City.
Circa: 1988–1990

This was a lesbian bar owned by Pam B and Sheila. The bar's specialty shots were "Crap Happens" and "What is it, Rose!"

Irene's Diamonds
3169 N. Halsted St.
Circa: 1984–1988

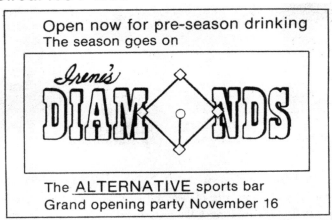

Open now for pre-season drinking
The season goes on

Irene's DIAM◇NDS

The **ALTERNATIVE** sports bar
Grand opening party November 16

3169 N. Halsted   883-9436

From left, Jack "Irene" McGowan and Harry Smith celebrated their 37ᵗʰ anniversary together at Irene's Diamonds. They were joined in the festivities by bartender Eddie.

Jack "Irene" McGowan opened the bar as a place for those playing in softball leagues to gather after games. The grand opening was November 16, 1985. Phillip Bernal told the authors, "It was one of the very first [gay] jock bars in the city. They would have the leagues and the baseball players would hang out there. They would come in in the summer all sweaty, and it was an amazing bar to hang out at. Big butch dykes would hang out there. It looked like a Cheers-type interior with sports equipment on the walls. One of the owners got sick, and they moved to California, where it was warm all year round. That's when they sold the bar."

The bar closed in December 1988.

This location was also home to Inner Circle and Lucky Horseshoe Lounge.

Iron Butterfly (see Butterfly)

Isle of Capri
14511 S. Western Ave., Dixmoor
Circa: 1968–1975

It's Here
2838 N. Broadway
Circa: 1982

It's Here was a non-alcohol bar.

This was also the location of Ann Arkee's and Le Trolls

J

Jacecosa's
3754 W. 26th St. (2nd floor)
Circa: 1984

The grand opening of this Latinx dance bar was February 3, 1984.

Jackhammer
6406 N. Clark St.
Circa: 1999-present

Jackhammer opened in 1999. The owners were Jimmy Keup, Joe J. Maggio and Joe's sister and her husband. Jackhammer is, or used to be, an anything-goes kind of bar. In its heyday, it was packed on weekends. One popular event was Gary Ward's Flesh Hungry Dog Shows with queer acts such as Jinx Titanic, Stewed Tomatoes, the Joans, Devin and the Straights, the

Artist Formally Known as Vince, Jen Porter, Fausto Fernos, Madge Weinstein, the Hellcat Hussies, and Retardos De La Mour. The Flesh Hungry Dog shows at Jackhammer ran from 2005 to 2012.

Jackhammer also hosted the Illinois Gay Rodeo Association's "King & Queen of Hearts Pageant" in February 2003 and the "Fat Tuesday Mardi Gras" party with underwear karaoke from Creagh in February 2002. Jackhammer was the home bar for the Roundhouse Pinochle Club. Jackhammer was bought by Mark Robertson and Mike Sullivan, who own SoFo and once owned Crew.

Also at this location were JJ's and Numbers.

Jackhammer pix by Sukie

Jack's Tap
901 W. Jackson Blvd.
Circa: 2001

Jack's Tap hosted many drag king events.

Jacquelyn's
4086 N. Broadway
Circa: 1985-1986

Jacqueline's was a men's dance bar.

This location was also home to Fosters on Broadway.

Jamee's
1157 N. Clark St.
Circa: 1964-1972

An ad in *Night Life* magazine February 1964 reads, "Opened, February 1964; Your hosts are Jerry-ALI-Joe." Dutch was a bartender there in 1966. Chicago mobster, James "The Monk" Allegretti, had a stake in this bar.

(New) Jamie's
1110 N. Clark St.
Circa: 1972–1975

In a *GayLife* article on August 1, 1975, Jamie's claimed he was being harassed by local car dealerships. The bar was first advertised in *Chicago Gay Crusader* in March/April 1974. An ad appeared in the June 2, 1972, issue of the *Mattachine Midwest Newsletter*, "Your Host Aggie." It also advertised "Go-Go Boys Nightly. Buffet Sunday at 6" and "The most unusual crowd in town." Bartenders were listed as Aggie, Feathers, Sadie, Mad Martha, Lenny, and Herb.

The Chicago Gay Crusader of November 1975 reported, "Jamie's was raided and 66 people are arrested on the evening of October 25. They were given November 14 court dates, although 31 were taken to holiday court the next morning, where all their cases were dismissed. Within two hours of the raid, Jamie's reopened, and by 4.30 am, one of those arrested had already returned to the bar."

Activist Richard Pfieffer told the authors, "It was a little bit of everything, probably like the Stonewall. You had street queens in there, you had transgendered people, you had leather people, you had everybody that could be anything ... it was a street type of bar.

This was also the location of the second incarnation of the Gold Coast.

Jamie's
1447 N. Wells St.
Circa: 1976

In March 1976, the New Jamie's bar reopened at 1447 N. Wells and advertised itself as, "Jamie's customers are the good, the bad, the ugly ... and the beautiful."

Jamie's Elsewhere (see Elsewhere)

JC's Touch
1942 W. 63rd St.
Circa: 1985–1986

JC's was a bar that attracted both lesbians and gay men.

Jeffrey Pub/Disco
7048 S. Jeffrey Ave.
Circa: 1966–1981

An institution on the South Side, the Jeffrey Pub has been around for years. According to bartender, Lee "Mr. Lee" Davis, it began as a straight bar, "Back in the early '60s ... across the street, there on the corner, there was a gay bar called Maxine's. And when Maxine's abruptly closed, even though this was a straight bar, gay people started coming here [instead]. By the mid-'60s, it was fully a gay bar."

Popular DJs include Stoney (born Terez Elmore), Eugene (Spuddie), and Ralph White. In 1980, mixologists were listed as Randy, Eddie, Sarah, Don, and Curtis.

Donna Rose told the authors, "I remember Maurice Hines, Greg Hines' brother, the dancer, the night he came in, I thought the boys were going to fall over themselves. You couldn't get a drink; they're muscling you out the way. They're all fawning over him, kissing his ass cherry red."

Jeffrey Pub/Disco
7041 S. Jeffrey Ave.
Circa: 1981–present

This is the second incarnation of Jeffrey's Pub.

Jeffrey's Pub not only serves as party central for Chicago's Black LGBT population, but it also serves as a community center, hosting fundraisers and organization meetings. Among some of the events the bar hosted were the PoW-WoW (Performers or Writers – Women on Women's issues), Chicago Black Gay Men's Caucus, Pre-Black Pride Kickoff Event, Brothers Health

Collective and the DVD release event for *Noah's Arc: Jumping the Broom*.

Jerry's Place
611 E. 63rd St.
Circa: 1960s

This was in the same location as the Kitty Kat Club.

Jessie's
1012 W. Lawrence Ave.
Circa: 1972-1976

Jesters
6654 S. Western Ave.
Circa: 1960s

One patron remembered, "It was owned by a lesbian couple, and they played Polish music. I went there for a year and didn't know the bartender was a boy."

Jimmy's Tap (University)
1172 E. 55th St.
Circa: 1960s-1970s

Bob Coale told the authors, "Jimmy's Tap at 55th and Woodlawn, in Hyde Park, was a noted place for gay University of Chicago people to meet in the pre-Stonewall days. It was also a sort of staging area for Hyde Parkers, for we would meet around 11:00 PM and have a drink or two before piling into taxis for a trip to the northern bars. My friend Cyril would tell the taxi driver to take us 'to fairyland,' and the driver would take us, usually without further discussion, to the corner of Clark and Division streets."

In late-1973, Jimmy's Tap requested, through attorneys, that they be removed from Chicago's Gay Directory.

Jimmy's 905 Club (see 905 Club)

JJ's
6406 N. Clark St.
Circa: 1983-1992

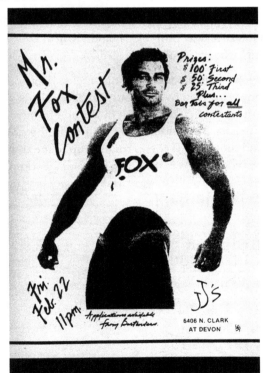

JJ's was a neighborhood bar with male dancers and drag performances such as the Miss Gay Northshore contest, and performances by Miss De De, Vikki Spykke, the James Girls (Stephanie and Audrey), Denise Carrington, Vikki Vague, Bili

Lundon, and themed parties including a Mr. Leprechaun contest. In 1983, the owner was Mike Campbell; in 1984, it was Ken Killian. In June 1984, JJ's advertised its first anniversary and the grand opening of its new patio. The bar closed in December 1992.

The space has also been home to Jackhammer and Numbers.

Photo courtesy of Gay Life
Just one big happy "family?" were seen recently at JJs. Clockwise Michael Campelli, Kenneth Killan, Kirk Matthews, Nancy Rocco, Henry Dilling.

JJ's Show Lounge
4601–4613 N. Sheridan Rd.
Circa: 1950s–1960s

This was a drag bar located on the ground floor of the Sheridan Plaza Hotel. It was run by JJ and owned by "Tony the Merchant," who was mob-connected.

Viki St. John remembered, "So, one night, JJ came back and said, 'Tony wants you to come out and have a drink with him.' So after the show, I go out and sit down, and he introduces me to some people. I'm chit-chatting with them. I go back to do the second show, and JJ comes running up to me and said, 'Do you know who that was, who you just had a cocktail with?' I said, 'No.' He said, 'That was [Mafia boss] Sam Giancana.' I said, 'Who the hell is he?'"

Jock's
432 N. Clark St.
Circa: 1978–1980

This was also the location of Marilyn's.

Jock's
3019 N. Clark St.
Circa: 1977–1980

The grand opening of Jock's was held on November 4, 1977. The bar closed temporarily but was open again in October 1979 and 1980 for its annual Corn Huskers Fest.

This was also the location of Big Red's, Locker, and Minkees.

Joe's Deluxe
6323 S. Parkway
Circa: 1940s–1954

Joe's Deluxe was a Black club with drag shows. It was owned by Joseph "Joe" Hughes. The club had a variety floor show produced by Dick "Mae West" Barrow. During World War II, Joe's Deluxe provided uninterrupted entertainment with female impersonator Valda Gray, and six chorines staged a skit called *Six Girls Named Flo*. The *Chicago Defender* wrote that the club's "sweetheart," Dixie Lee, started "stepping out with a line that pleases" and the "sinuous" Petite Swanson "tells the girls that it 'Aint Right,' and that they must love their sweeties with a feeling." Although none of Valda Gray's shows are known to have been recorded, one of its stars can be heard on two 78 rpm records recorded in March 1947 by Alphonso "Petite Swanson" Horsley on Marl Young's Chicago Sunbeam record label. The songs are "Lawdy Miss Claudy" b/w "My Jockey Knows How to Ride" and "I'm Sorry" b/w "Did You Ever Feel Lucky."

Frank Woods recalled, "Joe's Deluxe was a very nice but not an overly ornate interior. The shows were of a very high level of talent, and it was a great place to go but not that popular because of the racial feelings at the time. Several of the men in the shows there had their own long hair, and their costumes

and make-up were very tasteful and beautiful. They were very reminiscent of the elegance and class of Josephine Baker when she appeared at the Palace in New York ... The people who went there were, for the most part, established professional people who were literate and educated and not bothered by bigotry or stupidity. I think many of the patrons had probably traveled in Europe and were aware of the intellectual aspects of performing arts."

Joe's Deluxe closed in 1954.

Joe's on Weed
940 W. Weed St.
Circa: 1995-present
A straight bar that occasionally hosts LGBT events, such as "Proud to Laugh," a benefit for Gay Games VII.

John L's
335 154th Pl., Calumet City
Circa: 1980-2011

Johnny's
Location unknown
Circa: 1930s

Joie de Vine
1744 W. Balmoral Ave.
Circa: 2004-2021

Lori Ann Petrushkevich owned Joie de Vine. The bar was a cozy upscale, neighborhood wine bar, popular among lesbians and neighborhood straights. It also served craft cocktails. In July 2008, the bar hosted an artist reception for Bret Grafton featuring new art, martini specials, food tastings, and donations to benefit Chicago House. In October 2009, Joie de Vine hosted a Chicago Bliss Girls football team cocktail party benefit – the $10 donation went to Breast Cancer Awareness.

This is also the location of Nobody's Darling.

Jo-Jo's
22ⁿᵈ St. and Washtenaw Ave.
Circa: 1970s

This was also the location of Cookie & Shirley's.

Jokes on U
440 N. Halsted
Circa: 1996

This was also the location of Club Flamingo, Clubhouse, Redoubt, Jokes on U, Red No 5, and Rialto.

Julie's
2548 N. Halsted St.
Circa: 1976

In *GayLife* May 28, 1976, Rhonda wrote, "... formerly Mother's Other is packing them in."

This was also the location of Grapevine, Mother's Other, and Redford's.

K

K9 Club
105 E. Walton St.
Circa: 1920s–1934

The K9 Club was a speakeasy. In his book, *Chicago Whispers*, St Sukie de la Croix writes, "The female impersonators who worked there included Li-Kar, Billy Herrera, Johnny Mangum, Del LeRoy, Billy Russell, Art West, Billy Brennan Billy Richards, and Earl Partello, with Sylvia Rose as the MC. One night the club was raided by prohibition cops and the 'girls' fled the stage, out the back door and down the fire escape. At the bottom a solitary cop waited to scoop them up, but Herrera whacked him over the head with a beer bottle and they all lifted their skirts and escaped down an alley. When prohibition ended, the K9 Club went legit as a drag bar/restaurant with Chinese cuisine and music by Bill Lyles and his orchestra. In June 1934 the K9 advertised in the *Chicago American* as Chicago's 'Oddest Nite Club' with a breakfast show every morning at 5:00 a.m. Five months later an ad read 'PaLeeeze!! WHY SHOULD I BE MANNISH!' alongside a camp cartoon figure daintily waving a handkerchief.

On December 8, 1934, Mayor Edward J. Kelly revoked the K9's liquor, amusement, food and cigarette licenses; the *Chicago Tribune* report called the club an 'eccentric night life rendezvous.' Unable to find work, the performers scattered."

Ka-Boom
747 N. Green St.
Circa: 1990s

A 25,000 square foot multiplex nightclub venture produced by Cal Fortis of Neo and Ken Smith of Exit. When the club opened in May 1991, events were coordinated by Limelight's Richard Knight Jr., and Mark Reid acted as music director. KA-BOOM!'s Cabaret Room hosted films curated by David Risqué. According to one-time club technical director Joe Michelli, the venue also hosted popular disco theme parties. In September 1991, the club hosted a post-screening party of *Paris is Burning* to benefit the AIDS Foundation of Chicago. Several weeks later, AFC hadn't received a penny of the money.

Karma
318 W. Grand Ave.
Circa: 1995-2000

This popular mixed gay/straight club, owned by Srinivas Reddy and Rakesh Thakkar, lost its license permanently in early 2000 after numerous code violations.

This was also the location of Funny Firm.

K-Dron Club (see Hunger)

King's Inn
4156 N. Kedzie Ave.
Circa: 1965-1966

King's Palace
State St.
Circa: 1950s-1960s

The King's Palace staged drag shows. Jerry C remembered, "I went there with a couple of friends of mine on a Friday or a Saturday. This was in the '60s. They had contests there, and anybody could come in and play the piano or sing or do an act."

King's Ransom Pub
20 E. Chicago Ave.
Circa: 1968-1979

On February 4, 1976, *GayLife* described the King's Ransom as having a "Cozy open fireplace, exposed brick interior and minuscule dance floor. 'Intimate' is the word. Opens at 7:00 AM." *Gay Chicago Magazine* described it as a "Masculine lounge atmosphere with working fireplace. Large U-shaped bar, and a pop jukebox, and small dance area"

Glen Davis recalled, "You kind of went downstairs to it; it was sunken from the main storefront. It was crowded, small, noisy, a young person's hangout. A lot of people who were underage. I was one of them."

Monday was "Girls' Night," according to the *Damron Guide*.

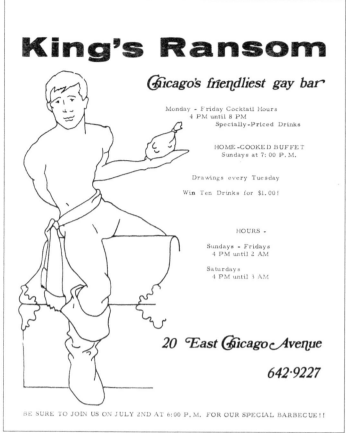

Kismet Club
200 State St., Calumet City
Circa: 1985

This was also the location of the Bank Vault, Ms. Behavin, and the Double RR Lounge.

Kit Kat Club
3700 N. Halsted
Circa: 2000-present

The Kit Kat Club is a restaurant serving dinner and brunch, and is known for its killer martinis (with at least 50 different varieties, including Snickerdoodle and Key Lime Pie). It features a small bar and an outdoor patio. Although it has a strong gay following, it is also popular with tourists and bachelorette parties. Everything is served with a side dish of drag performers. Among the performers are Delores Van-Cartier, Delilah Bouvier, and Madame X.

This was also the location of the LA Connection and Halsted's.

Kitty Kat Club
611 E. 63rd St.
Circa: 1950s-1960s

This was a Black jazz club. One patron remembered, "It was just like *Paris is Burning*, only it was on a smaller scale. Supposedly, it was a straight bar during the day and gay at night, but it was predominantly a gay bar. One of the bartenders was a lesbian, and they had a male singer there."

The Kitty Kat Club is featured in the 1961 movie *Raisin in The Sun*, starring Sidney Poitier and Claudia McNeil. The movie was based on the play by the same name, written by Lorraine Hansberry, a Chicago lesbian.

This was the same location as Jerry's Place.

Kitty Sheon's Little Club
3916 N Sheridan Rd.
Circa: 1944-1957

Kitty Sheon (born Kathleen Schert) opened this bar in the summer of 1944. Chicago's most prominent "fag hag" was a stout homely woman who, according to patrons of her bars, resembled Mayor Richard J. Daley in drag. Sheon's first bar was Cullen's Green Parrot, 3478 N. Broadway; it's not known if it catered to a gay clientele.

Like Sheon's later bars, this one featured a pianist. David remembered, "A woman named Eleanor Stat worked at the bar

Kitty Sheon

from 1955-1957, singing parodies of songs adding gay/vulgar meanings, songs with titles like, 'Wait 'Til Your Son Turns Nelly.'" Tony Simes and Mame also played piano at the club. Mame remembered, "I started to work for Kitty. Now, this would be in the '50s when she was up on Sheridan Road and Irving Park, and I played piano in there ... She eventually moved down to the Near North Side. We went to the grand opening, and it was there that Kitty uttered those immortal words, "I really don't like gay boys' but if it wasn't for them, I wouldn't have all these furs and jewels."

Sheon's bars were noted for their elegance, pink lighting, strict tie and jacket dress code, and a "no touching" rule. One reason Kitty Sheon's bars were popular with gay men is that they were never raided. Her husband, George, was formerly a policeman, and he kept the police away.

Kitty Sheon's Key Club
745 Rush St.
Circa: 1958-1978

In 1958, Kitty Sheon's Key Club opened. As with her other bars, she maintained a strict dress and conduct code.

Don related, "Even in the middle of the summer, you had to wear a shirt and tie. I had a friend of mine that came in from California one time, and he had been told about Kitty Sheon's, and he wanted to go. I said, 'Mike, you've got to put on a shirt and tie, and this is August. You don't have a shirt and tie with you.' He said, 'Well, I've got my uniform with me.' And yes, he did; he was a commander in the Navy. So, he put that on, and I put on my suit and tie, and off we went to Kitty Sheon's. Needless to say, we stopped traffic as we walked in."

Old Marlene remembered, "Did I know Kitty? Well, I went to her birthday parties and that, but nobody really knew Kitty.

We used to call her Mayor Daley in drag. Charlie was the piano player at Kitty's; he was there for years. He was a Black man in his late-50s, and he worked there for a good 15 years. ... Patty, her hostess, was the only person who got to know her well. Patty was a very stern person ... Kitty only made an appearance late at night, other than her birthday party, and that was by invite only. ... It was a different world at that time. All the ribbon clerks in Chicago used to go to Kitty's. You would see Field's and Carson's and Wieboldt's, and you could tell by the quality of their suits where they worked. ... Van Johnson, the movie star, used to go in Kitty Sheon's."

Kitty Sheon died on October 22, 1977, at seventy-four, eight years after her husband. They are in a mausoleum at Rosehill Cemetery. She left the bar to two of her bartenders, Nicky (last name unknown) and Eddie Jacobs; they operated for a few more years before closing the bar permanently.

2 ASK DAMAGES FOR BEATING IN RUSH ST. CLUB

Two men filed suit in Circuit court yesterday asking $25,000 damages each, alleging they were beaten without provocation Jan. 27 in the Kitty Sheon Key Club, Inc., 745 Rush st.

The plaintiffs are Richard C. Steffan, 40, and James McCoy, 39, both of 5455 Kenmore av. Their attorneys are Philip L. Howard and Robert F. Lisco.

Defendants are the key club and three persons identified as employes — William Sullivan, Edward Luther, and Samuel Schneider.

Kitty Sheon's
906 Ernst Ct.
Circa: 1980s

In 1978, Kitty Sheon's moved to Ernst Court. Joette Waters, a singer with vocal group Stardust, told the authors, "Kitty Sheon's was long and narrow like a boxcar of a train. It was a delightful place to work. For one thing, it offered some great eye candy. Sexy shirtless waiters with tight black pants and little bow ties. Kitty's had a very upscale and notable clientele, and since the entrance was in an alley, one could be very discreet. It was fine to hang out and joke around with some pretty powerful folks in the club, but what happened in Kitty's stayed in Kitty's. Mum's the word! I am proud to say that we performed there because Kitty Sheon's is such an important part of Chicago's gay history."

Other entertainment at the bar included Sam Horne, Ester Hana, and Ruth Allyn.

Kitty's Korner
2959 W. Irving Park Rd.
Circa: 1983–1986

Kitty's Korner was a lesbian bar that moved into the original location of Lost & Found.

Knight Out
2936 N. Clark St.
Circa: 1973–1985

The Knight Out was a neighborhood bar owned by Larry Brunicinni, then later, Harold Meyer. Attached to the bar was Chicago's first non-erotic gay bookstore, the Stonewall Memorial Bookshop. In 1980, Edmund White and Doric Wilson appeared to sign autographs.

Knob Hill
Hyde Park
Circa: 1950

Jim Wickliff told the authors, "Right across from the police station was a bar called Knob Hill, and again it was not totally gay, but it was more gay than straight. The straight people went in there to make out too, so there was no problem with gays and straights. Knob Hill was a jazz spot. A lot of the jazz guys would play there, so it attracted a lot of straight people. They ignored everything else. By the time I got to Hyde Park, it was gone, but the old Hyde Parkers told me about it."

Kokaine
1137 W. Fulton Market
Circa: 1979

Kokaine billed itself as Chicago's largest westernized cowboy and cowgirl disco bash.

Kona Winds
1114 W. Argyle Ave.
Circa: 1965–1969

After 1966, in the *Damron Guide,* it was listed as "KW (formerly Kona Winds)."

Krush Nightclub
1675 N. Elston Ave.
Circa: 2011

The Prop House/Rails was also at this location.

K's on Klark
2568 N. Clark St.
Circa: 1980

K's on Klark opened on January 14th, 1980. It was a small neighborhood bar owned by Joe Lyons. The manager was Lakeview-born Michael "K" Kucharski. This was also the location of Take One, Bughaus, Molly's Follies, Pourquoi Pas?, and Robert's Lounge.

Kustom Nightclub
1997 N. Clybourn Ave.
Circa: 2002

"Ritual" was the club's gay night with DJ Mark Anthony.

L

La Borsa
375 N. Morgan St.
Circa: 1996

In December 1996, Executive Sweet held their Christmas celebrations at La Borsa. Pamela Terrell and DJ Sheron Webb founded Executive Sweet, a women of color group that organized parties and fundraisers at different venues. In the late-1980s, it was taken over by Pat McCombs and Vera Washington.

La Cage Chicago
50 E. Oak St.
Circa: 1982-1983

One patron recalled, "It used to be a place called Huckleberry's, a straight disco run by the actress Barbara Eden, of all people. She was married to the publisher of the *Sun-Times*, I think. Whether she actually owned it or not, I don't know, but she was the name attached to it. Then they sold it, and it became La Cage, and I remember going to the grand opening, and there were pink feathers everywhere, and there were some drag queens. They would use a pink grand piano for a stage. They weren't open for that long. I don't even think it was six months. The IRS closed it down, like overnight, it was gone."

In January 1982, *Gay Chicago Magazine* wrote, "Starting Friday, Jan. 29, the bar will begin its new policy after many successful Sunday T-Dances and Tuesday gay nights. The weeknight cover charge has been dropped and only apply to Friday and Saturday evenings. Wednesday night will be dancing and romancing night and Tuesday, Thursday, Friday,

Saturday and Sunday there are two shows featuring Diana Hutton, Billy Blake, Ruth Dix, Lisa Eaton and occasional special guest artists."

Divine, Shanté (Alexandra Billings), Candy Slice, and Patti Kakes also appeared at La Cage.

The bar closed in November 1983.

LA Connection
3700 N. Halsted St.
Circa: 1986-1994

The grand opening of LA Connection was on April 17, 1986. It was owned by Norm Janus. It was a bar for younger gay men. The bar held events such as "Most Colorful Underwear Party,"

L.A. Connection owner Norm Janus with new barback and Randy Seens and manager Michael. Photo by Jack Sitar

"Winter Beach Party," and a "Steamy Nights in L.A. Party." There were drag shows featuring an Oprah look-a-like, Bernice Blew, and Lisa Eaton, Chicago's Judy Garland. In March 1994, the bar rebranded its back room as "Rear End," catering to the leather crowd.

This was also the location of Halsted's and the Kit Kat Lounge.

La Cueva
4153 W. 26ᵗʰ St.
Circa: 1972-2020

La Cueva was the oldest Latinx drag bar in the country, operating since 1972. It closed during the 2020 pandemic but was already under pressure from neighbors who wanted to shut it down, claiming it was a haven for prostitutes and drug users.

In 2011, La Cueva's manager was Ruben Lechuga. Miss Ketty performed there. Also at this location were Dolly's Place, and Stargazer.

Lady Bug
3445 N. Halsted St.
Circa: 1979-1986

The Lady Bug was owned by Marilyn Bohm and her partner, Vera Young. The bar opened in 1979. In August 1984, Young died from lung cancer. In later years, Bohm's daughter Kim worked behind the bar.

Ruth Ketchum said, "The Lady Bug was a small bar, but it was an important bar. A lot of women met each other there. It had a dance floor part and a pool table part, and if you couldn't decide between the two of them, there was this little stairway of about four stairs, and you sat on the stairway ... that meant you weren't involved, and you were looking, because everyone had to walk past you. And then they had these booths in the corner."

Kathy Edens told the authors, "I would say the Lady Bug was the first upper-class women's bar. Lady Bug was nicely done, nicely kept, and it was small."

The bar closed in May 1986.

This was also the location of Rick's Retreat.

Lakeview Broadcasting Co.
3542 N. Halsted St.
Circa: 2007

La Mere Vipère
2132 N. Halsted St.
Circa: 1976–1978

La Mere Vipère was owned by Noe Boudreau to compliment his other bar, the Snake Pit. The grand opening of La Mere Vipère was June 16, 1976. Describing the bar in *GayLife*,

columnist Rhonda wrote, "There is an upstairs lounge and a downstairs disco area where the blinking neon flamingos and palm trees are accented by streaks of neon lightning and a

revolving glass globe from one of Chicago's old hotels. The feel is all '30s, '40s, but the sound is pure 1970s. Many of the people who attended wore costumes. Safety pins, which have become a new form of jewelry in England, and are now for sale here in designer stores, were given out at the door. Much of the punk rock scene has overtones of S&M, sexual deviance, and general frustration, perhaps explaining why some gays relate well to this kind of sound."

In May 1977, another newspaper wrote, "Punk makes its debut in Chicago. The evening titled, 'Anarchy at La Mere' was sponsored by Sounds Good records and drew a crowd of 200 gay/straight/multi-ethnic to the bar. You could dance with a man, woman, or even by yourself, and no one thought anything of it. Some of the music played was by Blondie, Iggy Pop, David Bowie, Ramones, and Roxy Music."

LaMere Vipère was destroyed by a suspicious fire on April 27, 1978.

La Riviera
3216 N. Sheffield Ave.
Circa: 1972–1974

Lark Lounge
3441 N. Halsted, Chicago
Circa: 2017

Primarily a restaurant, it hosted an annual post-Pride parade women's dance.

This was also the location for Halsted's Bar & Grill, Madam B, and Voltaire.

Late Bar
3534 W. Belmont Ave.
Circa: 2011–2020

Lava Lounge
859 N. Damen Ave.
Circa: 2003–2006

"Flirt," the Lava Lounge women's night, featured an eclectic blend of electronica presented by female DJs.

La Vie En Rose
Calumet City
Circa: 1950

Leatherneck
209 W. Lake St.
Circa: 1997–1999

Leatherneck set itself up as "a kick-ass fag bar downtown," an alternative to the Halsted Street bars. In March 1999, an ad in the gay press read, "This aint no disco. The Cure for the Common Halsted." One newspaper described the bar as, "A multi-level erotic experience in the Loop theater district." Another wrote, "Right the heck downtown with masters, slaves, beer & booze, hooks, a cage, stocks, the El, and lots of parking."

Leatherneck was a bar downstairs and a dungeon upstairs.

John Birch owned the bar. The grand opening was in November 1997. Steve Cannon was a bartender.

This was also the location of Wet.

Left Bank/Right Bank
2140 N. Lincoln Park West
Circa: 1972-1974

Located in the Webster Hotel, there were two rooms, one on each side of the lobby. Mark remembered, "The bar on the left was the Left Bank, and one on the right was the Right Bank. They were both gay"

Gary Martin was a bartender there.

Le Kris
949 W. Diversey Pkwy.
Circa: 1984

An announcement in the gay press read, "March 1984: Le Kris holds its gala premiere with dancing, live entertainment, and free champagne."

Leo's Den
1200 E. 71st St.
Circa: 2003

Leo's Den hosted occasional LGBT events, such as a July 2003 benefit for Windy City Black Pride with a performance by nationally acclaimed spoken word artist Staceyann Chin, and an open mic with CC Carter and Tai Freedom Ford.

Le Passage
937 N. Rush St.
Circa: 2010

Le Passage hosted a monthly Glitter party. In June 2010, ChicagoPride.com and *Time Out Chicago* held an After-Pride Party at Le Passage, hosted by CT Hedden and Aurora Sexton.

Le Pub
1944 N. Clark St.
Circa: 1974-77

In May 1974, Le Pub came out as gay after years of being a straight dating and dining bar. Andy Cahill provided entertainment on the opening night.

David Honneger recalled, "At the grand opening of Le Pub, one of the owners of the Snakepit walked into the bar ... I don't know if there was animosity between him and the owner of Le

Pub, or whatever ... but he walked into the bar, looked around, took his dick out of his pants, pissed on the floor, and said, 'What a piss-elegant place."

Le Pub was owned by Danny Reilly and billed itself as "Chicago's Most Elegant Gay Bar." Among the performers who appeared at Le Pub were Billy Whitfield, Karen Mason, Bobby Duncan and Co., Pam and Jan, Tony Lewis & Co., and Karen Burns.

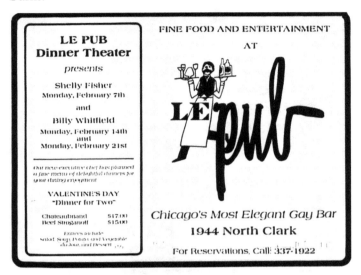

On Christmas Day 1977, Le Pub burned down, causing an estimated $150,000 to $225,000 damage. One bartender, Phil Scharpetta, smelled smoke coming from the basement. As the phones were dead, one employee ran across the street to a payphone to call the fire department. One fireman was injured.

David Plomin told the authors, "Christmas Eve 1977 I was there with a friend of mine, and all of a sudden smoke was coming through the vents, and everyone made a mad dash out for the exit door. Obviously, everyone got out OK because they had enough exit doors and that was probably about the time that all the gay bars left the Lincoln Park area and started moving further north."

Le Roma's Grand Ritz
1146 S. Wabash Ave.
Circa 1987

The gay press guides listed Le Roma's as a gay bar in 1987.

Let It Be
52nd Ave. and 32nd Pl., Cicero
Circa: 1972

(Nino B's) Le Trolls
2838 N. Broadway
Circa: 1978–1979

Le Troll's was owned by Peter Levine and Nino B. Heacox. In June 1979, the Bearded Lady performed there. Le Troll's advertised its 1900s period décor restaurant with, "We've got

beef for you. We've got chicken for you. We've got whatever you might want to put in your mouth."

On September 3, 1979, Le Trolls became Ann Arkees.

This address was also the location of It's Here.

Levin's Inn
3526 N. Lincoln Ave.
Circa: 1974–1976

This was a lesbian bar.

Liar's Club
1665 W. Fullerton Ave.
Circa: 1995–present

The mostly straight bar featured a hold-over following from previous incarnations as a gay bar, including Factory Disco, Music Factory, and Risqué.

Limelight
632 N. Dearborn St.
Circa: 1985-1988

In April 1986, Moving Molehill Productions presented a sneak preview and backers' audition of Tom Wilson Weinberg's *Ten Percent Revue*. In December 1988, Colt Studio model and film director, Gunner Hyde made an appearance. Richard Knight (AKA Dick O'Day) was in charge of special events. Sunday nights were gay night with an ongoing event called "Bent."

Reporting on the bar's opening in *Gay Chicago Magazine* in August 1985, Rick Karlin wrote, "The big news last week was the opening of Limelight. Many folks were more than a little peeved after waiting three or more hours to get in. It is rather tacky to invite people, then not admit them. In New York that may be chic; in Chicago, it's called rude."

The club was closed by the police numerous times.

This was also the location of Excalibur, Vision Nightclub, and Sanctuary.

Lips Chicago
2229 S. Michigan Ave.
Circa: 2020-present

The Chicago outpost of a chain of drag show dinner theaters.

Lite Factory
2500 N. Southport Ave.
Circa: 1979-1981

In August 1979, Jack and Gail Coutre opened the Lite Factory. It was a drag/trans bar with the buxom Robin Robins on the door, Spanish Rosa behind the bar, Juan Nieves handled the coat check (he later owned Madrigals), and Mysterious Marilyn read tarot cards on the floor. In October 1981, Danniel Lambert (The Dragon Lady), formerly of the Frog Pond, took over as manager. Gail Coutre died of a heart attack on August 25, 1981. This was also the location of Bird's Nest.

Lithium
1124 W. Belmont Ave.
Circa: 2001

This was a short-lived straight bar with a gay night. In December 2001, Monica Munro and guests performed at ALT Mondays.

Little Bits
2519 N. Halsted St.
Circa: 1976-1977

Little Bits opened in December 1976 and was owned by Albert "Little Al" Milaro. The bar was gay-owned and had an outdoor beer garden. It closed in October 1977, after failing to renew the liquor license.

This was previously the location of Carol's Coming Out Pub.

Little Club
6 State St., Calumet City
Circa: 1982

Little Hercules Disco (Herculito)
3477 N. Clark St.
Circa: 1980

Little Hercules was a Latino dance bar.

This was also the location of ?(Question Mark), and Sweets.

Little Jim's
3501 N. Halsted St.
Circa: 1975-2014

Little Jim's was opened in June 1975 by Little Jim Gates and Big Jim Slater. It was long credited with being the first gay bar on Halsted Street, but the Inn Between and Augie's – two women-owned bars – were on the strip before. Over the years, the bar hosted many fundraisers and events, including those supporting the Chicago House residence for people impacted by HIV/AIDS, in which all bar receipts and donations on the first Thursday of every month were donated. In August 1991, that monthly fundraiser reached a goal of $100,000.

Little Jim's was a popular neighborhood hangout for gay men. The long bar ran halfway back through the room, and beyond that was a small dance floor (later replaced by arcade machines). In the early days, the bar had a continuous slide show of male erotic images, later replaced by porn videos. For a

while, the bar featured go-go boys. In 1988, the manager was Guy Warner. Bill Mosier was the manager in 1980. There have been many bartenders over the years, including Rene Van Hulle, Tully Bertorelli, Matthew Gutowski, Richard Williamson, and Bill Scala. Sometimes the bar showed movies.

The bar changed ownership in 2014, and the name officially changed to LJ's.

Little Jim Gates also opened outposts of the bar in Phoenix (1984) and Fort Lauderdale (1983).

Lizard's Liquid Lounge
3058-3060 W. Irving Park Rd.
Circa: 2008-present

This was the location of Lost & Found Lounge. Liz Tomek took it over from Lost and Found owner, Ava Allen, when she retired. Tomek brought more of an edge and punk aesthetic to the bar. In August 2012, the bar hosted Queerpocalypse 2.0, and in July 2013, All That Glitters and Glows! starring Lucy Wak, Wanda Makeout?, Queerella Fistalot, Dahlia Fatale,

Holly Deck, Marci Vousplait, Phaedra Black, and Boy Gorgeous.

LJ's
3501 N. Halsted St.
Circa: 2014-2020

Little Jim's was opened in June 1975 by Little Jim Gates and Big Jim Slater. In 2014, the bar changed ownership and name to LJ's, but customers never acknowledged the change. The bar continued to operate until 2019, when the property was sold to the Howard Brown Health Center. The bar closed in July 2020. The building was demolished in August 2021.

Loading Dock
3702 N. Halsted St.
Circa: 1982-1994

The Loading Dock was the fourth gay bar owned by Steve Rempas, a local dentist; the other three were the Loading Zone, Scalawags, and Ozone. The bar was affectionately known as "The Dick Dock." In the first year of the bar's existence, Bart Lombard was the manager. Bar staff included Jeff Courtouise, Skip Howard, Tony Valdes, Bruce Fenn, Kevin M. Cole, Adam Cooley, Dave D. Jacobson, and Brad Boyd.

For *Gay Chicago Magazine*'s Garden Walk of Beer Gardens in July 1989, Loading Dock was described as, "No frills here. Concrete and lawn chairs are all you get (or need) for this late-night dance spot."

In 1992, David Boyer was the manager and, with DJ Ron Goodman, hosted Country & Western dances with lessons. In 1990, the Loading Dock was the first gay bar in the city to have a no-smoking area.

The bar closed in July 1994.

This location also housed the Latino gay bar, Vista Hermosa, the Aloha Bikini Lounge, and is now Cell Block.

Loading Zone
46 E. Oak St.
Circa: 1978–1986

The Loading Zone opened in November 1978, but the grand opening was January 1, 1979. Terry Castleman was the manager, and Don Cobbs was manning the door that night. The bar was owned by Dr. Steve Rempas. The bartenders in June 1980 were Fast Eddie and Fred Marr. Each year, in March, the bar celebrated "Greek Week" with a toga party, "Wear a

toga and your drinks will be 50c each from midnight to 5 a.m." In 1982, the bar celebrated with belly dancers Joseph and Valina.

In August 1981, the bar offered half-price poppers to customers who bought a Loading Zone T-shirt.

In 1982, the manager was David Williams.

Mark Palermo related, "The police came in and closed down the bar, a couple of days after Christmas, and this was for serving minors liquor. I just remember they came in, we had to shut up, be quiet, and had to line up against the wall ... the police frisked everybody, asked to see ID, and then one by one they let us out after asking us all kinds of questions about who we were and why we were there. That was in 1983."

This was also the location of TJ's on Oak and Scalawag's.

Loading Zone
3359 N. Halsted St.
Circa: 1991–1995

This was an attempt to move the Loading Zone up to the Halsted bar strip.

This was also the location of Cocktail, Men's Room, and Progress Bar.

Locker
3019 N. Clark St.
Circa: 1980

Jerry Bauman owned the Locker, and Bob Shields was the manager. Mike Scalzo was a bartender.

The Locker was listed as, an "Establishment for Men in or into Levis."

This was also the location of Big Red's, Jock's, and Minkees.

Loft
430 N. Clark St.
Circa: 1978–1979

Female impersonator Wanda Lust was a bartender at the Loft.

This was also the location of Punch's, Baton, Ramrod, Annex 2, and Sunday's (Children).

Logjam
2837 N. Clark St.
Circa: 1977

A report in the gay press in September 1977 read, "The hot event this week is the Ball Busting Grand Opening of Logjam, 2837 N. Clark St. The bar had formerly been known as Grandma's Receipts and all the previous patrons were invited by owners Bill Beck and Jim Szabo to attend the new Logjam featuring gay square dancing and clogging."

Rita the Shopping Bag Lady performed at Logjam.

The bar closed in December of 1977.

Lola's
1005 N. Western Ave.
Circa: 2002

This was a Latin restaurant, bar, and show lounge featuring drag performances.

Lolita's
4400 N. Clark St.
Circa: 2001–2002

Lolita's was nominally a restaurant. However, if you ordered food, they sometimes had to phone the chef at home to come in. It was really a Latin bar with a drag show.

This was also the location of Erotica.

Lolita's
4400 N. Clark
(773) 561-3356
(Clark & Montrose)

Chicago's Premier Latino Female Impersonator Review

with Shows
Wednesday thru Sunday
10pm and 12am
Dinner Shows
Starting at 8pm
Serving Exotic Mexican Food

DJs
Ramiro
and Trini

Lonnie's Skyline Lounge
135 W. 75th St.
Circa: 1966

St Sukie de la Croix's *Chicago Whispers* reads, "In April 1966, police raided Lonnie Doyal's Lonnie's Skyway Lounge, 135 W. 75th St., arresting Doyal and Gloria Smith, as co-keepers of a disorderly house, four waitresses, twenty-one patrons and five female impersonators. The 'girls' gave their names as Willie 'Shirley' West, Alphonso Dixon, stage name 'Alphonso Marlowe,' Charles 'Maggie' McNee, Harvey Williamson, and Raymond 'Rae Del Rays' Navarro, the only white 'girl.'"

Lost & Found
2959 W. Irving Park Rd.
Circa: 1965–1980

Arlene Halko, the owner of Piggen's Pub, recalled, "The first lesbian bar I went to was a couple of blocks west of California. It was owned by Ava [Allen] and Shirley [Christiansen], actually, Shirley owned it, and Ava was tending bar. It was in the old location then, on Sacramento and Irving. I don't think they had certified their romance at that time."

Tessie said, "It's like when I used to go to Lost & Found years ago. You would go into a bar, and the police would harass you. Women couldn't cross-dress; women couldn't wear pants with zippers in the front. You had to have pants with buttons on the side. You couldn't have men's shirts on. The buttons had to be, women are on the right, men are on the left, or they would actually come in and arrest you and put you in a paddy wagon, and you'd go to jail for cross-dressing."

This was also the location of Kitty's Korner.

Lost & Found
3058-3060 W. Irving Park Rd.
Circa: 1980-2008

This was the second incarnation of the lesbian bar, Lost and Found. One patron remembered the bar moving, "I used to go to the old Lost and Found, still on Irving Park Road but a block or so down from where it is now, and on the other side of the street. Ava Allen and Shirley Christensen always had a dream of opening a really nice bar, then they got this location two blocks down, where it is now, and it was much nicer. I was down there the night they moved; we closed the old bar at midnight and walked up the street and went into the new bar. The neighborhood policeman came and drove Ava and the money up from one location to the other. He was with her to escort her in, and he put the first quarter in the jukebox and said, 'Enjoy girls,' then he went out, got back in his squad car, and took off."

Another patron said, "This is a moment frozen in time for me. I went to Lost & Found and I was sitting there, the music was on, and people were dancing. All of a sudden, everything stopped, and Kate Smith's 'God Bless America' came on. Then the lights dimmed, and I had never seen it before, but there's an American flag high on the wall ... a spotlight shone on the American flag, and everybody stood up and started singing 'God Bless America' ... Am I in the middle of a Fellini film? I was completely freaked. I couldn't tell if it was camp, I couldn't tell if it was serious ... we looked around, and it was dead serious. I found out later that the early lesbian and gay movement were very patriotic. And this was, I guess, something that used to go on in the bars all the time. ... It was an amazing experience, because it was so completely out of my frame of reference."

On October 19, 1986, Shirley Christensen died after a long battle with cancer.

In 2008 owner Ava Allen sold the bar to Liz Tomek, who rechristened it Lizard's Liquid Lounge.

Louis Gage's Fun Lounge
2320 N. Mannheim Rd., Melrose Park
2340 N. Mannheim Rd., Melrose Park
Circa: 1940s-1964

Paul remembered the bar, "We always had fun at Louis Gages bar because you could push the bar, and the bar would move. There used to be a dirt floor. That bar was open 24 hours a day. Louis was a heavy-set person, and he was pretty nice, but his trouble was that he was for 18-year-old kids."

The *Chicago Tribune* reported on a raid on the club on Sunday, April 26, 1964. The headline read, "Teacher, 1 of 8 Seized in Vice Raid, Quits." The report went on, "One of eight suburban teachers arrested in a vice raid early yesterday morning at the Fun Lounge, a tavern at 2340 N. Mannheim Rd., Leydon Twp.,

resigned yesterday afternoon. A teacher in Lincoln Junior High School in Park Ridge quit although he denied any wrongdoing. Blair Plimpton, district superintendent, said his resignation would be accepted ... Many of the men arrested carried powder puffs and lipsticks and some of them wore wigs, according to Richard Cain, the sheriff's investigator. Arrested in living quarters in the rear of the place was the Lounge proprietor, Louis Gauger, 53, a 270-pound avowed friend of Tony Accardo, the 'elder statesman' of the crime syndicate.

"All those arrested were fingerprinted and photographed. The patrons were released on $25 bonds after being charged with having been patrons of a disorderly house. Gauger, the Fun Lounge proprietor, posted a $1,500 bond after being charged with sale of liquor to minors, possession of narcotics, and being the keeper of a disorderly house."

98 ARRESTED IN FUN LOUNGE RAID ARE FREED

Ninety-eight patrons charged with disorderly conduct in a sheriff's raid on the Fun Lounge, 2340 N. Mannheim rd., Leydon townsrip, were freed yesterday in West District court in Oak Park.

The state presented its case after attorneys for the defendants objected to the presence of photographers in the court and Judge Wayne W. Olson overruled the objections. Sgt. John Charconas of sheriff's police testified that when the lounge was raided April 25, he saw 10 or 15 male couples dancing and half a dozen male couples embracing. He said he could not identify them in the court room. The state rested its case and the judge dismissed the 98.

Seven other persons charged with disorderly conduct were not in court and the judge issued warrants for their arrest The cases of five other defendants were continued until June 26. They are Louis Gauger, Herbert Schieler, Robert Levy, Kevin Jenner, and W. G. Westby.

On January 29, 1960, the bar was destroyed by two explosions and a fire. The body of 27 year-old Robert Niewinski, a bartender, was found in the rubble; he was alone in the bar at the time. According to Capt. WJ McManigal of the Cook County police, the fire was caused by a gas leak. The Fun Lounge was rebuilt with an inconspicuous tile façade, no front windows, no sign and a thick steel door."

2 More Teachers in Raid Quit; Others Off Duty

Three Chicago area school teachers had resigned and two others and two school officials were off duty yesterday as the result of a vice raid early Saturday on the Fun lounge, 2340 N. Mannheim rd., Leyden township.

They were among eight school teachers and officials seized in the raid, in which 103 men and six women were arrested by sheriff's police under Richard Cain, chief investigator for Sheriff Richard B. Ogilvie.

Won't Renew License

Meanwhile A. L. Hornick, administrative assistant to Seymour Simon, county board president and liquor control commissioner for unincorporated areas, announced that Simon would not renew the liquor license for the tavern, which will expire at midnight Thursday.

It was announced that Norman Gee, 25, of 38 Washington st., Oak Park, has resigned as a 5th grade teacher in Longfellow Elementary school, Oak Park.

It was disclosed that Roger Born, 26, of 195 Harvey st., Wood Dale, quit his position as a teacher in Parkside school, Roselle.

Another of those arrested, Norris Angel, 24, of 2025 Pine av., Des Plaines, had resigned Saturday night as a teacher in Lincoln Junior High school, Park Ridge, altho he denied any wrong doing.

Board to Meet

Clair G. Grindstaff, 33, of 1637 Chicago av., Evanston, personnel director for elementary school district 39 in Wilmette, was reported "off duty" pending a meeting with the school board last night. It was reported he will be given an indefinite leave of absence.

John Kutcosky, 31, of 45 Forest av., Riverside, was granted a temporary leave pending investigation by the school board for Riverside-Brookfield High school, where he has been teaching.

Charles Rolinski, 35, of Lake Zurich, teacher in Palatine Junior High school, was suspended pending investigation by the school board and his court hearing.

It was announced that Herbert P. Jensen, 56, of 225 E. 1st st., Elmhurst, was being relieved of his duties as principal of Jackson Junior High school, Villa Park, pending investigation of his arrest in the raid.

Melvin Anglin, 30, of Algonquin, teacher in Dundee Community High school, Dundee, another of those arrested, continued teaching. School officials said they were convinced he would be acquitted, and that he claimed all he knew was that he was going to a night club.

Will Appear May 15

The 109 persons arrested are to appear in West District court in Oak Park May 15, most of them on disorderly conduct charges. The proprietor, Louis Gauger, 53, avowed friend of Tony Accardo, crime syndicate figure, will face several charges.

Col. John Bucher, police director of personnel, said he was investigating the arrest in the Fun lounge of one of his clerks, Michael Gavigan, 26, of 8432 Throop st. Forest preserve district officials said they were investigating the arrest there of a painter employed by the district, Robert Zahnen, 41, of 5712 N. Moody av.

The Chicago board of election commissioners said George A. Kapellas, 24, of 7700 Cornell av., would be dismissed as a Democratic election judge in the 20th precinct of the 8th ward as a result of his arrest.

Lucky Clover Lounge
2315 W. Fullerton Ave.
Circa: 1979–1980

The grand opening of Lucky Clover Lounge was held on November 10, 1979. One gay newspaper described the bar as "An Irish bar with a Latin flavor." The owner was Toni, and the bartenders were Janis and Anne. Every Friday night, there was a live DJ and belly dancers for entertainment. On Sunday nights, they hosted an amateur dance contest with cash prizes.

Lucky Horseshoe Lounge
3169 N. Halsted St.
Circa: 1989–present

Ben Allen originally planned to open the bar as a new location for his Clark St. bar, the Inner Circle, but then decided to rebrand it. After extensive renovations to the former Irene's Diamonds, he opened in 1989 with a bar focused on male dancers, with a stage in the center of the room, with a bar encircling it. His partners in the venture were bartenders Rene Van Hulle, and Larry "Sophie" Graham.

Photos by Terry Gaskins

Although the primary focus was on the dancers, the bar hosted theme nights. In March 1994, "Doug's Rock 'n' Roll Funhouse" with classic rock all night, or the August 1991, "Ronnie's Krazy Kiddie Karnival Birthday Party."

On July 21, 2001, the bar was attacked with pepper spray or mace. Sophie suffered a heart attack and died the following day at age 58. Rene Van Hulle died of AIDS complications on February 27, 2007. When Ben Allen died September 13, 2016 – he left the bar to his husband, Micah Hilgendorf who also has a partnership in @mosphere and North End.

Spider, a dancer at the Lucky Horseshoe recalled, "I danced at the Horseshoe a long time ago. But one thing I never did was let them stick a buck or any money down my G string. Cuz they want to grab and touch, like ... Oh no ... It was like, stick in my boot, or put it in my hand."

This was also the location of Irene's Diamonds and Inner Circle.

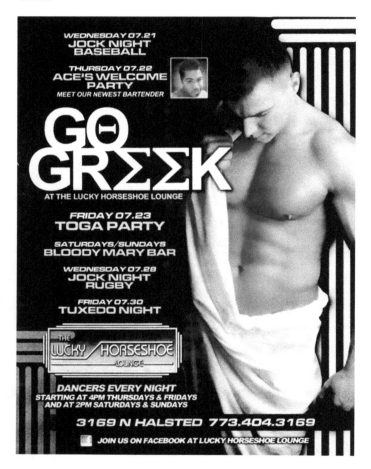

M7
3641 N. Halsted St.
Circa: 2016-2018

This was the front bar of Circuit which was also known as Rehab and Fantasy. This was also the location of the Halsted Street Café.

Machine
4363 N. Sheridan Rd.
Circa: 1973-1975

The Chicago Gay Directory, 1974-1975 Fourth Edition listed the Machine as semi-gay, with no alcohol. In the December 1973 *Chicago Gay Crusader,* the paper described the bar, "It's a beautiful place, two stories, two dance floors, with a disc jockey playing music, strobe lights, dancing, looks like a lively bar. But there's a difference; there's no age limit, no sex discrimination."

Macho/Chicago
3724 N. Clark St.
Circa: 1978

Macho/Chicago was a short-lived leather bar.

This was also the location of Giovanni's.

Madam B
3441 N. Halsted St.
Circa: 1998

In April 1998, this restaurant advertised in the gay press, "Brunch with a female impersonator revue." Madam B was described as, "The spirit of Puccini, or at least the high drama of opera, lives at Madame B. Pacific Rim influences produce dishes that are as exotic as they are delicious and could easily inspire the singing of an aria or two. The setting is at once rich, ethereal and theatrical."

This was also the location of Voltaire, Halsted's Bar & Grill, and Lark Lounge.

Mad Bar
1640 N. Damen Ave.
Circa: 1999

In April 1999, this straight/gay-friendly bar hosted the Sister Sense Spoken Word event for women.

This was also the location of Amadeus.

Madrigals
5316 N. Clark St.
Circa: 1994-2003

Opened in July 1994 by Juan Nieves, Madrigals was originally a piano bar/restaurant. Some of the performers were Freddy Allen, Honey West, Michael James, David Hamilton, and Victoria LaMarr, a female impersonator who could sing "Hotel California" in Vietnamese. Later in the year, they changed over to male dancers. An ad in February 2003 read, "Brad, JJ, RC, Giano and Christian strip down to the bare essentials and dance on the pole at Madrigals."

Main Drag
2401 N. Milwaukee Ave.
Circa: 1998

This was a straight bar with a gay night.

Mama Jan's
2659 W. 21st St.
Circa: 1977–1980s

The grand opening of Mama Jan's was in May 1977. Female impersonator, Kay Howard and his "Fantasy in Pantomime" were regular performers at this lesbian bar.

George FH described Mama Jan's, "The bar had been closed a long time when I began to notice women going in there. I knew at once that I wanted to go in and welcome her to the neighborhood and wish her success, but these lesbians looked pretty rough, and I chickened out. The area was old and conservative, and the women were laying low and playing it cool, so for a long time, the bar went unnamed. In fact, I never saw any sign there. The entrance was at the corner, but the bar faced Fairfield. Mama was older, the maternal type with vast bosoms and a very sweet expression – a perfect mother figure

for lost terrified chicks just coming out. There was one party, maybe her farewell, the racket was unbelievable. There were even two motorcycles out front. After that blast, she seemed closed. Closed, but I think she had a network and would only open on occasions – everyone knew and showed up. I can't remember when she closed; in the mid-'80s perhaps?"

Mama Lion's
3600 N. Pulaski Ave.
Circa: 1976–1977

Mama Lion's, owned by Lucy and Rose, had pool and bowling tournaments and occasional drag shows. When it opened, *GayLife* newspaper columnist Christopher reported, "My very good friend Lucy is one of the owners, joining Rose in operating Mama Lion's. They have three female and two male bartenders. Lucy assured me that everyone is welcome. Her bowling league was there (all of them) and they all had a ball. They'll be doing fun things, like a bowling tourney (where else ... on their pool table). And they'll give a trophy to the high-score winners. Sounds like Mama Lion's is going to liven up an otherwise staid area of Chicago."

In 1977, Kay Howard performed there.

Manchester Grill
473 E. 31st St.
Circa: 1940

The *Chicago Defender* reported on November 2, 1940, "Now that Valda Gray, America's most outstanding sepia female impersonator has taken control of things at Cyril Richards' Manchester Grill has taken on new life. Francis Dee, another well-known impersonator, and Anita Brown, the glamour girl of nightlife, are being featured at this ultra-smart spot. Horace Malcolm and his swing masters furnish the music."

Maneuvers
118 E. Jefferson St., Joliet
Circa: 1982-2019

Maneuvers was opened by Fred Schramm on July 10, 1982, with Mark Rodriguez as bartender and DJ Steve Freshwater. In 2011, the bar celebrated the 25th anniversary of the Miss Gay Joliet contest. The bar is most known for the drag shows, with stars such as Regina Upright, Angelique Munro, Phoenix Envy, and Soroya.

In April 1986, the bar held a benefit for the Howard Brown Memorial Clinic starring Odessa Brown with Grace LeRay and Brian Winston, from Club Victoria.

This was also the location of Continental Club East.

Maneuvers
pics by Kirk

Manhandler
1948 N. Halsted St.
Circa: 1980-2020

On August 15, 1980, *Gay Chicago Magazine* reported, "On Friday, August 15, 1980, a new 'western-style bar' opened ... The warm paneled room with fireplace is enhanced by one of the most comfortable beer gardens/patios in town with plenty of foliage, a three-tiered fountain, and cushioned lounge chairs." The fountain was installed by the manager Paul Wirts and the bartender on the opening night was Jay Wells." Other popular bartenders included Joseph "Texas" Butler, James Owen, Danny Johnson, Brian Arsenault, and Butch Toland. *Gay Chicago Magazine*'s Garden Walk of Beer Gardens in July 1989 reported, "Perhaps the largest, and at times, the lushest garden."

The bar, owned by Jerry Armstrong and Peter Kalamaras, maintained its western theme for 40 years and referred to its garden as "the back 40." On May 25, 2016, it hosted a Bear Pride Party, the first official event of Bear Pride 22.

The Manhandler closed in 2020.

Manhole
3458 N. Halsted St.
Circa: 1990-1998

Jeff Tesler, a straight man who owned the building, was the brother-in-law of Steve Brahill and his partner Pat Kasaras, co-founders of Christopher Street, which preceded Manhole in this space. After Steve and Pat succumbed to AIDS, Jeff brought in Ben Pohl to run the bar, along with the new concept. The bar was known for its underwear parties and leather-only back room.

The DJs over the years included Mark Vallese, Tim Cleary, and Boom Boom.

This was also the location of Hydrate and Christopher Street..

At the Manhole's "Underparty," a lucky Tony Marchese is sandwiched between two hot hunks, Edwin D'Valle and Carlos Fuentes.

Photos by Terry Gaskins

Manhole
3200 N. Halsted St.
Circa: 2014

An attempted reopening of the old Manhole – by the group that owns Hydrate – in the basement of Spin was not successful and only lasted a few weeks.

This was also the location of Spin, Foxy's, VII, Den, Whiskey Trust, and Eons.

Manor
42 E. Superior St.
Circa: 1999

The Manor, a cabaret drag bar, had a grand opening in February 1999. Kathryn Payne and Michael McAssey performed there, as did the Divas of Delight drag show.

Maria's Lounge
3037 N. Halsted St.
Circa: 1987

Maria's Lounge was listed in the gay press as gay-friendly.

Marilyn's
432 N. Clark St.
Circa: 1976-1978, then 1980-1981

The grand opening of Marilyn's was on November 3, 1976. Allan Rodman was the owner, Cathy "Milky" was a bartender, and Nancy Reiff was the manager. Reiff also worked at Punchinello's, Le Pub, Mr. Kelly's, *Gay Chicago Magazine*, and was Gay Liaison for Mayor Daley in the 1990s. In January 1978, the Harlettes, Bette Midler's backup singers, visited Marilyn's to wish Nancy Reiff a happy birthday.

Nancy Reiff explained how she became involved with the bar, "I was working at Sundays and Allan Rodman, the owner, and I, were very, very good friends, and one day he approached me and said, 'I really want to do a women's bar, do you want to run it for me?' I said, 'I think it's a great idea, let's do it.' So we opened up November 4, 1976, and it was a success. He had premises already, which was the little space between the Baton and Sundays, and then we started planning the whole thing, the visuals, decorating it, the sound system, hiring staff. Anna, who [later] owned the Swan Club, was hired to be one of my bartenders. The bar was absolutely fabulous inside. I am biased, but I have to say it was probably the best women's bar the city of Chicago had ever seen. It was a women's bar, but we didn't keep men out. We had Sundays there, we had the Bistro over on Dearborn, the Gold Coast across the street, and we had the Baton next door, and we always had a nice amount of men in the bar. So we never kept men out. There was a reciprocal thing, the bartenders from the various bars would come in for cocktails. A lot of the guys would come out with their female friends, and they'd come in, then they'd go off to the Gold Coast or wherever. The girls would stay, and the men would come back later to pick them up. So, we always had men in and out.

"Marilyn's was a disco, but periodically, we would have bands appearing. Judy Roberts was a phenomenal pianist and vocalist. I hired her a few times to perform. And there was a women's band, and I can't remember the name, but they were regular customers of mine, and they would sometimes come and play.

We would do salsa on Sundays, because I had a large Latina crowd, and that music has always been a favorite of mine.

"The owner sold Sundays and Marilyn's both to a guy by the name of Sam from Madison, Wisconsin. Sam came in and changed things around a lot. I think I quit and went back, then Allan bought it back from Sam. It was a mess. The bar closed, then reopened ... the first time it closed was '78, '79. Then he opened it again as Marilyn's for something like six months, but it didn't work." Jock's was also at this location.

Mark III
73rd St. and Cottage Grove Ave.
Circa: 1973–1977

Donna Rose remembered, "The Mark III, which was on 75th and Cottage Grove, and that was a stomp down daddy bar, but when I was at high school, I was afraid to go in. I would sit with a couple of friends, and we would just watch these women going in and out, and I mean Cadillacs, fur coats, mini-skirts, halter tops ... 'Oh baby, I can't wait to be older' ... when they first started doing FM Radio, like BMX, that was the underground radio station, they used to have a blurb, an advertisement, and Deni was one of the DJs and I can't think of the other woman's name, but the way the thing went was, 'Sisters, come on down to the Mark III, the Mark III, the Mark III.' So that was pretty out there in '77."

'Bridegroom' Peaches hugs new bride after ceremony.

Two Females 'Married' In Chicago—To Each Other

Two women, Edna Knowles and Peaches Stevens, were wed in Liz's Mark III Lounge, a gay bar on

Martini Club
3124 N. Central Ave.
Circa: 2010

In July 2010, the Martini Club held a First Fierce Gay Party hosted by Zachary Thurmond. The bar offered a free pick-up limo-bus from the corner of Belmont and Halsted.

Martin's Corner
1900 W. Lake St.
Circa: 1940

This Black drag bar was owned by James C. Martin. When the Cabin Inn closed, the performers moved to Martin's Corner, including female impersonator Valda Gray and song and dance man "Joan Crawford."

Martin's Den
5550 S. State St.
Circa: 1976–1980s

This Black disco dance bar was owned and operated by Henry Martin and featured "Up-and-coming disco DJ WaKu who spins Thursday through Sunday." Other DJs at Martin's Den were Craig Cannon, Craig Loftis, and Michael Ezebukwu.

In 1983, Henry Martin hosted a series of workshops entitled, "HIV and Health in the Gay Community."

The bar closed when Martin died.

Marty's Martini Bar
1511 W. Balmoral Ave.
Circa: 2012–present

Marty's Martini Bar is a tiny neighborhood bar featuring crafted cocktails and fine wine. *Time Out* wrote, "This upscale Andersonville martini lounge burns through olives and vermouth faster than a steakhouse does. These Don Drapers come in all types, but it seems the straight folk tend to show up first for a predinner cocktail and the gay crowd comes later. Like gentrification, but in reverse."

Mary's Attic (see Hamburger Mary's)

Mashed Potato Club
316 W. Erie St.
Circa: 1996–2002

The Mashed Potato Club was a restaurant with drag shows. Sean Parnell of the Chicago Bar Project wrote, "Canary yellow paint and a flashing pink neon sign outside give a prelude to the potpourri of glitz on the inside. This is a place where all the waiters are flamboyantly gay, and the menu urges you to flirt with them. The walls are painted with huge, colorful murals of naked men and women, Mr. Potato Heads and pink flamingoes are scattered around the room, and the high ceilings are bedecked with disco balls, upside-down Christmas trees, and more tinsel, tulle, and colored lights than you can shake a stick at. Additional decor includes walls of bookshelves and fake

animal heads, one of which is eating someone. The bar is longer than most I've seen and is complete with a giant martini glass at the far end."

The Ultra Glam shows' performers included Tina Stefano, Sassy Trade, Angelique Munro, and Regina Upright.

Matchmaker
740 W. Madison St.
Circa: 1976–1978

The Matchmaker opened on December 17, 1976, with an all-male burlesque revue. It was across from the Holiday Inn in Greek Town.

Maxbar Chicago
2247 N. Lincoln Ave.
Circa: 2010

The bar hosted a post pride parade T-Licious T Dance with "lickable go-go boys" and DJ Matthew Harvat (Circuit Mom).

Maxine's (Boulevard Room)
79th St. and Langley Ave. or Jeffrey Ave. near 71st St.
Circa: 1967–1968

Maxine's was raided in May 1968.

Maxine's New Living Room Lounge
744 E. 83rd St.
Circa: 1981

On December 24, 1981, a listing in the gay press read, "'JR' Proudly Presents Jazz & Glamour on Revue featuring Ms. Margret, Ms. Pisces, Ms. Theresa Stella Kingston, Roberta Wilson, and Andrea, at Maxine's New Living Room Lounge, 83rd St. Music by DJ Gene Taylor, and lights by Oscar Grant."

Michal Brody remembered, "Maxine's was on 79th and Langley. I remember it as a long, narrow storefront with the bar as a long, narrow island in the middle. It was a very congenial place, mostly women, but some gay men, some neighborhood hookers, a few straight men. It would get very crowded on the weekends, and there wasn't much room to move around. Dancing wasn't allowed. The hot dance that summer was called the Pearl. We did it on our barstools. I heard that the place had gotten raided one night, and Maxine herself went down and bailed everyone out. That was an extraordinary and generous thing to do, quite unheard of!"

McKie's Club
6325 Cottage Grove Ave.
Circa: 1960

On September 20, 1960, there was a Jewel Box Revue cast party at McKie Fitzhugh's gay-friendly McKie's club, where they held "Ladies' Fancy Pants Night" for masculine women. The resident singer at McKie's was gay celebrity Wilbur "Hi-Fi" White, who also sang at the Kitty Kat Klub.

Meat Rack
2479 N. Clark St.,
Circa: 1978

A listing in the gay press from May 1978 reads, "The Meat Rack is New Town's newest bar with hosts Aggie, Regina, Casey, and Kojak." This was also the location of Pepper & Salt and Park West Lounge.

Medusa
3133 N. Halsted St.
Circa: 1982

A precursor to David "Medusa" Shelton's legendary after-hours club on Sheffield.

Medusa Chicago Nightclub (see Mission)

Medusa's Music Hall
3257 N. Sheffield Ave.
Circa: 1983-1993

A late-night after-hours hangout featuring alternative music. It didn't serve alcohol, so it was also popular with underage kids. The club often featured live music such as a personal appearance by the Violent Femmes in May 1982. Other headliners included Divine, Ministry, Red Hot Chili Peppers, and Sheila E from Prince's band. In February 1988, live bands, original films and video, art painting and photography displays, performance art, and a fashion show were all featured in a multi-media event. It was put together by students from Columbia College and the School of the Art Institute of Chicago as a benefit for Howard Brown Memorial Clinic.

On June 22, 1986. A Blow Out! Party featured DJs from gay bars around the city, including Mark Hultmark (Christopher Street), Frank Lipomi (Gold Coast), Mark Stephens (Medusa's), Michael Fowler (Loading Dock), Teri Bristol (Orbit Room), and Tom Parks (Hunter's).

Ray Thomas recalled, "I worked lights for Medusa's. Medusa had long curly hair; that's why everyone calls him Medusa. Have you heard the name Blue? There was another guy named Blue. Blue was a part of that and Bob Anderson. ... they were all on the same party circuit."

After losing his lease, Medusa moved his events to the Congress Theater until November 1993 before opening his own club called Mission in his hometown of Elgin.

Meeting House Tavern
5025 N. Clark St.
Circa: 2018-present

This bar opened in a brand-new building, right before the pandemic struck, so it didn't have much time to build a following. It's owned by Mark Robertson and Mike Sullivan of the 2 Bears Group, which also owns Jackhammer and SoFo Tap.

This was also the location of T's and the Gold Coast.

Melodies
3174 N. Clark St.
Circa: 1976

In 1976, *Gay Chicago Magazine* wrote, "Stained glass and live plants accent this completely gay-owned establishment. Another of the new breed of mixed bars, they feature a large disco dance floor with the DJ. Away from the disco is a separate lounge with a short-order kitchen. Special cocktail prices nightly."

Men's Room
3359 N. Halsted St.
Circa: 1985-1991

The grand opening of the Men's Room took place in May 1985. The bar was owned by Dr. Steve Rempas, who also owned Ozone, Scalawags, Halsted's, Loading Dock, and Loading Zone. Tommy Parks was a DJ there, and Michael K and Tommie Rogers were popular bartenders.

The Men's Room closed in April 1991.

This was also the location of Loading Zone, Cocktail, and Progress.

Photo by Dan Di Leo

The Men's Room staff helped promote the Black and Gold party held up the street at the Loading Dock. Helping them out that night was Jim Dohr (second from right).

Metro
3730 N. Clark St.
Circa: 1982-present

One of the largest dance clubs in the city. How gay it is, depends on the night and performers scheduled, since it's also a concert venue (Lene Lovich, Amy Ray, and Iggy Pop for example). Metro regularly hosts a post Pride parade tea dance as a benefit for local gay NFPs.

In 1990, the owner of Metro was Joe Shanahan.

In December 1988, one gay newspaper described Metro as, "Chicago's only Rock 'n' Roll fag bar." In May 2016, Metro hosted the Grabby's, the annual adult film awards show, hosted by Chi Chi La Rue and Honey West.

This location also houses Smart Bar and was once home to Center Stage and Stages.

Miami Moon
4500 W. Washington St.
Circa: 1949-1954

The Miami Moon was a drag bar. From St Sukie de la Croix's book *Chicago Whispers*, "The Miami Moon ... a roadhouse saloon with a troubled history: the Miami Moon was closed down and robbed on numerous occasions; on Nov 1, 1949, five shotgun blasts came through the front window narrowly missing the owner James Scallon and several customers; in 1950 Scallon sold the bar to James J. Cleary and his wife Marie for $55,000; Cleary sold it again in 1953; on March 4, 1954, Cleary was charged with murder in Reno, Nev. He asked Margaret Jenkins, a Western Union clerk, if telegraphed money he was expecting had arrived. When she said 'No' he fatally stabbed her in the neck with a screwdriver."

Miami Show Lounge
2822 E. 55th St.
Circa: 1940s-1950s

This drag club was owned by Neal Cooper.

Michelle's Sports Bar
7225 W. Grand Ave.
Circa: 1998

Wednesday was gay and lesbian night at this straight bar.

Midget Inn
Kedzie Avenue near Montrose Ave.
Circa: 1950s

Marge Summit, interviewed by historian Owen Keehnen, said, "The first floor of that place was a straight bar, and then you went through the bar, and up the stairs and there was a big room for gay women with a jukebox and a bar. When it got raided, the cops had to come through the bar and up the stairs, so there was time to get out. We kicked out the screens to the windows and jumped from the second floor and started running."

Mike's
W. 63rd St. and S. Harlem Ave.
Circa: 1978

Mike's Aragon Lounge
1113 W. Lawrence Ave.
Circa: 1973-1979

This was also the location of Sharon's Side Track.

Mike's Terrace Lounge
1137 W. Granville Ave.
Circa: 1973-1987

Mike's Terrace Lounge was owned by "Irish" Mike Costello. In May 1983, Joanne Bishop was the manager. Bishop owned the bar back when it was called the Hi-Ho Terrace Lounge.

On July 12, 1974, Daniel Powell, Jr., a bartender on the night shift, was murdered at the bar. His body was found the next day when the daytime bartender arrived for work at 11 a.m. Powell, whose hands were tied behind his back, was stabbed at least five times, and $1,500 was missing.

This location was also the Hi-Ho Terrace Lounge and the Granville Anvil.

Minibar Ultra Lounge and Café
3341 N. Halsted St.
Circa: 2005-2016

Minibar was opened in 2005 by John Dalton and Stu Zirin. In 2016, it was owned by Robert Brumbaugh. It attracted a young crowd, mostly gay men. In February 2010, members of the touring cast of *Rent* performed at Minibar. In July 2010, Minibar hosted a male burlesque show. In July 2012, Cyon Flare presented the Chicago Black Gay Men's Caucus' United in Pride, featuring live performances, appetizers, spoken word, and house music.

In 2013, *Out* magazine included Minibar in their list of the "200 of the Greatest Gay Bars in the World." The magazine said of the bar, "Attentive and, more importantly, hot modelesque guys serve your every whim – from delicious cotton candy martinis to paninis. In the heart of the gay-filled Halsted Street, walk upstairs and tilt your head back for a stunning light show in this attractive, modern lounge."

This was also the location of Felt.

Minkees
3019 N. Clark St.
Circa: 1980-1981

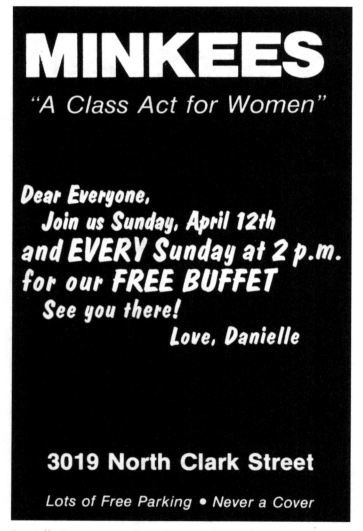

Danielle Lewis opened Minkees on December 27, 1980. One of its first ads read, "Dear Santa, I've waited all year ... please bring me the best sound, the friendliest women and a place that will warm me inside and out – please give me Minkees. XXX OOO Danielle."

On Sundays, they hosted a wet T-shirt contest, where all the women were soaked.

Jan Wills told the authors, "We used to go there all the time, a bunch of women, one was called Mafioso Debbie, Pinky, Tuna.

That bar didn't last long, but that was a fun place. A totally lesbian bar."

This was also the location of Big Red's, jock's, and Locker.

Missing Link Pub
3011 N. Mannheim Rd., Melrose Park
Circa: 1975

The Missing Link Pub wasn't open very long – just a few months – but in June 1975, the bar hosted a fundraiser for the ailing newspaper, *The Gay Crusader*, with special guests Euneda Hose from the Linoleum Sisters and Bertha Butt. It cost $1 to get in. The Bearded Lady made an appearance on the opening night.

According to a report in *The Gay Crusader*, the bar's owner, Fred (no last name given), who was 22 and said to be the youngest person to obtain an Illinois liquor license, was robbed, badly beaten, and suffered a black eye and fractured facial bone. His head bartender, Billy, ran the bar while Fred was in the hospital.

Mission
4746 N. Broadway
Circa: 1993

Mission (Medusa Chicago Nightclub)
209 E. Chicago Ave., Elgin
Circa: 1998-2020

After losing the lease on his Chicago location, Dave "Medusa" Shelton moved his after-hours club to Elgin. He operated the club until it closed due to the COVID pandemic in March 2020. After Shelton died of natural causes in July 2020, the club shuttered permanently.

Moda VIP
2409 N. Mannheim Rd., Franklin Park
Circa: 2009

This was also the location of Texas Ranch.

Molly Maguire's Lounge
131st St. and Cicero Ave.
Circa: 1984

Molly's
2935 N. Broadway
Circa: 1974

Molly's was a non-alcohol juice bar.

Molly's Follies
2568 N. Clark St.
Circa: 1980

At the grand opening of Molly's Follies on August 18, 1980, there was a buffet and a raffle for a TV. A popular figure in the community, Sophie, served drinks – later, he was a bartender at Lucky Horseshoe Lounge. Molly's Follies was run by Chicago Molly (born Lawrence Berlandi). In his *GayLife* column, the Polish Princess (born Ron Helizon) wrote, "The joint was jumping as the new camp bar Molly's Follies held its grand opening. Seen enjoying the colorful balloons and sipping champagne were Marge of His 'n' Hers, and her delightful new bartender Hazel, Scotty of the Carnival, Chicago's only non-alcohol bar, Wes & Bob of Checkmate II, and Charlie of the New Flight." The Polish Princess also said, "She [Molly] was like a Mother Carol, she was heavy, and she did drag. She was in that mold of Michael K."

On May 9, 1993, Lawrence "Molly" Berlandi died.

This was also the location of Take One, Bughaus, K's on Clark, Pourquoi Pas?, and Robert's Lounge.

Mommy-O's
39th St.
Circa: 1950s-1960s

This was a lesbian bar.

Mona's
3358 N. Broadway
Circa: 1971-1975

Monte Carlo
6320 S. Cottage Grove Ave.
Circa: 1932

Walter Winston, who performed under the name the Sepia Gloria Swanson, was in residence at the Monte Carlo in the early part of 1932.

Mother's Other
2548 N. Halsted St.
Circa: 1975-1976

Mother Carol (born Richard Farnham) opened Mother's Other on December 29, 1975. The grand opening featured female impersonators Jackie Knight, Terri Paige – the Pantomime Rage, and Tillie the Dirty Old Lady.

This was also the location of Redford's, Grapevine, and Julie's.

Mousetrap
Skokie Hwy. and Belvidere Rd., Park City
Circa: 1973

Mr. B's
606 Stateline Rd., Calumet City
Circa: 1950-1992

According to *Gay Chicago Magazine*, in 1976, Mr. B's was the fourth oldest gay bar in America. It was owned by Richard Bronkowski. A report in the *Chicago Gay Crusader* of June 1975 read: "Mr. B's marks 25 years in business at the same location ... Richard Bronkowski successfully fought for the gay community in confrontations with city and state agencies for the rights of our 'community' to have a gathering and drinking spa; a right that most citizens have always taken for granted in their daily lives. In 1967, Mr. B's won a memorable decision in Cook County Circuit Court that no bar is responsible for the actions outside its premises. ... Much bad publicity was involved in the case, which ended successfully for the rights of gay people to gather in a bar for mutual social pleasure and drinks."

The bar changed ownership to Don Zuzevich in December 1992 and closed shortly afterward.

Photographer Allan Zlatarich recalled, "It was June of '68. I'm showing my age. Mr. B was behind the bar, and I'd never been in a bar before, let alone a gay bar. It was the night of my 21st birthday, and Mr. B checked my ID and gave me a free drink. His bar was there for 45-50 years. His parents had a bar there before him... At that time, in '68, he had a piano bar at the back, but I don't ever remember anyone being back there. It was mostly local people that went there. Dick used to play cards at the end of the bar with a bunch of his older friends; they had a

little desk light. That was my very first bar and that was right on State Line. State Line has Hammond on one side and Calumet City on the other. The liquor laws in Hammond were strict, so all the bars were in Calumet City." Richard Bronkowski died, aged 85, on April 19, 2007.

This was also the location of Ups and Downs..

Mr. T's
5244 N. Sheridan Rd.
Circa: 1969

Mr. T's was a piano bar.

This was also the location of Dancers.

Ms.
661 N. Clark St.
Circa: 1973-1975

Marge Summit and Chee Chee opened Ms. in September 1973. It was a lesbian bar. Sharon Haines remembered, "Marge Summit and Chee Chee had Ms., and I remember that being raided. I loved Ms., that was on Huron and Clark, a big bar, great dance floor, great music, a variety of women. You would walk in the door, and there would be Chee Chee in a big muumuu and a couple of Doberman's, and there would be Marge behind the bar serving drinks and cracking jokes. Always a good time."

Donna Rose related, "When I walked up into Ms. I was like ... there was tall, short, fat, skinny, black, brown, red, yellow, blue, pink, orange, and just all these women dancing, and it looked like just a big warehouse."

On a 1974 Pride parade float for Ms., there was a naked woman painted in gold. The *Chicago Gay Crusader* noted that the lesbian community had various reactions to the Ms. float in the parade, ranging from outrage to delight. The lesbian newspaper *Lavender Woman* condemned the float with a label of "most insulting to women" and "most messed up lesbians of 1974."

This was also the location for O'Banion's, PQ's, and Saturday's.

Ms. Behavin
200 State St., Calumet City
Circa: 1986-1987

This was also the location of the Bank Vault, Double RR Lounge, and Kismet Club.

Music Box
3735 N. Southport Ave.
Circa: 1977-1978

The Music Box opened on December 28, 1977, as a lesbian bar. Soon afterward, it became a mixed lesbian/men's bar with drag shows by Mr. Kay Howard and His Fantasy in Pantomime. Michelle Faithe performed there, singing her "Ode to Anita," about Anita Bryant, and Sonny Santiago was the cook in the sandwich shop.

Music Box
1632 S. Indiana Ave.
Circa: 1984

Music Box
326 N. Lower Wacker Dr.
Circa: 1985

Music Factory
1665 W. Fullerton Ave.
Circa: 1983-1985

Mike Macharello was the DJ at Music Factory. He later owned Circuit.

This was also the location of Factory Disco, Liar's Club, and Risqué.

My Brother's Place/Oasis
111 W. Hubbard St.
Circa: 1975-1993

This bar/restaurant was owned by Bob Cochran. On the first floor was the bar Oasis, with the restaurant upstairs. *GayLife* reviewed it on February 4, 1976, "A quiet little restaurant with exceptional food ... not cheap, but good. Also close to other near-north bars for later dancing. Reservations suggested for late diners."

It closed in March 1993.

This was also the location of Belfry.

JERRY AND JIMMY, perform as good waiters at MY BROTHERS PLACE.

Mycroft's
2900 W. Belmont Ave.
Circa: 2002

In October 2002, former *Nightlines* columnist, Kathie Bergquist, hosted Rock Star Karaoke at Mycroft's with free food and "singing lesson" shots.

My Place
551 E. 79th St.
Circa: 1977-1980

This was also the location of Other Bar and Ronny's.

N

Nanny's
3000 W. Chicago Ave.
Circa: 1983

Name of the Game
2616 E. 75th St.
Circa: 1973-1977

Neo
2350 N. Clark St.
Circa: 1979-2015

The bar attracted a young crowd dancing to alternative music. Although not strictly a "gay" bar, LGBT folks were always evident, especially for DJ Dave Roberts and his Planet Earth nights. Dave Awl described Neo as, "the Island of Misfit Toys. It's for all the people who don't fit in with the other bars and clubs."

On the history of Planet Earth night, Awl remembered, "Planet Earth didn't start out at Neo; its birthplace was the old Club 950/Lucky Number on Wrightwood near Lincoln in 1994, and it moved to Neo in the year 2000 after it had already

been running successfully for many years. And after leaving Neo, it moved to Late Bar in Avondale. DJ Dave Roberts began his career as a DJ in the late 1970s at some of Chicago's earliest punk nightclubs, like La Mere Vipere. He launched his New Wave/Punk dance night Planet Earth Chicago in 1994 at Club 95 ... At the end of 1999, Dave Roberts and Planet Earth left Club 950 following a break with the owners due to some bad business decisions they were making, which eventually led to Club 950's closure. Planet Earth moved to the Spin nightclub at Halsted and Belmont for a few weeks ... but Spin wasn't a

Waiting for the mothership to take them back to Planet Earth at Neo
Every Thursday

Pix by Sukie

good fit due to the size and layout of the club. So, Planet Earth moved yet again, arriving at Neo sometime in the spring of 2000, where it continued on Thursday nights for most of a decade. Once it moved to Neo, I started attending on a weekly basis and helping DJ Dave with promotions, like starting an online community for fans and running ads in *Nightspots*. Planet Earth left Neo sometime around 2006 or 2007 ... and then there was a gap for a year or two, punctuated by some special events at Subterranean in Wicker Park. In 2009, DJ Dave Roberts and his collaborators opened their new club Late Bar in Avondale. They relaunched Planet Earth there on Saturday nights. Planet Earth and DJ Dave have been a Saturday-night tradition at Late Bar ever since."

Neo closed in 2015. Though closed, the sign painted on the side of the building identifying the club remains.

This was also the location of Hoots.

@ Neo's Planet Earth

Pix by Kirk

Nevin's Pub
1450 Sherman Ave., Evanston.
Circa: 2002–2017

Primarily a straight tavern, but hosted LGBT performers such as Ellen Rosner, Dylan Rice, and Super 8 Cum Shot.

New Flight
420 N. Clark St.
Circa: 1977–1988

The New Flight was co-owned by Bob and Howard Goodman and their sister Harriet Freeman. Howard Goodman died in October 1980, and Bob took over running the bar. In July 1977, the bar held its grand opening. However, it had been open since the previous year when Al Lee Evans was the bar's contestant in the 1976 Mr. Windy City contest. On April 23, 1988, it held a farewell party, having lost its lease.

THE NEW FLIGHT

SUNDAY, MARCH 26
Easter Bonnet Parade
PRIZE FOR BEST HAT
BIG EASTER BUFFET

420 N. CLARK   467-5551
A Friendly Place To Meet People

The bar was described in *Gay Chicago Magazine* as having "an attractive décor with a lounge featuring mechanical games, a pool table, and a pop and easy-listening jukebox that attracts a very leisurely, conversational crowd."

Mark Palermo remembered, "It was always fun to see people there, just watching the older men talking with the young boys, and money being passed, and people walking out of the door ... who knows what was going on. It was just part of the scene back then because a number of the bars were down there."

Wally recalled, "The bar closed ... as soon as the lease was up, they wanted to triple his rent, and he said, 'No way.' That was the end of the bar.

"The Flight was known as a hustler bar, which is what it was, but we took care of our people. If there was a bad hustler, we would not let the person work the bar, but by the same token, if there was a bad john, we'd make sure they were not welcome. That's the way we kept the house clean, and pretty soon the johns realized they couldn't pick anybody up, or the hustler couldn't pick anybody up, so they just stopped coming in."

New Swinger's Lounge
1221 E. 87th St.
Circa: 2002

This mixed gay/straight club often held LGBT events, such as erotic poetry readings by CC Carter and Paul Gee and Sex-O-Matic, featuring a lingerie show.

New Variety Cabaret
400 N. Clark St.
Circa: 1992

Nexus North
178 W. Randolph St. (5th floor)
Circa: 1984

Nexus North was a dance bar that hosted lesbian events.

Nice 'N' Easy
6213 N. Broadway
Circa: 1966

Nicky's Bar & Grill
3203 N. Clark St.
Circa: 1983

Night
223 W. Chicago
Circa: 1992-1993.

Nine-O-Five (See 905)

Nite Life Lounge
933 N. State St.
Circa: 1940s-1980

Nite Life opened in the 1940s and catered to gay/straight and tourists. It was a drag bar owned by Ira Gruenberg. One patron remembered, "Gayle Sherman worked there before she had the operation ... Kay Leslie, Roby Landers worked there, and Vicki Marlene ... she had a fantastic act, she would jump from the stage in her big heels onto the bar, and then walk the bar doing the Can-Can."

Joey recalled, "The Nite Life was very small, and at that time, it had a lot of the mob characters there. I met a guy who killed people for a living. That type of thing. Dan Dailey, the old

actor, used to go in there and date a couple of the guys in drag. It was a different era in the early '60s."

Gayle Sherman was Chicago's premier drag queen. After her transition, she changed her name to Brandy Alexander.

The bar burned down in early 1973 and reopened circa October 1973.

GayLife, on February 4, 1976, reported, "Nite Life and Blue Dahlia, plus a number of other places run for 'touristy' types, are not recommended."

On June 21, 1979, a birthday party for Gender Services founder John Prowett was held at the Nite Life Lounge. In October 1978, Gender Services of Chicago celebrated four years of service to Chicago's transvestite/transsexual community with a benefit at the Nite Life Lounge.

This was also the location of the Walton Street Water Works.

Niteline
3320 N. Halsted St.
Circa 1987-1989

Niteline opened on October 16, 1987, and billed itself as "The newest Video Dance Bar." The owner was Mark Woolard.

This was also the location of Bugle Boy, Carrs Halsted Street Cabaret, G-Spot, Bushes, Gentry on Halsted, Bugle Boy, and Scarlet.

Nobody's Darling
1744 W. Balmoral Ave.
Circa: 2021-Present

An upscale neighborhood wine and craft cocktail bar, primarily lesbians. Black-owned and operated by Renauda Riddle and Angela Barnes, the bar's name was inspired by an Alice Walker poem, *"Be Nobody's Darling."*

This was also the location of Joie de Vine.

Noche de Infierno
1579 N. Milwaukee Ave.
Circa: 1995

In August 1995, this Latin bar hosted a fundraising event for the Minority Outreach Intervention Project. It was a caliente party with caliente music, caliente entertainment, caliente hors d'oeuvres, and plenty of icy beverages to keep you cool.

Noche de Ronda
2626 N. Halsted St.
Circa: 1973

Owned by Frank Lopez.

This was also the location of the Tilt Inn and Prodigal Son.

Nocturnal
1111 W. Lake St.
Circa: 2001

Hosted occasional lesbian events sponsored by Chix Mix promoters, such as the "Black Bra Party" and "Tanked," a high-energy dance party with "thousands of women in sexy tank tops."

No Exit Café
6970 N. Glenwood Ave.
Circa: 1958-2000

A small coffee-house vibe (although wine and beer were served), which had a variety of owners. Mostly laid-back hippies, then hipsters, LGBT friendly, hosting many events such as Scott Free's Homolatte and *The Partly Dave Show*, a variety show hosted by Dave Awl.

No-Name
1123 N. State St.
Circa: 1983

This gay-friendly piano bar literally had no name.

This was also the location of Steve and Eddie's Saratoga.

Normandy
744 N. Rush St.
Circa: 1970-1971

Although gay bars had sometimes allowed same-sex dancing in the past – most often by locking the doors – the police considered it obscene and cause for arrest. After pressure from the Gay Liberation Front, the Normandy was the first bar in Chicago to allow same-sex dancing. In *Chicago After Stonewall*, by St Sukie de la Croix, he wrote, "The Normandy Inn on Rush St., the largest gay bar in the city, held 500-600 people. On April 24 and 25, 1970, the Normandy was picketed. The protest emptied the bar. On April 29, the Bar Committee of GLF met with Wally and Jerry Fleischmann, the owners of the Normandy. They promised to 'do everything in their power' to obtain a dancing license. They would apply for it on April 30, and, if granted, the bar would allow dancing. If not granted, they promised to fight for it. In Northwestern University's Special Collections, a GLF leaflet entitled 'What the hell does Gay Lib think it's doing?' reads, 'The oppressive atmosphere of the Normandy must be removed. The right to dance, any tempo, any style, is thus a crucial step towards our personal and collective liberation.'

"The boycott was suspended until May 15. On May 14, both parties met again, by which time the bar owners had acquired a license and agreed to allow same-sex dancing, both slow and fast. They also threw out the draconian dress code. Customers could now wear sunglasses, sleeveless T-shirts, and shorts in the bar. All were previously banned. Other concessions included banning discrimination against women, a pledge that drink prices would remain the same. There would be no minimum, no cover, and no pressure on customers to buy drinks. Before this, customers at the Normandy were required to cradle a drink in their hands at all times.

"The following night, gays danced together for the first time in the Normandy. Still, when a slow number was played and couples drew closer, security stepped in and separated them. The owners reneged on the deal and the no-touching rule was reinstated. The Fleischmann brothers explained that a new district police commander started that morning and they were waiting to see where he stood on the matter. The call went out from GLF, 'Now it's time for some gay power! This Friday night (22nd) is D-Day! Invade the Normandy! Join us and dance (any way you want to)! ... Do it! Dance! Brothers and sisters, dance!' On May 21, the Fleischmanns backed down and permitted slow dancing."

Normandy
5246 N. Broadway
Circa: 1971

The second incarnation of the Normandy was even larger than the location on Rush St.

This was also the location of Coconuts.

Normandy
Entrance on 3400 N. Clark St.
Circa: 1983–1991

Normandy was a Latin bar owned by Angelo Rios. In 1990, Pat Mooney was listed as co-owner. The bar had many events over the years. On April 10, 1984, a male dance contest MC'd by Tina Ray. In September 1986, live from Las Vegas, it was "A One Wo-Man Show featuring female impressionist Alana Russell. In May 1987, an ad for a regular "Amateur Hour" every

Tuesday read, "Please no baton twirlers, or tap-dancing bears." And in August 1991, Miss Ketty presented her Latin Revue.

This was also the location of Deeks and the El Palacio.

Photos by Dan Di Leo
Above are contestants at The Normandy's Male Strip Contest Finals held last week and below is the winner, Jeffery, who won $500. A new contest begins this week.

Norma's
3729 N. Halsted St.
Circa: 1979–1985

Norma's was a quiet neighborhood bar. Its grand opening was in November 1979.

This was also the location of Big Red's, Bobby Love's, Dandy's, In Between and Augie's.

North End
3373 N. Halsted St.
Circa: 1983–present

The grand opening of North End was December 10, 1983. The bar was owned by Rudy Johnson, Ken Eschenbach, Jack Conti, Bob Nicholson, Michael Pawlowski, and Scott Tietje. Over the

COME DANCE
COME LISTEN
ROCK
THE NORMANDY
348-9806
3400 N. Clark
Starting APRIL 12
BLONDIE
Fleetwood Mac
ROLLING STONES
the Beatles
Bob Seger
Led Zeppelin
the WHO
Journey
... and many more
ALL DRINKS $1.00
NO COVER D.J. ALL NIGHT

WE'RE NOW OPEN
THE NORTH END
3733 N. HALSTED

years, North End has hosted everything from cabaret acts to screening sports games to hosting drag shows, including in April 2012, the Sisters of Perpetual Indulgence first Mud Wrestling event. It has also sponsored several sports teams and welcomed politicians to the bar for meet and greets. In January 1996, the manager was Paul Weisman. George Nichols was a popular bartender there for years. In October 1990, North End hosted the Chicago Gay Men's Chorus "New Members Party" and, in 1994, hosted a monthly Cockpit BBS party. Paula Sinclaire and Vikki Spykke presented drag shows regularly in the 1990s. The bar also hosted concerts by Kenned & Carl.

Photos by Terry Gaskins

No Zone
4740 N. River Rd., Schiller Park
Circa: 1990-1991

Fred Hands was the manager. He co-owned Trianon. In March 1991, model/stripper Beau Beaumont made an appearance, and on Sundays, there was an "Oldies T-Dance." The grand opening was November 15, 1990. The bar closed in July 1991.

Numbers
3110 N. Broadway
Circa: 1976

Numbers was a restaurant and disco catering to the gay crowd.

Numbers
6406 N. Clark St.
Circa: 1993-1996

The grand opening of Numbers was on January 29, 1993, with Tillie the Dirty Old Lady attending. It was co-owned by Rudy Johnson, Bill Wood, Jerry Sanders, Jimmy Scullens, and Dennis "Teddy Bear" Graf. In November 1993, Dennis' Playmates male dancers performed. In May 1993, Daisy Mae and Vikki Spykke put on a show. And in December 1996, Lance Krystopher performed as Marilyn Monroe.

This was also the location of JJ's and Jackhammer.

Nutbush City Limits (Nutbush)
41 S. Harlem Ave., Forest Park
Circa: 1976-1991
7201 W. Franklin Ave., Forest Park
Circa: 1991-2007

Nutbush City Limits opened in September 1976. From 1976 to 1991 the entrance was on Harlem Avenue, but after that, it was advertised as being on Franklin St. It was owned by Mike Zych and Bob Zabel. Nutbush was a neighborhood gathering spot for more than 30 years. The bar followed the trends, offering disco, C&W dancing in the late 1980s and early 1990s, and alternative music. In August 1994, Rene Van Hulle was bartending. Other bartenders were Jimette Jean and Mickey Powers. In the 1990s, it became well-known for its troupe of drag performers headed up by Miss Peaches. On July 23, 2005, the club celebrated its 29th anniversary with strippers and a buffet. Rich Jentzen explained the appeal of

Photo by Sherman Heinrich
Mr. Nutbush 1985 Steve Cox is flanked by co-owners Mike Zych on his left and Bob Zabel on his right.

Nutbush, "One wonderful thing about suburban bars is that people ... you don't have leather bars, and you don't have drag queen bars ... everybody's all together ... old, young."

The bar closed when the building was sold. It was later demolished, and a strip mall was built on the lot.

This was also the location of the Bus Stop Lounge and Adron's.

Oasis
1745 W. Howard St.
Circa: 1954-1970

Rob C. related, "The Oasis on Howard Street was a gay bar. It was very low-key and served great hamburgers at the bar. (You had to keep your) hands-on the bar and 'kneeseys' below. You had to be careful not to go to the washroom at the same time. Surreptitious eye contact and 'knees' action, and you would meet in the parking lot out back by leaving through the rear door. The bar was located on the south side of Howard Street, a block west of the El station."

Oasis (see My Brother's Place)

O'Banion's
661 N. Clark St.
Circa: 1977-80

The grand opening of O'Banion's was in October 1977. It was owned/managed by Russ Cramsey with a crew that included Mark, Alan, Butch, Sophie, and Feathers. In April 1978, an ad for O'Banion's read, "A Man's Bar."

Johnny Bash recalled, "O'Banion's was popular during the punk era, and we would go there and slam dance. That's where you literally slammed into each other. That was quite a time."

This was also the site of PQ's, Saturday's Girl, and Ms.

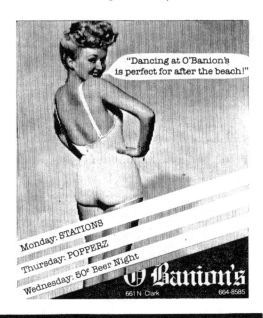

O'Bar
3343 N. Clark St.
Circa:1998

In 1998, O'Bar had an open mic for women.

Obsessions
325 N. Jefferson St.
Circa: 1995

The grand opening of Obsessions was on January 18, 1995, with DJ Earl Pleasure.

OBSESSIONS
Grand Opening
Wednesday, January 18th

DJ • Earl Pleasure   Door • Byrd Bardot

325 N Jefferson tel 312•258•0523
Opening reception 10pm-12am. Open every wednseday 10pm-4am.

Odyssey
1415 E. New York St., Aurora
Circa: 1983-1984

Opened by Doug Clark on July 22, 1983, the bar featured male dancers.

This was also the location of Galaxy.

Odyssey Bar
3231 N. Clark St.
Circa: 1973

In December 1973, a listing in the gay press announced, "A new gay bar, the Odyssey, opens, where Wednesday nights are Carmen Miranda night: everyone in platform shoes gets drinks for 50¢."

This was the location of Ruthie's and BJ's.

Off Broadway
1004 W. Belmont Ave.
Circa: 1986-1987

The bar held its premiere on December 31, 1986. By January 1987, it was under new management and held another grand opening on March 20, 1987. In August 1987, a pre-Mr. Windy City Contest party was held featuring Mr. Off Broadway, Kevin Hammer. The bar closed shortly thereafter.

Office
4636 N. Broadway
Circa: 1965-1979

Gary C. remembered the Office, "The owner was John Healey. He was a regular guy, but if you crossed him, you were on his shit-list. The Office was a dump. You had to watch who you spoke to, who you went home with. It was a rough place. I never had any trouble there. ... 'Do you want to come home and fuck?' That was the whole attitude. The Office was that kind of place. They had a jukebox in the bar, but nobody ever played it. That was a men's bar. The hustlers would come in there, and 'straight' guys ... trade."

This was also the location for Quenchyurs.

Off the Line
1829 W. Montrose Ave.
Circa: 1993-1997

Off the Line opened as a women's sports bar on July 29, 1993. They put in the TV monitors, so people could watch sports. Maria, a bartender at Off the Line told the authors, "Off the Line was owned by two young women, Marie and Diane, and I met Diane at the cooking school I was working at; she was taking a restaurant management class there. I actually introduced Diane to Deborah Rae and Barb, owners of Suzy B's. Deborah called me up and said, 'In case you know anyone in the business, we're trying to sell the bar.' So, I introduced Diane to Barb and Deborah Rae, and she bought the bar.

"Off the Line was not a dancing bar; it was a drinking bar where people would have a lot of conversation and a lot of singing. In fact, I remember the moment I knew I was getting older; I was standing behind the bar, and all these regulars came in, and they put this '70s CD on, and they all stood up and started singing the song from the Brady Bunch. They knew all the words, and I just looked around and thought, 'Oh my god! I have no idea who these people are.'"

In 1996, new owners took over, and the bar closed a few months later.

Angie Colella remembered, "It was kind of artsy, it had an open mic area, guitar and poetry and all kinds of stuff. It was more like a coffee house atmosphere in a way, for a bar ... it was your Generation X–er lesbian types."

This was also the location of Scot's, Ravenswood Tavern, Wee Frog, and Suzie B's.

Omar's
10 N. Clark St.
Circa: 1950s

Omar's is where Charles "Chuck" Renslow's leather group started. It was a predominantly Black bar that welcomed White men. William Rydwels remembered, "The first time I saw leather was in New York, but here in Chicago, it was around 1957 or 1958 at Omar's. I went in Omar's because it was very open, it was Black and White, and there were a lot of very handsome Black guys, and it was very convenient, because it was near the Clark movie theater and the Monroe movie theater, and if you didn't make out there, you'd go to the bar afterwards."

Chuck Renslow said, "Omar's was a cafeteria during the daytime, and they would close around 6 o'clock and reopen about 8.30 as a gay bar. It was on Clark at Madison, in the basement, and it was on the west side of the street. The first leather group we tried to organize met in Omar's. It was not classy; you could wear Levi's. You could almost say it was a low-class gay bar."

The leather-clad group was asked to leave Omar's, and so they moved to another bar down the street, called the Gold Coast.

One More Time
3420 W. Grace St.
Circa: 1983

One More Time opened in August 1983.

This was also the location of the Abbey Pub.

Ontourage
157 W. Ontario St.
Circa: 2005-2006

In May 2005, Ontourage hosted the Hearts Foundation "Hot Tea" dance with DJ Paulo.

Onyx (Marvin's)
6344 S. Cottage Grove Ave.
Circa: 1987

Probably a straight club, but in 1987 Wednesdays was lesbian night.

Oo-la-la!
3335 N. Halsted St.
Circa: 1996

Primarily a restaurant, but on Saturday after dinner service, it was "Boys Nite Out" with DJ Dirk.

Opal Station
6655 N. Clark St.
Circa: 1981-1986

A neighborhood bar run by Michelle Fire and owned by Ted Hoerl. It was a lesbian bar that welcomed gay men. Its grand opening was December 31, 1982 (although calendar listings appear as early as April 1981). It had a cabaret showroom that featured local performers such as Tricia Alexander and Lori Noelle, Mary Lynn Morrison and Bill Muzillo, singer-comedian Russ Tremayne, Jan Hobson & Her Bad Revue, Mandel & McVeigh, Lance Brown, Sharon Carlson, and Ginni Clemmens, and the all-women band, Surrender Dorothy, with Toni Armstrong Jr., Paula Walowitz, and Laurie Lee Moses. In March 1985, Romanovsky & Phillips performed.

The bar closed in November 1986.

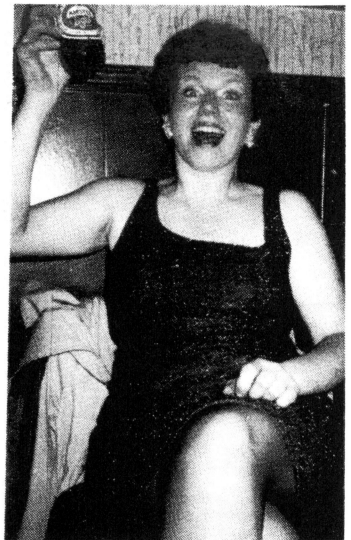

Photo by Sherman Heinrich
Michelle Fire, Opal Station's manager, offers a toast.

Orange Cockatoo
2850 N. Clark St.
Circa: 1964-1965

The Orange Cockatoo was a mob-controlled drag bar. Mame recalled, "[They had a] piano there, but I never saw anybody play the piano, and you know how it got the Orange Cockatoo name; it was originally a Chinese restaurant. I think they were too cheap to change the sign."

Val Camelletti added, "The very first gay bar I walked into was probably in the mid-'60s, and that was a guy's bar called the Orange Cockatoo. They used to have dancers, transsexuals or drag dancers, in these ... they looked like bird cages. ... that was probably 1964 or '65."

Orbit Room
3708 N. Broadway
Circa: 1986-1988

Opened by Medusa and Nunzio, this bar is remembered fondly. It closed because the property was sold to developers, who tore it down and built a strip mall. It was featured throughout much of the first season of the TV series, *Crime Story*, as an off-duty haunt for the series' characters.

Randy Gray remembered, "It was state of the art on Broadway. Video screens all over the place playing music videos. Met Michael J Fox there. Kind of punk clientele."

The Orbit Room closed in April 1988.

Photo by Jack Sitar
Orbit opening. Left-right, DJ Terri Bristol, manager Kevin Tuszynski and bartender Valerie Scheinpplug. Mondays and Tuesdays are men and women's night.

Orphans
2462 N. Lincoln Ave.
Circa: 1978-1981

A small gay-friendly concert venue, the crowd changed depending on who was playing. Faith Pillow and Karen Mason performed there.

Other Bar
551 E. 79th St.
Circa: 1976

This was also the location of My Place and Ronny's.

Other Side
3153 N. Broadway
Circa: 1980-1982

The grand opening of the Other Side took place on September 28, 1980. The entertainment that night was Leslie Rajeanne "Miss Gay Chicago," and Harriet and The Hairlips. The show was MC'd by Deluxe. Robbie Crystal was the manager. The original plans for the bar were to have a bowling alley with a gay bar in the middle of it.

The Other Side was billed as "New Town's newest cruise bar." In February 1982, Joseph Heflin and Michael Wilcoxen were the DJs. Danny Goss was also the DJ for a while.

In 1982 they opened their sundeck.

Photos by Dan Di Leo
GRAND OPENING CELEBRATION OF THE OTHER SIDE

This was also the location of Club Victoria and Crystal's Blinkers.

Other Side
3655 N. Western Ave.
Circa: 1992-1998

The grand opening of Other Side was held on August 8, 1992. In February 1994, the bar held its 2nd annual Beach Party with a limbo dancing contest.

Our Den
1355 N. Wells St.
Circa: 1974

On May 28, 1974, an ad in the gay press read, "It's the Grand Opening of Our Den, the new bar and restaurant catering to the gay community. Among the delicious meals on the menu are beef stroganoff with spinach noodles, shrimp crepes in a white wine sauce, stuffed pork chops in sour cream, and coconut lamb curry."

The February/March 1975 issue the *Chicago Gay Crusader* reports that Our Den – "Old Town's Boogie Bar" – advertises in *Chicago,* published by WFMT, describing itself as "the bar that's for us, by us." There's a small lambda in the corner of the ad.

This was also the location of Carol's Speakeasy and Den One.

Our Place
1658 S. Throop St.
Circa: 1975-1976

Our Way (Gallagher's)/Our Place
706 Stateline Rd., Calumet City
Circa: 1968-1979

Allan Zlatarich recalled, "Our Way was owned by lesbians at the time ... I believe they were lovers. They had a dance floor, but in the late '60s, early '70s, guys couldn't dance together. So, if there were girls in the bar, we would all dance together on the floor, but if there were no girls there, you couldn't get up and dance. They had drag shows there at weekends, and it was funny because it was right across from the hospital in Hammond, and people on the night shift would look out the windows, and there'd be drag queens and dancers on the sidewalk taking a break. They'd wave to the hospital people across the street. They got a big kick out of seeing these drag queens on the sidewalk having a cigarette." In 1979, an article in *GayLife* reported, "An early morning fire destroyed Our Way disco, 706 State Line Rd., Calumet City ... Fire Chief Stanley Skiba told *GayLife* the fire was apparently caused by a frayed extension cord in a storeroom that linked Our Way to a second tavern. Spreading from there, the fire reached into both taverns, virtually destroying them both." This was also the location of Bells and Club.

Our Way II (Kelly's)
648 State Line Rd., Calumet City
Circa: 1980-1989

Our Way II was possibly owned by Dennis Kelly and Dean McCracken. Although, it's thought they were working for somebody else.

In January 1989, Kelly's Our Way II hosted a series of safer-sex presentations in cooperation with Cook County Department of Health's HIV-AIDS prevention program. The first was called "Hot and Healthy Times."

In April 1989, a gay newspaper noted that Kelly's Our Way II was "unexpectedly closed."

MR. KELLY'S OUR WAY CONTEST
Sunday, July 12th
1ST PLACE
Trophy & Cash Prize plus sponsorship in
Mr. Windy City Contest

1ST RUNNER-UP
Trophy & Bar Tab

2ND RUNNER-UP
Trophy & Bar Tab

Kelly's

Come see the newly remodeled beer garden.
A Sure Pleasure!

**648 N. STATE LINE
CALUMET CITY**

Our Way on Wells
1437 N Wells St.
Circa: 1984-1985

In May 1984, the bar held a Mr. Our Way on Wells contest. The bar closed in May 1985.

This was also the location of the Butterfly.

Outer Limits 1 and II (See Steppin' Out)

Oz
1770 W. Greenleaf St.
Circa: 1980

Oz had a disco and DJ playing new wave and punk rock.

This was also the location of the Greenleaf.

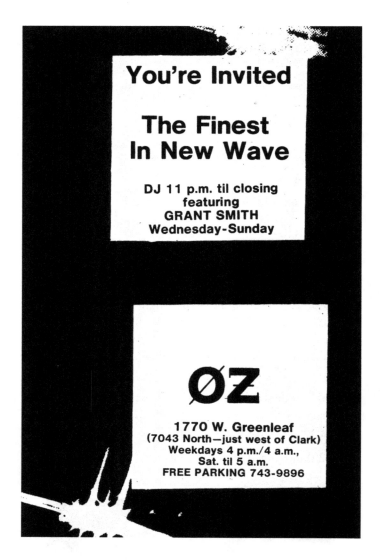

You're Invited

The Finest
In New Wave

DJ 11 p.m. til closing
featuring
GRANT SMITH
Wednesday-Sunday

ØZ

1770 W. Greenleaf
(7043 North—just west of Clark)
Weekdays 4 p.m./4 a.m.,
Sat. til 5 a.m.
FREE PARKING 743-9896

Oz Again
112 W. Hubbard St.
Circa: 1980-1981

The slogan was "Oz Again, where you are 'in with the in-crowd.'"

This was also the location of Druids, Ozone, White Elephant Bath Lounge, IC Station, and Ranch.

Ozone
112 W. Hubbard St.
Circa: 1981-1983

The Ozone opened on April 16, 1981. Dr. Steve Rempas was the owner, and Larry Seewald was the manager.

In September 1982, Sylvester performed at Ozone. Bert Thompson remembered, "I was a member, and I enjoyed it as the only place we've ever had with leather men who danced. It would be very crowded indeed ... What I most clearly remember is seeing Sylvester in live performance – yes, THE Sylvester, the disco god, not long before he died. He had a lot of energy, sang for a pretty long set, and even reached down and sucked the fingers of those in the front row who were standing and waving their arms. Rather wild, actually. This was in the long, main dance room, and he simply stood on the bar at the far end and danced and sang there."

Vicki Sue Robinson and Paul Parker also performed at Ozone. Mark Hultmark was a regular DJ.

David Honegger recalled, "It was still very much like the old bars, where you went in the alley, you didn't go in from the front side. Its back room was always dark, and you could feel the walls, and it had that flocked French wallpaper ... I don't know if it was red, black ... (laughs) ... you could never tell because the room was always dark."

The Ozone closed on December 10, 1983.

This was also the location of Druids, Oz Again, White Elephant Bath Lounge, IC Station, and Ranch.

Packinghouse
4859 S. Wabash Ave.
Circa: 1980

The bar ran an ad for All That Jazz Disco on May 10, 1980.

Palette Bistro
2834 N. Southport Ave.
Circa: 2011

Palette Bistro hosted a monthly gay night.

Palm Gardens
743 W. North Ave.
Circa: 1950s–1960s.

Palm Gardens was a lesbian bar. In the book *Chicago Whispers* by St Sukie de la Croix, he wrote, "It was run by Henry Bevier. In 1955 it was one of the last holdouts to serve German beer in what was once a heavily Germanic neighborhood. The Palm Gardens' problems started Sept. 25, 1960, when it was raided and closed down. Bevier was arrested for keeping a disorderly house, and 14 customers, eight men, and six women were charged with soliciting for prostitution and resisting arrest. Then on Nov. 14, 1962, three people were shot in the bar. The incident started when a woman named Edith Shields was stabbed in the alley behind the bar; the suspect was another woman. The 25-year-old Shields was helped into the bar by Nancy Davis, the owner's daughter, who tended her wounds. That's when Robert Wilson walked in and opened fire, shooting Davis, Barbara Kramer, and Robert Miller, the bartender. What the incident was about is unknown to the author, but the result was that Palm Gardens lost its license again. It reopened Feb. 13, 1964, under the name of a new licensee, Marvin Mykytyn, formerly of Little Falls, N. Y. This didn't fool Comdr. John McDermott of the Chicago Ave. police who criticized city officials for renewing the bar's license, saying Mykytyn had no money to buy the bar and 'may not be' the owner. The Palm Gardens closed soon afterward."

One patron remembered, "A straight German guy owned that bar ... in the middle of it, on the inside of the bar was an organ... You went in there to drink, and all these big bull-dykes were in there.

3 SHOT IN BAR ON NORTH SIDE; HUNT SUSPECT

Robert Wilson, 35, of 1519 Warren blvd., was sought last night for the shooting of three persons in the Palm Gardens tavern at 743 North av. The victims are Mrs. Nancy Davis, 43, daughter of the owner; Barbara Kramer, 23, of 749 North av., and Robert Miller, 26, also of 749 North av., the bartender.

The shooting followed the stabbing in the alley back of the tavern of Edith Shields, 25, who gave the tavern as her address. In County hospital, she told police that she was stabbed in the abdomen by a Dorothy Collins, who is sought.

She was carried into the tavern, Mrs. Davis was attempting to bind her wounds, when Wilson entered. Mrs. Davis ordered him out. He returned a moment later and began shooting. Mrs. Davis, Miss Kramer and Miller were taken to Henrotin hospital.

Pangea
3209 N. Halsted St.
Circa: 1989

Pangea opened on July 26, 1991. The bar was owned by Samuel F. Davis and Robert Yeaworth. Davis also co-owned Clubhouse and Deeks. Pangea was operated and fronted by David Wilshire, a former Mr. Windy City.

In May 1992, Joan Jett Blakk hosted Pangea's Dating Game.

This was also the location of Guzzlers, Happy Hours, and Stars.

Paradise
2848 N. Broadway
Circa: 1982-1986

Dion & Co. manager John Cattone (center) is surrounded by some of his waiters and cooks, from left, Art, E.J. and Al. Dion's is now located in the alley bar of Paradise and serves meals nightly from 5pm to 3am. They still have pickup and delivery service as well.
Photo by Sherman Heinrich

This dance club was opened shortly after Bistro closed and involved many of the same people: Eddie Dugan, DJs Lou di Vito, and Jeff Berry, among others. In September 1983, Sylvester celebrated his birthday at Paradise. Other musical performers included Paul Parker, Eartha Kitt, Pamala Stanley, and Hazell Dean.

"It was all young beautiful hustlers and older men, and groups of lesbians who went there to dance," remembered Ruth Ketchum.

While Steven August Papa recalled the décor, "The second part they finished was like a cityscape with bricks. One of the walls was painted with a cityscape and an alley, and those old escape ladders from apartment buildings. That's how the whole thing was done in there. It was gritty, and they had a tiny dance floor, then when they opened the third part of the bar, it was almost like a 1940s nightclub. It was very beautiful. It was on two different levels, and it surrounded a gigantic dance floor. My favorite memory of going there was that they used to have these New Year's Eve packages, where you could go and there'd be tables and food, cocktails, and champagne. Then at midnight, they'd play Madonna's 'Into the Groove,' which was the big

song, and they let all these balloons and confetti down from the ceiling. It was really a wonderful bar."

This was also the location of Paradome and Phoenix.

There's no such thing as a stranger in...

Paradise
2848 N. BROADWAY

Paradome
2848 N. Broadway
Circa: 1990

A December 1990 listing in the gay press read, "Michael Kudesh presents Paradome, a savage dance club grand opening with the Strawberry Champagne Ball at 2848 N. Broadway."

This was also the location of Paradise and Phoenix.

Paris Dance
1122 W. Montrose Ave.
Circa: 1985-1997

Paris Dance opened in September 1985. This upscale lesbian bar was owned by Linda Rogers and Barb Bancroft. It had beautiful mosaics on the floor made with vinyl tile. There was a large dance floor and a smaller room off to the side. It had once been a bait shop and had porthole-type windows. It looked like a ship. In July 1988, the bar added the Luna Park Café, billed as

"The only café in Chicago designed with women in mind. Cappuccino, espresso, appetizers, and desserts, open on Saturdays and Sundays 10 a.m. – midnight."

Benefit Fashion Show
Sunday, December 15
For Sarah's Circle
A drop in center for homeless women

$5.00 donation at the door
proceeds and percentage of bar donated to Sarah's Circle

Bar opens at 2pm. Fashion show 3pm.
food/appetizers

Clothes	Accessories
Monica Rezman	Stacy Kinetyk
Robin Richman	
L.V. Jordon	**Hair**
Paul Sisti	Gayle Johnson
Phillip Cantrell	Robin Sinclair
Linda Darabi	Nicci Dumas

women of the world unite in Paris
1122 W. Montrose   769-0602   parking available

In February 1990, the bar hosted a celebrity auction to benefit the Association of Women's Music and Culture with a special guest appearance by the Washington Sisters with Melanie Monsur. In August 1991, Test Positive Aware Network and the Illinois Gay and Lesbian Task Force presented "The last outdoor event of the summer," a picnic and dance.

Lori Weiner remembered her first time at Paris Dance, "It was probably about 1985. I was 16 and driving a 1976 Oldsmobile Delta 88. Interestingly enough, I never wanted to go in the bar; what I did was sit outside writing poetry in a little red notebook. The door lady who worked there ... her name was Mary ... befriended me, and she would bring me Cokes, and sit out and talk to me. It was really cool. It was actually one of my first and fondest memories of my gay adolescence ... doing this weird stuff, and being a real individual, at the same time getting a foothold in the community and seeing what it was like."

Arlene Halko said, "Paris was wonderful. Linda and Barb, when they opened it, did a great job. It was a place for people who wanted to go to a sophisticated club. Barb sold out several years later to Linda. And I think Paris Dance served a real purpose in this community. It was a wonderful bar. I had many a good time there, and it was a nice group of people. Always pleasant. None of this fighting crap."

Paris Dance closed in November 1997.

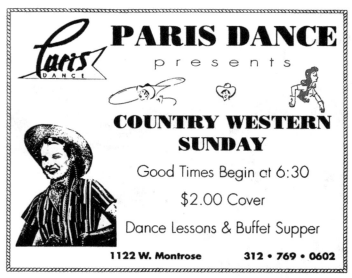

Parkside
51st St. and Cottage Grove Ave.
Circa: 1972-1975

Parkside was a Black gay men's bar. One patron remembered, "There were a lot of married men with children but doing their little creeps on the weekend. It was all that way."

Alvin remembered, "I used to go over to this little sleaze bar called the Parkside, and that was a gutbucket bar. The Parkside was a dump! It was a little cocktail bar, and you could sit down in a booth and chit-chat, or whatever."

Ken recalled it differently, "I never went to the Parkside because that was the 'in-crowd,' people who thought they were high class: fur coats, the cocktail set. I went to Lynn's, which was a low bar, and you would run into rough trade in there."

Park West Lounge
2479 N. Clark St.
Circa: 1978

This was also the location of Meat Rack and Salt & Pepper..

Parlour on Clark
6341 N. Clark St.
Circa: 2010-2014

Parlour was opened in August 2010 by Jennifer Murphy of Girlbar, and Nikki Calhoun. In November 2010, Parlour hosted Northern Lights, a dance party and queer performance with DJ Erik Roldan and the Northern Lights go-go gothic dancers.

When the bar closed in August 2014, Murphy told ChicagoPride.com, "[co-owner Nikki Calhoun] and I took a rundown tavern in an area of the city that we loved and turned it into a space that would provide a home for artists, musicians, comedians, drag queens, and many amazing dance parties."

This was also the site of Badlands, Dan's on Clark, and Pelican.

Party Party
3474 N. Clark St.
Circa: 1983–1984

Tony Mongello and Kathe Kimmerie were bartenders at Party Party.

This was also the location of Christy's on Clark, Studio 69, Zo Ran, and The Factory.

Party Time Lounge
1004 N. Clark St.
Circa: 1989–1991

The grand opening of the Party Time Lounge was August 26-27, 1989. The bar featured male dancers. The bar was owned by Dewey T. Gray, who also owned Stop 65. Gray died from a stroke in April 1991.

Patch
201 155th St., Calumet City
Circa: 1971–2006

The Patch was a legendary lesbian bar owned by Elizabeth Tocci, (AKA Toc). Sue Kroll explained the importance of the bar to many women, "For huge numbers of us, the Patch was where we 'found' ourselves. Each of us can vividly remember our first time entering this nether world. Many (probably most) of us were underage that first time. We were scared and hesitant to venture into unknown territory. After that first visit,

however, we knew we had found home. We were only mildly surprised to run into friends and acquaintances who were already regulars. The Patch will always be known to us by a number of names: 'T's' 'Tocci's' or simply 'The Bar.' Sometimes, when we heard it referred to as 'The Patch,' we had to remind ourselves that was actually its name. For years it was where you met friends, cooled down after a softball or football game, or just stopped by for a cold one. It was the place to party for a birthday, anniversary, wedding, or just to get away from it for an hour or two. It was both a destination and a refuge. It was where we went for comfort in times of trouble or tragedy. It was a place to fall in, or out, of love. It was like a favorite easy chair; it was a consoling hug. Simply, it was 'home.'"

While Rene S. related, "We have been served by a lot of hardworking, patient ladies: Tocci herself, Laura, the manager, Jo Tocci, Angie Picchetti, Jeanette, Laurie Santell, Shelley, Karen Dearing, Val Peterson, Jo Mama, Amy, and my apologies to those I may have missed. Through the years, Tocci maintained an honorable reputation that has made her a respected person in this city and its community. She has received an award from the Gay and Lesbian Alliance, and another from Mayor Daley."

In July 1998, Nicole Maaskant took over as the bar's new owner.

Pat & Donna's Stop Inn Lounge
1812 W. Montrose Ave.
Circa: 1975-1976

This lesbian bar was the center of a scandal reported in the January 1976 issue of the *Chicago Gay Crusader*, "Donna Smith, 40, was beaten and stabbed to death in an alley near her home at 4801 N. Bell Ave. on November 6, 1975. She was an employee and close friend of Patricia Hurley, operator of the Stop Inn Lounge, a neighborhood lesbian and gay bar at 1812 W. Montrose Ave. Smith was the mother of two children. The victim's ex-husband, Eugene Smith, who operates a tavern down the street from the Stop Inn, and his friend Sandy Barr, an ex-policeman, were arrested while driving in a car shortly after the murder. Barr had been discharged from the police force earlier in 1975 after being charged with breaking the windows of Hurley's bar. Eugene Smith and Barr were arraigned on murder charges December 15."

Peanut Butter & Jelly
659 W. Diversey Pkwy.
Circa: 1974

In *Chicago Gay Crusader*, August 1974, it reads, "No, What's the truth? Two rumors. Peanut Butter & Jelly is going to be a new superbar, and the other is that it will be a day-care center."

Pelican
6341 N. Clark St.
Circa: 1985-1989

One patron recalled, "There was never a whole lot of business up there. I think they wanted to be a leather bar, but they weren't, although some of the bartenders wore leather. But it was really just a neighborhood dump."

Two bartenders who worked there were Orville "Butch" Toland, who also worked at the AA Meat Market, Manhandler, and North End, and Don "Wheezy" Crenshaw, who also served drinks at Cheeks, Company, Manhandler, and BJ's.

This was also the location of Badlands, Dan's on Clark, and Parlour.

Photo by Sherman Heinrich
Pelican bartenders Glendoara, left, and Teddy right, the "Bent Elbow Sisters."

Penguin
75th St. and S. Yates Ave.
Circa: 1973-1976

This was a mixed gay men/lesbian bar.

Pepper & Salt
2479 N. Clark St.
Circa: 1978

On October 6, 1978, in *GayLife*, Ira Jones wrote: "Also, the Pepper and Salt, previously referred to as the Meat Rack Bar - not without good reason - now claims to be straight." This was also the location of Meat Rack and Park West Lounge.

Pepper's
1502 W. Jarvis Ave.
Circa: 1970-1989

In June 1977, Peppers was sold to John Moretten. In January 1979, the bar hosted an auction to benefit the Rogers Park/Edgewater Gay Alliance.

Popular bartenders included Jim Christner and Jim Foley.

The bar closed in July 1989.

This was the location of Chalmers and Charmers.

Toasting Peppers' fifth anniversary are, from left, Rockwell Hunt, Robert Harvey and Kevin O'Brien of Gay Chicago Magazine.

Photo by Jack Sitar

Pepper's Lounge
3441 N. Sheffield Ave.
Circa: 1996

In April 1996, an ad in a gay newspaper read, "Pepper Lounge, Saturday. You: tall, gorgeous, dark hair, eating Jamaican lamb chops w/two male friends. Me: blond, glasses, eating Red Pepper Ravioli & drinking Chocolate Martini w/friend. Our eyes kept locking; something about you intrigued me. I kept hearing 'I Feel Pretty.' Wouldn't it be fun if next time we were dining together?"

Petunia's
2559 N. Southport Ave.
Circa: 1976-1978

Petunia's was owned by Pat Connors and Judy "Jay" Theorin. It opened in April 1976. In December 1976, some of the staff were Cherie, David, and Diane.

A *GayLife* ad in 1976 read, "A Bit of 1950s for His & Her Enjoyment." In June 1978, Petunia's held a cookout to benefit Gay and Lesbian Pride Week, and in May 1979, the Lesbian Community Center celebrated its first anniversary at Petunia's.

Trish Koch recalled, "It was very dark, and there were tables along the side that had liquor labels shellacked into them, and then there was the big bar, and there was a little dancefloor in the back. On occasion, the police would come in and check the licenses on the jukebox, the pinball games, and cigarette machines, and make sure everything was cool. Occasionally, they would pick a couple of people out of the crowd who looked particularly young, and that's when the bartenders or Patti Petunia would make sure that I was way in the back in the darkest area, knowing that I was underage. It certainly wasn't a dress-up bar, by any stretch of the imagination. The line dancing, that was appropriate for the time, like the Bus Stop and the Hustle, and things like that. It was a mixed crowd."

In 1980 the Déjà Vu was at this location.

A Bit of the 1850's for His and Her Enjoyment

Petunia's
NEW SUMMER HOURS

| Monday | Tuesday | Wednesday | Thursday | Friday | Saturday | Sunday |
| 7 p.m.—1 a.m. | 7 p.m.—1 a.m. | 7 p.m.—2 a.m. | 7 p.m.—2 a.m. | 7 p.m.—2 a.m. | 3 p.m.-3 a.m. | 3 p.m.—1 a.m. |

2559 N. Southport   Chicago

Peyton Place
116 E. Pershing Rd.
Circa: 1960s

A Black club where gay celebrity Wilbur "Hi-Fi" White performed.

Phoenix
2848 N. Broadway
Circa: 1990

In August 1990, the Phoenix held its grand opening, with 25% of the net profit going to the fight against AIDS. Rudy de la Mor, Memory Lane, and Judy Tenuta, all attended the opening.

This was also the location of Paradome, and Paradise.

Phoenix Bar & Nightclub
1932 E. Higgins Rd., Elk Grove Village
Circa: 2014-2019

Phoenix was owned by Robert Brumbaugh. This dance bar took over the space that formerly housed Hunters and made extensive renovations. In December 2014, Phoenix hosted "Fire and Ice," an elegant catered affair with a $500 balloon drop, music by DJ Laura B, hot go-go boys, and a champagne toast at midnight. $25 at the door.

The city of Elk Grove Village bought the property in 2019 and demolished the bar in 2020.

Picasso's
3948 N. Lincoln Ave.
Circa: 1993

A straight dance club with Climax Thursdays as gay night with host Orlando and DJ Freddie Bain.

Piccadilly Club
2652 S. Indiana Ave.
Circa: 1920s and 1930s

This was a speakeasy and a Black pansy parlor in Bronzeville. Female impersonator, Gilda Gray, performed here.

Piccardy Club
4300 block of Cottage Grove Ave.
Circa: Unknown

Piggen's Pub
674 W. Diversey Pkwy.
Circa: 1982-1989

At various times, Piggen's Pub was owned by Chipp Matthews, Arlene Halko, and Andy Antoczyk. It was a neighborhood gay bar and restaurant with sidewalk seating. It opened in January 1982. Its small kitchen turned out meals such as fish and chips,

butt steak, and fried chicken. Popular bartenders included Steve "Missy" Allman, Clarence Smith, and Antonio Lazzara.

This was also the location of Dickies, Cesar's, and Cocktails and Dreams.

Pit
Towertown
Circa: 1920s

In his book *Hobohemia*, Frank O. Beck, a Methodist minister, wrote about Professor Lant who ran a club for homosexuals called the Pit. Beck wrote, "Here, night after night, huddle the sexually distorted and perverted, the uncouth forms, the pathological misfits: that melange of middle sex which nature started but never finished. Prepare for consummate disgust for, in such vile and loathesome spots the 'stripper' is omnipresent and there are everywhere evidences of grossly radical sex practices."

Pits
2628 N. Halsted St.
Circa: 1981

George and Martha were the hosts of this juice bar.

This was also the location of Carnival and Snake Pit.

Place
1840 N. Wells St.
Circa: 1968

A calendar listing in the gay press from September 1968, reads, "It's the Grand Opening of Bert's bar the Place at 1840 N. Wells with a buffet and your hosts Bert, Roy, Eddie, and "Boom Boom." The Place was managed by Howie and Bert, who also operated Club 69 and Alameda.

This was also the location of Hugo's.

Plan B
1675 N. Milwaukee Ave.
Circa: 2009-2010

Mixed gay/straight with gay nights. In September 2009, Plan B hosted Boy's Room featuring a performance by Jade of *Ru Paul's Drag Race*. And in September 2010, Kiss A Girl Fridays, for sexy and stylish LGBTQ women and men.

Pleasure Inn
505½ E. 31st St.
Circa: 1920s-1930s

The Pleasure Inn was run by James Pleasure and was one of several Black "Pansy Parlors" on the South Side of Chicago. Most of the club's success was due to a resident female impersonator known as "the Sepia Gloria Swanson" (born Walter Winston). His theme song was Fats Waller's "Squeeze Me," to which he added spicy lyrics. Winston was born in Atlanta on May 23, 1906. On May 20, 1930, the Sepia Gloria

'Female Impersonators' Rule Many Floor Shows

By HILDA SEE

Female impersonators supply the main draw in cafes now, according to a survey made by a well known critic. To prove his point, he talks at length about what is happening in Chicago and then moves along to Harlem for a discussion of conditions there. His main "star" discussed was Gloria Swanson, one of the first of the "impersonators" to hit the stroll in Chicago and now a featured entertainer in New York's Harlem. Since then the Mae Wests, Peggy Joyces, and others have come along to make their way but the popularity of such players were first made known here in Chicago at old Pleasure Inn.

Talent Scarce

Look into the thing as the average cafe owner has and you will find that good female impersonators are scarce. You will find quite a few who can dress and look the part, but in most instances they have no stage ability. A few of them can sing, but cannot dance; others handle their feet well on the floor but cannot sing and it really requires a combination of dance and song to win a place in one of these floor shows of today.

Chicago has one cafe that features this kind of entertainment, but the owners will tell you that it is hard to find players when you want them. "Most of them are huge jokes," one of the managers of this particular cafe told your author. And travel to New York or any place else where they are used, and you will learn the same thing. They are all seeking the three or more "stars" Chicago has, and isn't willing to turn loose.

Swanson was the "Mistress of Ceremonies" at the Pleasure Inn with celebrity guests such as boxer Jack Thompson, and cabaret singer and actress, Caroline Snowden, who co-starred with Stepin' Fetchit in *Old Kentucky*, reputedly the first movie depicting Black on Black romance.

Polly Esther's
213 Institute Pl.
Circa: 1998

Polly Esther's Boys Night Out was every Wednesday night.

Polly's Tea Room
Wabash Ave., opposite Marshall Field's
Circa: 1930s

Poppa Marks
State St. and Division St.
Circa: 1953–1954

Poppa Marks was a restaurant with a bar at the back.

Poppy's
Broadway at Surf St.
Circa: 1975

Pour House
103 155th St., Calumet City
Circa: 1973–2000s

The bar celebrated its 25th anniversary in November 1998 with the "Touch of Class Show" with male dancers. An article in June 1978 *GayLife* read, "One of the popular bars in Calumet City is the Pour House, owned by Ernie Taliani. It's a disco bar with a young crowd of both men and women who find the music and atmosphere very congenial. The Pour House provides its patrons with frequent social events, including a recent Fever Dance Contest and a Mardi Gras Costume Contest. A modern disco light and sound system has been installed by Dave Morrison of Stereo Components

and the Pour House has a DJ 7 nights a week."

The bar was remodeled in September 1986. Tamara Lee was a regular performer there.

Pourquoi Pas?
2568 N. Clark St.
Circa: 1978–1979

Pourquoi Pas? was a short-lived neighborhood tavern. Jack Witten was the manager. It opened in June 1978, with a benefit for the Frank M. Rodde III Memorial Building Fund. Then in February 1979, it was listed for sale.

This was also the location of Take One, Bughaus, K's on Clark, Molly's Follies, and Robert's Lounge.

Powerplant
1015 N. Halsted St.
Circa: 1982

In November 1982, Frankie Knuckles left the Warehouse to open his own club, the Powerplant. "I felt I had reached a point where I couldn't go any further with the Warehouse," Knuckles explained.

This space was also home to Riverside Club and Rockers.

PQ's
661 N Clark St.
Circa: 1972-1973

PQ's was the first live DJ gay disco in Chicago. It opened in the spring of 1972 and advertised as "The IN place to go." On July 22, 1972, a bus departed from PQ's for something called the Allison Woods GayFest. Tickets were $3. It was advertised in the October 1972 edition of the *Mattachine Midwest Newsletter*.

Ray Thomas remembered, "The first bar I actually went in was PQ's' which later became O'Banion's. It was the most incredible energy dance bar, it was really a small club, and it was in a four-flat type of building, but it was the length of the first floor. The dance floor was by the back door, and ... there were drag queens, gay boys, everything there just dancing ... having a good old time, and I was completely drawn to it. The guys didn't dance together until the early '70s. Stonewall was in '69, and in the early '70s, it took off at PQ's. PQ's was one of the first bars that I was aware of where you could actually dance together. That was early in '72. PQ's opened just before the Bistro, and it was great."

Johnny Bash recalled, "It was an old, original, '20s bar. What I heard was that it had been a speakeasy at one time, and it had all these tunnels underneath; it was a mob hangout. Supposedly, the mob built a tunnel system under the downtown area of the city where they ran booze during prohibition. This bar had been built pre-prohibition, then through prohibition, it was a speakeasy. Once the Bistro opened, PQ's died."

This was also the location of Saturday's Girl, O'Banion's and Ms.

Price Is Right Lounge
5035 N. Sheridan Rd.
Circa: 1988

The bar opened in 1988, and you entered through a door on Carmen Ave.

Primary Night Club
5 W. Division St.
Circa: 2012

In an ad in the gay press in December 2012, Primary Night Club hosted the Wednesday Night Creature Feature where Jo Jo Baby welcomed you to the Underworld.

Primrose Path
1159 N. Clark St.
Circa: 1946

LeRoi remembered, "It was a gay bar, but it was frequented by a lot of straight people; it was 1946. It was on Clark St., just south of Division ... That block had several stores, and the one in the middle was Primrose Path. It was a bar, with overtones of gay, with this gal that played the piano behind the bar, up on the stage. Joy Page was from Minnesota."

Page sang "dirty ditties" and told risqué jokes.

Prodigal Son Bar & Grill
2626 N. Halsted St.
Circa: 2002

Prodigal Son Bar & Grill hosted performances by queer punk bands, the Rotten Fruits, Scott Free, and Boys' Entrance.

It was also home to Noche de Ronda and Tilt Inn.

Progress Bar
3359 N. Halsted St.
Circa: 2013-present

When it opened, Progress Bar had two owners, Justin Romme and Robert Brumbaugh. In July 2013, "Billboard dance sensation," Crystal Waters, performed. In April 2014, an ad boasted, "Progress Bar Gives Back with 30% of all sales to Test Positive Aware Network and About Face Theatre." In May 2015, Christian Owen hosted special porn star appearances of Rocco Steel, Alexander Gustavo, Armond, Rizzo, Dakota Wolfe, and Seth Santoro.

Progress bar got into hot water when the owner, Justin Romme, told DJs to stop playing rap music in the bar. As a result, the bar was picketed by the Chicago Black Gay Men's Caucus and Lighthouse Church of Chicago members.

This was the location of Loading Zone, Cocktail, and Men's Room.

Prop House/Rails
1675 N. Elston Ave.
Circa: 1990s-2000s

A mixed gay/straight Black club. Rails was its gay night. Prop House was a dance club with DJs Steve Miggedy, Steve Maestro, Spen, Kurt Robinson, Ron Carroll, and Lego.

This is also the location of Krush Nightclub.

Pub & Grub
175 N. Clark St.
Circa: 1972-1976

A notorious cruise bar in the old Greyhound bus station, which was torn down in 1988. The bar was undoubtedly gay in 1972-1973 but was described as semi-gay in 1974. An ad in the June 6, 1972, *Mattachine Midwest Newsletter* read, "Your Host Kenny Farmer invites you to a buffet at 5:00 pm Sunday." Another ad in the August 4, 1972, issue read, "Now has hosts Chris and Sandy and is 'The gayest spot in the Loop.'"

Raw Bar
3720 N. Clark St.
Circa: 1996–2001

Primarily a restaurant. One gay newspaper wrote, "Raw Bar. A cozy, intimate room to dine, listen to the live musical performance, or to play pool." On November 13, 1996, Honey West made her Raw Bar debut.

Razmataz
4174 N. Elston Ave.
Circa: 1987–1990

Razmataz was a lesbian bar owned by Ellen O'Donnell and Gwen Meyer. It opened in June 1987 and closed after being gutted by a fire in December 1990. Some of the bands who performed at the bar were Krystal Moon, Bare Necessities, Fantasy, and Strange Brew. Claudia Weglarz, Faith Matthews, and Jean Leigh were bartenders there.

Red Dog/Boom Boom Room
1951 W. North Ave.
Circa: 2001

The Boom Boom Room was gay night at Red Dog, a predominantly straight club. Silky Jumbo and Jojo were the hosts with London Broil and DJs Freddie Bain, Lego, and Orlando. The door diva was Byrd Bardot.

Redford's
2548 N. Halsted St.
Circa: 1978–1982

Redford's was a jazz club. Sandy Andina performed there in September 1980, Mary Lynn Morrison and Bill Muzzillo, and Kyle Nash, entertained in January 1981. In 1982 this location became the Kingston Mines.

This was also the location of Grapevine, Julie's, and Mother's Other.

Red Line Tap
7006 N. Glenwood Ave.
Circa: 2011–2020

Red Line Tap was a gay-friendly neighborhood bar and music venue. Many LGBT artists performed there, including Ripley Caine.

Red No 5
440 N. Halsted St.
Circa: 2002

This was also home to Club Flamingo, Clubhouse, Jokes on U, Redoubt, and Rialto.

Redoubt
65 W. Illinois St.
Circa: 1976–1982

The Redoubt was a leather bar owned by Jim Flint. The bar was located around the corner from the Gold Coast. Downstairs in the basement was the Stockade. Bert Thompson remembered the staircase, "The stair rail going down the stairs was hand-carved from wood, and the end of it was shaped like a great big, circumcised dick ... which, of course, had been polished to a high sheen by everyone rubbing the rail as they walked upstairs.

the Stockade
CHICAGO'S ONLY WESTERN BAR
Where the Nickels Are Still Wooden!

WOODEN NICKEL POLICY!
One wooden nickel with each drink.
Six wooden nickels buys a free drink.
(Only in the Stockade.)

OPEN
WED. THRU SUN.
AT 10 PM

REDOUBT

65 WEST ILLINOIS STREET   CHICAGO   644-6029

Photo by Mike Williams

Three happy faces all in a row! These happy faces were seen at the opening of the New Redoubt. They are managers (left to right) Jim Russell, Dan Neniskis, and owner Jim Flint. They recieved their 4am license only hours before the opening.

YAHN

REDOUBT

Our 6th
Anniversary

65 W. ILLINOIS ST. · CHICAGO

NOW
FOR THE BIG ONE
MR. REDOUBT

Tuesday May 5th 9pm

CONTEST IS AT THE BATON
436 NORTH CLARK STREET

NO COVER
NO MINIMUM

1st   2nd   3rd   4th
$250 $150 $75   ONE WAY
                          BUS TICKET
                          TO PEORIA

Special
Guest:
Colt
Model
Clint
Lockner

chicago's newest and finest
REDOUBT
LEATHER & LEVI BAR

Special Prices

ALL CLUB MEMBERS
wearing colors

OPEN at 12 NOON
10 PM 'til Closing
LEATHER or LEVI

65 West Illinois Street
CHICAGO, ILLINOIS, 60610 · 644-6029

A TOAST TO
THANKSGIVING

SUN
NOV 22
4-8pm

TURKEY DINNER WITH ALL
THE TRIMMINGS

DRINKS 75¢ EACH

FREE TICKET FOR A 10 LB
TURKEY DOOR PRIZE

DONATION
LPL MEMBERS $1
GUESTS $2

AN LPL EVENT   at the **REDOUBT**

RESERVATIONS CALL: 280-0163 / 935-7299 / 565-0609

MR REDOUBT 1980

REDOUBT

OPEN: NOON TO 4 AM

65 W. ILLINOIS ST. 644-6029

There was a back room that went behind a staircase, under the staircase, you had to go through a very narrow passage, about 10 to 12 feet long, and it opened into a small room that was totally dark, no light, no nothing."

This was also home to What's Up.

Redoubt
440 N. Halsted St.
Circa: 1982–1986

Managers at the second incarnation of Redoubt were Jim Russell and Dan Neniskas. It was owned by Jim Flint.

An anonymous man related it was "a huge building that was practically a barn, and it was a new incarnation of the old Redoubt. I think urban renewal forced him out. And when he moved over to Halsted St., it really never did well. It was a huge place, and there was a downstairs that never really drew much of a crowd. I suspect it was too far out the way."

In May 1984, the Redoubt served lunch. The menu included shrimp Newburg/confetti rice, roulade of ham and asparagus/ mushroom benedict, and supreme of chicken apricot.

This was also the location of Clubhouse, Rialto, Red No 5, Jokes on U, and Club Flamingo.

Redoubt
1315 W. North Ave.
Circa: 1993–1994

This was the third incarnation of Redoubt. It was managed by Dan Neniskas. Frank Kellas bartended. In May 1994, John Birch of *Metropolitan Slave* magazine held a Rest in Hell "Poko" party. Original John Wayne Gacy artwork was on display.

In August 1994, Redoubt closed.

Reflections
217 Ruby St., Joliet
Circa: 1978

Reflections
3169 N. Broadway
Circa: 2005

Primarily a straight bar, but LGBT friendly and gay-owned.

Rehab (see Circuit)

Replay Andersonville
5358 N. Clark St.
Circa: 2015–present

A mixed gay/straight neighborhood bar featuring vintage arcade games.

Replay Lakeview
3439 N. Halsted St.
Circa: 2016–present

A neighborhood bar featuring vintage arcade games.

This was the location of Bucks.

Rhinoceros Club
1221 W. Diversey Pkwy.
Circa: 1975

Rhumba Room
3631 N. Halsted St.
Circa: 1996–1998

Rhumba took over the space of Vortex and was a restaurant and bar with performances by Charlene Ungar (born Peter Mohawk), Honey West, and Samba Bamba. It served brunch and dinner and then turned into a dance club after food service.

This was also the location of Fusion.

Rialto
440 N. Halsted St.
Circa: 1990

The grand opening of the Rialto was March 30-31, 1990.

This was also the location of Club Flamingo, Clubhouse, Red No 5, Jokes on U, and Redoubt.

Rialto Tap
14 W. Van Buren St.
Circa: 1970s–1990

A report in the gay press December/January 1979-1980 notes, "Police raid the Rialto Tap, 14 W. Van Buren, and arrest 100 men on various charges. The bar has a largely Black clientele. One customer was arrested for offering to perform sexual acts with an undercover cop for cash. Four bartenders were arrested for keeping a disorderly house and ninety-five others for being inmates of a house of prostitution."

The Rialto Tap was a lively Black, gay pick-up bar that became a center of house music in the late 1980s under Michael Ezebukwu. Willie Watson was a DJ there in 1979; he also provided the sound system for Martin's Den. The bar's other DJs included George Alexander and Nick Lewis. Music started at 6 p.m. and lasted until 4 a.m.

According to Ezebukwu, "Rialto was a very wooden, traditional-looking bar." The DJ equipment was set back near the liquor. DJ Mystic Bill recalls dealers at the tavern openly offering patrons a wide range of drugs, including LSD.

The bar was torn down in 1990 to make way for the city's new Harold Washington Library.

3445 N. HALSTED, CHICAGO   **281-3336**

IT'S FIRST ANNIVERSARY TIME AT
RICK'S RETREAT

Tuesday & Wednesday
June 23rd & June 24th

Would you believe . . .

☑ **IT'S PARTY TIME . . .**

☑ **IT'S THANK YOU TIME . . .**

75¢ Well, Wine Draft
Both Days — All Day

Barbeque on GEM of a PATIO
7 to 9pm both days

And with Joe there,
who knows what else . . .

Rick's Retreat
3445 N. Halsted St.
Circa: 1986–1989

Joe Esposito owned Rick's Retreat after Little Ricky died. Madame Rhodesia de Halsted (born Gerald Myers), Jim Hughes, and Burt Gates were popular bartenders. Female impersonator, Alana Russell, often performed. *Gay Chicago Magazine*'s Garden Walk of Beer Gardens in July 1989, describes Rick's Retreat as, "An exceptionally well-tended garden and creative design (by our own Dave Myler) make this retreat a favorite."

Rick's Retreat hosted many charity events, such as in February 1990, when German shepherd puppies were auctioned off for Direct Aid – Mr. Windy City, Alan Naparella, bought one of the dogs.

In June 1988, on the night before the Pride parade, twenty-five cheering and clapping fundamentalist Christians were greeted by the Rick's retreat crowd singing "We Shall Always Cum," their version of "We Shall Overcome."

This was also the location of Lady Bug

Risqué
1665 W. Fullerton. Ave.
Circa: 1979

Risqué was a lesbian club, above the Factory Disco.

This was also the location of the Music Factory, Factory Disco, and Liar's Club.

Ritz
1300 N. Rush St.
Circa: 1972

Ritz
937 N. State St.
Circa: 1975–1981

In November 1977, the Ritz installed a new disco with a sound system and light show. A 1975 ad in *GayLife* touted, "Quad sound disco-dancing" noon until 4 AM, seven days a week." *GayLife*'s Fun Guide described a "rustic interior, open beam ceiling," and "a good-sized dance floor" that was "well used."

A front-page article in *GayLife* in September 1981, reported, "Fires on June 1 and September 2 at the Ritz, ...were both the result of arson, according to police investigators. Detectives of the Chicago Police Department's Bomb and Arson Unit determined the origin of the September 2 fire by observing burn patterns in the dance floor area. When floorboards were pulled up, they said gasoline that had seeped through was discovered." The bar's owner was Bill Jacobs.

MP remembered, "By 1976 [it] was a predominantly Black gay bar. The music was out of sight; I think the DJs name was Larry Fox. In the back, by the bathroom, people would smoke weed and snort coke. Then they would go to the dancefloor and sniff poppers. I had a bike whistle hung around my neck, and I would blow on it at the appropriate moment, while Donna Summer's 'Bad Girls' played. The Ritz was a pick-up bar. I would go there on a Saturday night, with friends, and we'd make bets on who would score before last call, that would be about 4:45 AM."

Fred Morris took over the bar in October 1980. On July 23, 1981, the Mr. Black Midwest contest took place at the Ritz. The winner was Kenneth Eric Hoskins.

Craig Cannon was a DJ, he recalled the crowd, "It's twenty minutes to four, and I cut the music off, and they just kept dancing. They would stomp their feet, they would clap their hands. One guy would take two of those big round metal ashtrays and play it like it was a tambourine. I kid you not."

Ritz Manhattan
910 W. Buena Ave.
Circa: 1989–1995

Robert Schultz III told the authors, "For a brief two year maybe three year period there was a Black gay bar in Buena Park Uptown called Ritz Manhattan. We lived directly across the street when it opened. It was a tiny place. It was the only time in my life that I lived directly across the street from a gay bar and a Black one at that! I had recently moved to Chicago so having the bar there affirmed I had made the right move."

River Edge Cabaret (see Deroma's Riveredge)

Riversedge
325 N. Wells St.
Circa: 1977

The restaurant and lounge had outdoor seating by the river, boat docking, and was available for private parties. John and Darwin were your hosts.

Riverside Club
1015 N. Halsted St.
Circa: 1982–1983

The Riverside Club was a private, non-alcohol, membership club for men.

Bert Thompson remembered, "It was truly a membership club; I still have my key. I'm number 675, so there must have been at least that many men who paid to join. It was basically a warehouse floor that was turned into an after-hours club for gay men who still wanted to dance after 4 a.m. The décor was non-existent; a card table selling soda pop, a DJ on a slightly raised platform, a coat closet, a toilet, and perhaps a few old sofas. The rest of the space was available to dance, on the bare wooden floors, without even a designated dance floor marked off from the rest of the club space. There must have been some tracer lights and a mirror-globe, too, but I wouldn't swear to it. It was an OK experience, but nothing compelling enough to make me want to go all the way down there, to a spooky, deserted commercial district, in the hours before dawn."

This space was also home to Powerplant and Rockers.

Riviera Club
4747 N. Broadway
Circa: 1989

The Riviera Club was primarily a concert venue, but when it first reopened, it was an old movie palace, then a dance club with a gay night on Sundays called Thrust. DJs were Farley Jackmaster Funk and Mike Ezebukwu.

Roadhouse
61 W. Hubbard St.
Circa: 1981

In January 1981, an ad read, "*Gay Chicago Magazine*'s Ralph Paul & Mike Williams invite you to join them every Saturday and Sunday at the Roadhouse, a friendly neighborhood bar atmosphere in the heart of Chicago's GAY NIGHT LIFE."

This was also the location of Stars.

Robert's Lounge
2568 N. Clark St.
Circa: 1979

An ad in *Gay Chicago Magazine* read, "Never strangers always friends." Michael "K" was the bartender.

This was also the location of Take One, Bughaus, K's on Clark, Molly's Follies, and Pourquoi Pas?

Robert's 500 Room
301 E. 63rd St.
Circa: 1979

In 1979, the club presented a "Christmas Extravaganza" with female impersonators.

Robert's Show Lounge
6622 S. Parkway
Circa: 1957

A Black club owned by Herman Roberts. It was a large nightclub with extravagant drag shows, such as the Jewel Box Revue. It featured such well-known entertainers as Tony Midnite, James Tai, and Jene Korday, "the boy with the million-dollar legs."

Rossee related, "The audience wasn't necessarily gay; it was like pre-Baton."

Meet the Boy-ological Experts!

They Took Show Business for A Boy-Ride!

The first Jewel Box Revue was co-produced in 1939 by Danny Brown and Doc Benner. Recognizing that female impersonation is true art, and not the burlesque it had come to be, they decided to bring back the glories of a neglected field in entertainment. Since then, Danny and Doc have skyrocketed to the very tops in their producing profession. Combing the country for the very finest talent, they have staged some of the most lavish and spectacular reviews ever to be seen in show-wise metropolitan cities. They have discovered and sponsored innumerable young men who have achieved stardom through their critical encouragement and interest.

Rocks
3320 N. Halsted St.
Circa: 1986–1987

The grand opening of Rocks was held on December 5, 1986. Every Friday, Miss Lori Hammel performed at 10:00 p.m. Bartenders were Gail Rossow and Michael Shadley.

This was also the location of Carr's Halsted Street Cabaret, Bugle Boy, G-Spot, Scarlet, Niteline, Bushes, and Gentry on Halsted.

Rockers
1015 N. Halsted St.
Circa: 1982

This location was also home to Powerplant and Riverside Club.

Rogers Park Social
6920 N. Glenwood Ave.
Circa: 2014–present

As the bar's website points out, "Intended to reflect the soul of the neighborhood, Rogers Park Social offers a unique and inviting venue featuring craft beers and freshly prepared cocktails – lovingly created and served by your friends and neighbors. Founded and operated by neighborhood residents, we strive to mindfully infuse the spirit of community, diversity, and service in all that we offer."

This was previously the location of Sidecar Bar.

Ronny's
551 79th St.
Circa: 1977

This was also the location of My Place and Other Bar.

Ronny's
2101 N. California Ave.
Circa: 2008

In May 2008, genderqueer rappers, Scream Club and Actor Slash Model, performed at Ronny's.

Rooster Blues
811 W. Lake St.
Circa: 2002

A straight bar that occasionally booked gay acts such as the lesbian band, Stewed Tomatoes.

This was also the location of Club Reunion.

Roscoe's
3354-3356 N. Halsted St.
Circa: 1987–present

Opened on April 1, 1987, by Arthur Johnston and Pepe Pena of Sidetrack, with Jim Ludwig and Ed Norris. Jim Ludwig is still the owner. Roscoe's is a landmark on the Halsted strip. In 1991, the DJs were Donovan Depass, Michael Macharello, and Jim Belanger. In April 2001, VJ Russell and DJs Jungle Jorge, Bobby Marley, Kevy-B, and Louis Herrera ruled the roost. In the early 1990s, Dane Chase, Chicago's best Dolly Parton impersonator, hosted a country night at Roscoe's.

The bar has hosted everything from political candidate meet and greets to game shows and viewings of hit TV shows, in addition to countless fundraisers. Among the organizations benefitting from fundraisers were Windy City Gay Chorus, Bonaventure House, and Direct Aid, among others.

In the 2000s, Amy Armstrong and Freddy Allen entertained. Honey West hosted karaoke.

In 1991 Roscoe's boasted three areas, Roscoe's Tavern (the front bar), the Stables (dance hall and pool room) and Roscoe's Café, in addition to the gardens. *Gay Chicago Magazine*'s Garden Walk of Beer Gardens in July 1989, described Roscoe's, "Designed by Schema and tended by the staff of Roscoe's, as two gardens that make the most out of limited space and also offers a glassed-in year-round atrium.

Roselle Inn
1330 N. Clark St.
Circa: 1933

This was a bar for "women who dress as men." It was raided and closed down during a clean-up of the city for the Century of Progress World's Fair.

Roundup
3419 N. Broadway
Circa: 1977

R. Public House
1508 W. Jarvis Ave.
Circa: 2013-present

An intimate neighborhood tavern. In January 2014, R. Public House began hosting a weekly Q&A Quiz with Kwizmaster Kirk Williamson. The first prize was a $25 certificate to the bar.

Rudy's (Checkmate)
2829 N. Clark St.
Circa: 1971

Rumors
7522 W. Madison St., Forest Park
Circa: 2008

The grand opening was in October 2008.

Rumors
2433 Des Plaines Ave., North Riverside
Circa: 2009

In July 2009, R-Rated porn stars Ricky Sinz, Ray Daniels and Rocco appeared at Rumors. In September 2009, Miss Foozie hosted a Labor Day potluck.

Rusty's Show Club/Lounge
1723 N. Halsted St.
Circa: 1991

In July 1991, an ad in a gay newspaper read, "the best female impersonators in town."

Ruthie's
2833 N. Clark St.
Circa: 1960s

Jim Dohr remembered, "My first gay bar was Ruthie's, and Eddie Dugan was the bartender, and the reason I remember that, it's so impressed in my brain, is because it was the first time anybody had bought me a drink. I was underage at the time. It had to be '68 or '69."

Ruthie's
3231 N. Clark St.
Circa: 1970-1973

Mark Sherkow remembered, "The first bar I went to was Ruthie's. There was a bouncer who would walk around the bar and make sure everyone was drinking something – they did not want people to just be in the bar without spending money. At one point, everyone near the back of the bar seemed to be facing in the same direction and not moving. The person I was standing next to told me that sometimes when there were a lot of people in the bar, people would stand like this and if somebody would start, people would end up groping each other. Nothing like that happened then, that I was aware of."

This was also the location of BJ's and Odyssey.

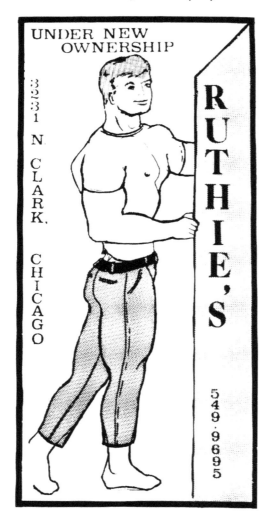

S

St. Regis
520 N. Clark St.
Circa: 1979

St. Regis was a restaurant and lounge.

This was also the location of Bus Stop.

Sam's
1205 N. Clark St.
Circa: 1940s-1970

This bar was owned/run by the Fleishman brothers, Julius and Walter. They also ran the Normandy, at 744 N. Rush St. JD remembered, "It was a long room with an elongated O-shaped bar, with not much room between the bar stools and the walls, just barely standing room. Going to Sam's on a Friday or Saturday night was quite a thrill in the early '60s. You went there, generally speaking, for one purpose, sex. When the front door opened, and someone was making their entrance, all eyes turned to inspect the person coming in. There was jukebox music but not loud and not much conversation. Voices were muted, heavy with strained anticipation. At times there was an abrupt cessation of all talk if someone who was particularly attractive opened the front door and made an entrance."

Nick Kelly added, "It was a very typical bar of that era, small, a circular bar, you could walk around the bar. Tiny little windows at the front that no-one could see out of, and no-one could see into. If you went by a bar and if it had two tiny windows, and it was dark and dismal, that might be a gay bar."

David met a celebrity, "Sitting at Sam's one Saturday night at 2 o'clock in the morning, I met Leonard Silman. Leonard Silman produced New Faces of 1952 on Broadway and went on to produce New Faces of 1956. His sister was June Carol ... she was one of the actors in New Faces of 1952. I remember meeting them in Sam's ... June Carol was wearing diamonds like I've never seen, and I think I asked her if they were real, and she said, 'Yes.' and I said, 'Then you shouldn't be wearing them in here.'"

Sam's
2540 N. Clark St.
Circa: 1981-1985

Sam's was owned by Sam Ohlin. In August 1984, the bar was burgled, and sound equipment and cash was stolen. The bar held a closing-down sale on October 14, 1985.

Sanctuary
632 N. Dearborn St.
Circa: 2013

Also at this location were Vision Nightclub, Excalibur, and Limelight.

Sandy's Corner
8501 S. Cottage Grove Ave.
Circa: 1983-1985

Alvin related, "There was a bar over on 85th and Cottage Grove called Sandy's. It was in a small shopping mall about a block long, and it was a little storefront bar. They used to pack the house up in there. I heard about it in '83 and that only lasted for about two years, if that long."

Saturday's Girl
661 N. Clark St.
Circa: 1976–1977

Saturday's Girl opened in January 1976. On October 9, 1976, it hosted a futuristic disco. In November 1976, it opened an art gallery space and advertised, "Saturday's Disco invites all local artists to display and sell their paintings in the club's newly designed gallery. Submit your artwork for consideration to Don or George." The Disco opened from 10 p.m. 'til 4 a.m. When it first opened, the host was Daffy (Ralph). The bartender was Jeff, formerly an employee of the Annex.

In 1976, its contestant for the Mr. Windy City contest was Keith Nick. In May 1977, Saturday's Girl advertised, "Saturday's offers live entertainment in the piano bar and a new dance floor, comfy tables and chairs and pinball and bowling games in the back room.

This was also the location of PQ's, O'Banion's, and Ms.

Scalawags
46 E. Oak St.
Circa: 1977

In May 1977, Scalawags advertised as "Chicago's most extraordinary gay bar" and offered "all drinks at $1 from noon 'til 8 p.m." It was owned by Steve Rempas. The bar closed in December 1977.

This was also the location of the Loading Zone, and TJ's on Oak.

Scarlet
3320 N. Halsted St.
Circa: 2007–present

Opened November 2007 and in a report in a March 2009 article by Amy Wooten and Matt Simonette in the *Chicago Free Press*, "On Friday evening, Scarlet Bar co-owner Paul Cannela stood inside the wreckage of his Halsted Street bar before workers boarded up the fire-damaged building.

"'I'm still in shock,' Cannela said, looking around at the smoky and soaked space in disbelief.

"Earlier that morning, the three-story building at 3320 N. Halsted St. that housed the relatively new bar (it just celebrated its one-year anniversary in December) went up in an extra-alarm blaze that, at one point, over 100 firefighters tackled the fire at once."

Cannela eventually reopened the bar. Some of its DJs were Lawla, Greg Haus, Lego, and Luis. It's house DJ of late is Phil DaBeatz.

Other bars that operated at this location were Bugle Boy, Carrs Halsted Street Cabaret, G-Spot, Niteline, Rocks, Bushes, and Gentry on Halsted.

Scarlet Ribbon
Clark St. and Belden Ave.
Circa: 1950s

Scarlet Ribbon was a men's bar with a drag show.

Schuba's
3159 N. Southport
Circa: 1989–present

A mostly straight gay-friendly neighborhood bar and concert venue. Among the LGBT performers there were Laurie Geltman, Norah O'Connor, Catherine Smitko, Moviegoers, Plunging Necklines, Ellen Rosner, and Thomas Negovan.

Fausto Fernos and the Radical Fairies performed their Feast of Fools at Schuba's.

Scooter's
1177 N. Elston Ave.
Circa: 1987

The bar offered boat rides on the Chicago River for $2.

This was also the location of Fire Island and Bridge.

Scorpie's
6301 S. Harlem Ave.
Circa: 1977–1980

A 1978 gay guide described the bar, "Scorpie's is a friendly spot with an intimate dancefloor. Mother Sullivan serves the cocktails." In February 1978, neighborhood thugs broke the windshields of the customer's cars.

Scorpie's held Halloween parties with Diana's Dames.

This was also the location of Escapades and Inn Between.

Scot's
1829 W. Montrose Ave.
Circa: 1997–2018

The grand opening of this neighborhood tavern was April 6, 1997, with owners Bill Houlihan and Tom Scott – Scott described the bar as "the Cheers of the Midwest" or "the little gay bar on the prairie." One of the popular events at the bar was the annual January 1 pajama party.

In January 2008, Scot's fell victim to a watermain burst and sinkhole. Dan Gambony, a manager at Scot's told Andrew Davis at *Windy City Times,* "At first, it just looked like a water main had burst and the street had been flooding, and the city thought it was under control; I didn't know ... Then, around 1:30, it just blew. Water was everywhere. We were standing in the front window and the street just disappeared."

This was also the location of Wee Frog, Ravenswood Tavern, Off the Line, and Suzy B's.

Sculpture Room
6403 S. Martin Luther King Dr.
Circa: 1976-1979

Donna Rose remembered, "It was quite grand, an upstairs and downstairs and a huge fountain (of course) ... some male nude, spouting water in the middle of the room when you first came in on the first floor, hence the name... Invariably there would be a fight/shooting at the bar up there. It was the domain of the butch/femme doctrine."

Alvin added, "It was interesting, they would play cards and stuff. Bid whist games. They used to do the same thing at Martin's Den; most of the Southside bars they had that going on, to attract a crowd. A lot of Black gays were into playing card games. They had tournaments. Martin's Den had a tournament ... whoever won so many games won a prize, and the bars would play each other."

This was also the location of the Edye Room.

Second Story Bar
157 E. Ohio St.
Circa: 1985-present

This is a quiet neighborhood tavern, located on the second floor, above a restaurant, just off Michigan Avenue. When it opened, it was owned by John Tessler. Popular bartenders include Doug Hinkie, Terry (Moosh), Henry Ott, and Danny Williams.

In December 1986, Second Story Bar hosted a meet & greet with Ron Sable, 44th Ward Ald. Candidate. On December 3, 1987, the bar held a raffle night to benefit Strike Against AIDS.

(Shirley's) Set Lounge
6539 W. Roosevelt Rd., Berwyn
Circa: 1972-1977

Sewer
620 N. Clark St.
Circa: 1949

Shadows
6255 N. McCormick Blvd.
Circa: 1992-1993

A short-lived attempt to start a gay night (on Tuesdays!) at a straight club.

Shakers on Clark
3160 N. Clark St.
Circa: 2014

Shakers opened in August 2014. A listing in a gay newspaper read, "Help welcome the new kid on the block (in the former 3160 space) with $11 mix-n-match buckets, and $4 Jager shots. 6:00pm - 2:00am.

This was also the location of Annex 3, 3160 Club, and Teddie's.

Shanty Inn
716 N. Clark St.
Circa: 1940s

Described by St Sukie de la Croix in the book, *Chicago Whispers*, as, "A shoddy saloon licensed to Syd Rosenthal and Jerry Abraham."

Shari's
2901 N. Clark St.
Circa: 1972-1980

In December 1980, Shari's manager was David Jacobson and Frankie T was the owner. In September 1977, Shari's "family" included Ken Taylor, Frankie T, Danny Hurling, Jim Phelps, Jim Boyce, and John Leslie.

Tim Cagney recalled, "The door was in the corner, there was a bar on the left, a lot of people standing along the right-hand side. It was scary, standoffish ... maybe they just appeared scary to me because I didn't know what was going on in there. It was a pick-up bar, a cruising bar. That was the only thing you had back in those days."

Jerry added, "At that time the bars were run by the Mob. If they weren't run by the Mob, they were paying off the Mob. I remember going in Shari's and ... you'd see this big Cadillac or big Buick pull up in front and one of these big burly guys would get out and, all of a sudden, walk out with an envelope."

Shari's burned down in early December 1980.

Sharon's Side Track
1113 W. Lawrence Ave.
Circa: 1980

This was also the location of Mike's Aragon Lounge.

Shay's Tap
746 N. Clark St.
Circa: 1972-1973

Sheffield's
3258 N. Sheffield Ave.
Circa: 1980-present

A gay-friendly straight neighborhood tavern. In 2003, Larry McKeon and Michael Bauer chaired a BBQ fundraiser for Commissioner Mike Quigley and Alderman Tom Tunney at the bar.

Shelter/Quench
564 W. Fulton St.
Circa 1992-1993

Quench was the gay night (Wednesday) at the club with DJ Ralphi Rosario. It became the "in" party quickly and developed a diverse following. A benefit for Stop AIDS in October 1992 featured "An Evening with Bob Paris & Rod Jackson" with entertainment by the Patricia Barber Trio and Lori Noelle."

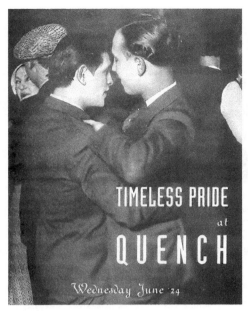

According to Byrd Bardot one of the event's creators, "Quench was gay, queer, queen, leather, lesbian, drag queen etc! We made sure the staff covered all of the categories and nationalities. You had to be gay to be part of Quench. We had major DJs wanting to be part of us but they weren't gay so they couldn't. We had huge performers, but we couldn't cause we had that same rule. ... This was a different time, and we knew what we were trying to do! We did something that wasn't done! We brought the underground scene up to the downtown street level!"

Quench event cancelled in March of 1993 and Friday night "Kingdom" parties started in 1994.

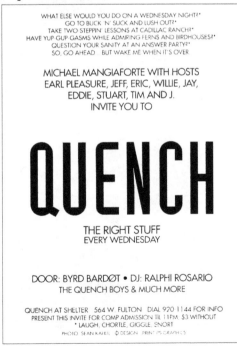

Shoreline
7650 South Shore Dr.
Circa: 1973–1975

Shoreline 7
7 W. Division St.
Circa: 1940s–1960s

It was a common misconception that the Shoreline 7 was owned by Ralph Capone, it was actually owned by ex-boxer Johnny Campbell and managed by Ralph Marco. The bar was really called the Shoreline, but on the matchbooks, it said, "Shoreline, then underneath 7, then West Division," so many called it the Shoreline 7. It specialized in comic drag.

Blondina told the authors, "As the guest person there, and I did the payoffs. I always had white envelopes, since I had the front door, the police captains and the police officials and the politicians would come in and I would hand them their envelopes. I never looked inside but I knew it was a lot of money, there were a lot of payoffs there. We had big names come in there, a lot of them. The back was more reserved for syndicate men and their girlfriends, or cops or politicians."

Dee LoBue, one of the drag performers at the bar, recalled,

SHORELINE 7
Proudly Presents
ENTERTAINMENT
? ? ? ? ? ? ?
Your Host
JOHNNY CAMPBELL
7 WEST DIVISION STREET
WHitehall 4-8735

"The dressing room of the Shoreline 7 was in the back room and there were two big copper kettles, maybe they held 500 gallons, and they were for wine-making. ... Papa Ralph and his brother would put cheap vodka in those kettles, add water, then redo the bottles.

"The Shoreline 7 was a long bar with the stage in the back and you had some tables on the side. Blondina was the bartender, and they did shows there ... Roby Landers was there, Pearly Mae, Blondina, CC Collins, Terri Page, and Tony Leigh."

COP ARRESTS 5 IN RAID AT 7 W. DIVISION

Five persons were arrested early yesterday in a raid on the Shoreline 7 lounge, 7 W. Division st., staged by Policeman Frank Guerra of the East Chicago Avenue district's vice detail.

Miss Annie Hicks, 29, was charged with soliciting for prostitution. The bartender, James Watson, 23, of 5012 N. Winthrop av., was charged with contributing to solicitation for prostitution, and the licensee, John J. Campbell, 74, was charged with being the keeper of a house of prostitution. Two men, described as female impersonators and dressed in women's clothing, were charged with being inmates. They are Vernon D. Lay, 25, and Eillie R. Watts, both of 2459 N. Halsted st.

Showcase One
959 W. Belmont Ave.
Circa: 1985–1986

The grand opening of Showcase One was held on February 15, 1985. The manager in the piano lounge was Todd Dayton, the general manager was Robby Dayton, and the general manager in the dance bar, Scott Resch.

Bert Thompson described the bar, "It was in the 2nd-floor space that had also been a hair salon and a tanning salon. You entered from the staircase which goes right up to the rear of the space. The main (showroom) bar, to the west, had a small stage,

Photo by Jack Sitar

Mr. Showcase One, Lee Stevens, is surrounded by fellow winners and the emcees of the Mister Contest. From left, back row, assistant manager Gary Trayman, Stevens, manager Scott Foreman; front row, Quincy Gaines, second place; and Mark Garcia, third place.

raised only about one step, on the inner (south) wall, with a tinseled backdrop but no arch or curtain. The fairly modest bar proper was in the northeast corner of the room, and most of the space was taken up with table seating: bar stools and high tables a step or two up, along with the windows on the north (street) side, and regular chairs and tables on the floor. I usually stood up, since I was there alone and had no money to buy a lot of drinks (they had a waiter or two). They did charge a modest cover. The crowd was the usual New Town crowd, mostly gay white men under 40, but with a scattering of everybody else, too. There was also another, smaller, bar room, sort of a lounge, in the space to the east of the stairs from the street."

Entertainment was provided by "Boylesque Review," Alana Russell, and "A Night with the Stars" with Patti Kakes as emcee and starring Shanté aka Alexandra Billings (Miss Gay Illinois 1985-86), Ginger Grant (Miss Gay Chicago 1985-86), and Candi Stratton (Miss Gay Indiana 1985-86). In May 1986, Mimi O'Shea wrote, "The incomparable Ethel Herman pulled out her nylons and all the stops in her recent return appearance at Showcase One. Dressed in black chiffon and string pearls, Ethel sang to an enthusiastic crowd at last week's Monday night talent search."

The small lounge was often used as a cabaret room, booked by impresario Ralph Lampkin.

This location was later Avalon.

Shrimpie's
North Ave, near Sheffield Ave.
Circa: 1968

Si, Como No
Sheffield Ave. near Barry Ave.
Circa: 1975

Short-lived Latin bar with Louis from the El Dorado pouring the drinks.

Sidecar Bar
6920 N. Glenwood Ave.
Circa: 2012

The bar hosted some benefits and a night of stand-up comedy featuring LGBT comedians. This would later become the location of Roger's Park Social.

Sidetrack
3349 N. Halsted
Circa: 1982-present

The bar was opened in 1982 and owned by Rocco Dinverno, who died soon after the opening while visiting Key West, Fl. It was, for a short time, owned by his mother, Fran London, before being taken over by Arthur (Art) Johnston and Jose Pepin (Pepe) Pena, with Chuck Hyde as managing partner from 1989-2016. Brad Balof took over as manager in 2017.

Originally one-storefront of less than 800 square feet, it expanded into neighboring properties in 1984, 1988, 1994, 1999 2001, and built an enclosed back patio and second-floor roof-top deck for a total of 20,000+ square feet. In 1999, a front courtyard was also added. It was one of the first video bars in the country and certainly the first catering to a gay clientele. It was one of the first successful bars on Halsted between Belmont and Addison and helped pave the way for the gentrification of the neighborhood. Steven August Papa said, "They were the true pioneers who enticed people to the neighborhood."

It is known for its numerous fund-raising events for LGBT and neighborhood charities. It is also a popular spot for visiting celebrities and the casts of Broadway touring companies, among those appearing at Sidetrack, have been Bea Arthur, Margaret Cho, and Scott Thompson.

Sidetrack was also the place politicians would appear to meet their gay supporters and constituents. Among those appearing at Sidetrack have been Sen. Howard Dean, Chicago Mayor Lori Lightfoot, Illinois Governor Pat Quinn, and many others.

It is best known for its sing-along show-tunes, Academy Awards, and Mardi Gras parties. For years, its signature event was "Night of 100 Drag Queens" which began as a birthday party thrown by *Gay Chicago Magazine*'s entertainment editor, Rick Karlin. The first year, two drag queens, Vikki Spykke and Paula Sinclaire performed on a stage made out of a sheet of plywood atop a stack of beer cases. For 25+ years the event grew to a multi-stage event with dozens of performers and the entire staff done up in drag. The event has raised hundreds of thousands of dollars for charity. Among the performers have been Samantha Sinclair, Carlotta Nerve, Daisy Mae, Frida Lay, Memory Lane, Honey West, Charlene Ungar, Gina Taye, Tina Tech, Jaye LeBow, and the She-Devils.

On February 22, 1990, Sidetrack hosted Lionheart Gay Theatre's production of *Bar None* by Perry Brass, a one-act play set in a bar before Stonewall, when it was illegal to serve "known homosexuals"

Sidetrack owners Pena and Johnston have a policy about the brands they sell, "We do not sell any product that the [drink] owners and/or distributors do not put money back into the community, period." Evian water is sold at Sidetrack because Evian is a major sponsor of LGBT-related sports events, teams, etc. Conversely, "Rolling Rock was non-responsive to our suggestion that they support things in the gay community, so we stopped carrying (it)."

Popular bartenders and DJs include Jeff (Boner) Bivona, Boom, Tommy O'Connell, Kathy Edens, Randy D'Agostino, and Brian Banahan.

Pepin Pena and Art Johnston of Sidetrack.

Siegelman's Allegro
2828 N. Clark St.
Circa: 1978-1979

Siegelman's Allegro was in the Century Mall and was owned by Ed Siegelman. "Pina Coladas or strawberry daiquiris were 95¢ on Thursdays.

This was also the location of Allegro International and Century Disco.

Simon's
Rush St. near Oak St.
Circa: 1930s

Owned by Ann and Sal Simon.

Slippery Slope
2357 N. Milwaukee Ave.
Circa: 2015

Slippery Slope hosted a gay night the third Thursday of the month.

Smart Bar
3730 N. Clark St.
Circa: 1983-present

A small dance club in Metro. It attracts a young crowd and features alternative dance music. In December 1992, Smart Bar listed in the gay press, "The first Tuesday of every month D3 Productions presents 'Decadence,' a night of fornicators and voyeurs fucking off on the dancefloor to the wicked sounds of DJs Teri Bristol, Ralphi Rosario, and Donovan DePass." And in January 2015, a tribute to late house-music pioneer Frankie Knuckles took place, "'For Frankie! A Celebration of His Life and Birthday' ... Among those slated to appear and/or perform were David Morales, Louie Vega, Tony Humphries, Derrick Carter, Michael Serafini and Garret David, among others. Tickets were $15 each.

Snake Pit
2628 N. Halsted St.
Circa: 1973-1977

The Snake Pit opened in October 1973. In September 1975, a woman took 2nd place in the Mr. Snake Pit contest. In January 1976, *GayLife* described the bar as, " ... the trashiest, tackiest, most garishly decorated bar in Chicago. It's now a western bar with western décor and two surrealistic white horses." Also in January 1976, it was announced that the owners of the Snake Pit were opening another bar called La Mere Vipere.

In October 1977, the Snake Pit closed after failing to renew its license.

This was also the location of Carnival and Pits.

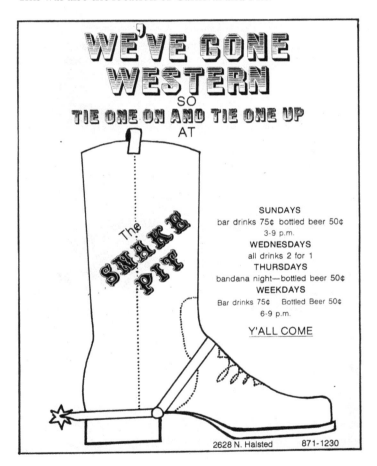

Sofo Tap
4923 N. Clark St.
Circa: 2007-present

Sofo Tap is a neighborhood tavern in Andersonville. In 2011, Mark Robertson, Mike Sullivan, Steve Milford, and Brian Wells, acquired all the shares of Sofo, according to a press release. Milford and Wells were principal owners of Crew. The bar is currently owned by Mark Robertson and Mike Sullivan of the 2 Bears Group, which also owns Meeting House, Jackhammer, and 2Bears Tavern.

In March 2011, Sofo Tap hosted its inaugural comedy event. Performers included Amy Eisenberg, Brian Henning, Kristin Clifford, Maggie Jenkins, Marla Depew and Thomas Bottoms. In November 2012, the bar advertised, "D.I.L.F. The hottest monthly event for sexy daddies and the guys who want to f#ck them. Daddy Jason Hendrix hosts with Daddy DJ Marc 'Moose' Moder on decks. The place to be in Chicago for MEN over 35 and the men who want them."

This location was formerly home to Different Strokes.

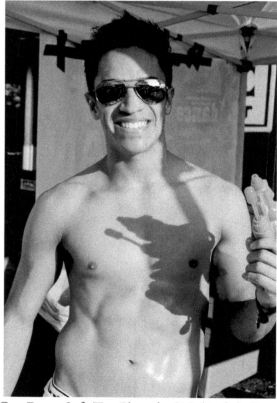

Gun Fun at Sofo Tap. Photo by St Sukie de la Croix

Sound Bar
226 W. Ontario St.
Circa: 2004-2015

Sound Bar was a mixed gay/straight bar that hosted LGBT events. It had two levels, two dance floors, and four lounges. In May 2004, "Hot Tea 4" at Sound Bar benefitted the Leather Archives and Museum. In May 2015, the bar held IML's Black and Blue Ball with DJs Barry Harris and Steve Henderson, and host Mr. Chicago Leather 2014 Miguel Torres.

Other popular DJs include Mark Picchiotti, Ralphi Rosario, Chris Eterno, Luis M, and Earl Pleasure.

South Pacific
Lake Park Ave. and Hyde Park Blvd.
Circa: 1950s

Jim Wickliff related, "The South Pacific was a bar in the old Hyde Park hotel; it was real, real old and it had been a very elegant hotel. And it had become a little better than a flophouse. They had a piano player in there, a woman that sang up on a stage. The bar was in the center of the room, and a lot of straight people went there, but I'd say it was about 85 percent gay, and cruising gay. It was fun, people sang, and every now and then she [the piano player] would do some risqué lyrics. It was a predominantly White bar. In the '50s there wasn't a lot of crossover."

Southside Workingmen's Club
5228 S. Parkway (basement)
Circa: 1951

The club was raided and closed down with charges of contributing to the delinquency of a minor, but all charges were dropped when the minor refused to testify.

Sparrows
5224 N. Sheridan Rd.
Circa: 1970-1972

Sparrows opened in October 1970. Charles "Chuck" Renslow owned this drag bar. Among those appearing were Wanda Lust, Roby Landers, Jackie Knight, Kay Leslie, Virginia Slim, Ebony Carr, Audrey Bryant, Jill Christie, Tanya Terrill, ED Lloyd, Artesia Welles, and Shelly Michaels.

Renslow reported, "In '71, we had the first float in that parade from Sparrows. What we did was ... Gary Chichester was the coordinator ... since they had no floats and they wanted floats, we took a flat car we rented, one of these flat trailers you pull, and we put this artificial grass on it. Somebody had a trellis and we mounted that and put all the drag queens on it."

JC remembered, "I used to go there all the time when they first started out. I thought that was the best drag bar in the whole city. They had a bigger stage, and the people in there were friendlier. I knew most of the drag queens at that time. I remember Roby Landers, and his friend ... I can't remember his name ... but they used to sit on the swing and do 'the swing song.' They had a swing in there and he would sit on the swing in his beautiful gown, and he would sing a song as he was swinging. It was so cute!! That was everybody's favorite. I do remember Ebony, and he did Etta James a couple of times. Sparrows was a pretty big place; they had the bar at the front and at the back there was tables and the stage. It was there for a year and a half. I wish it had stayed because we always had a good time there."

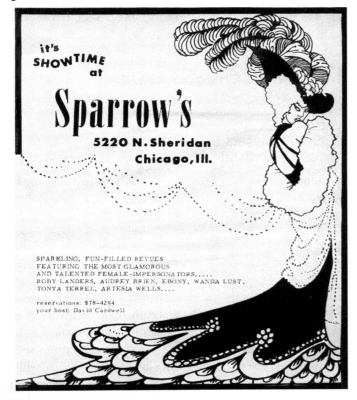

Speakeasy Supper Club
1401 W. Devon Ave.
Circa: 2004

A supper club featuring performers such as Alexander Billings and Amy Matheny.

Spectrum Disco
7 S. Stolp St., Aurora
Circa: 1976-1979

Spectrum was in the basement of the Leland Hotel. Before opening as a gay bar, they asked gay people to turn up on September 9, 1976, at 8 p.m. to see how many gays in the area would frequent the bar.

Obviously enough did, Spectrum advertised itself as Aurora's first gay disco. In 1979, the Aurora Gay People's group held a monthly bingo social event at the bar. On October 15, 1978, Maxine King did three shows in one night.

Spice Tree
2811 N. Central Ave.
Circa: 1982-1983

The Spice Tree disco and dance lounge opened as a private membership club on October 27, 1982. On March 5, 1983, the "Spice Tree Revue" starred Patricia De Roma, Tata, Peaches, Lady B., and some surprise guests. All drinks were 50c.

Spin
3200 N. Halsted St.
Circa: 1995-2014

The bar opened in 1995 with owners Larry Ciupak and Earl Wallace. Dave Gassman, a straight real estate developer bought the property and Spin in 1996. Among some of the events, in addition to dance parties and shower contests, were benefits for Asians and Friends and the Chicago Anti-Bashing Network, Daisy Mae's Drag Queen Bingo, and a bear shower contest. In 1999, DJs and VJs included Freddy Bain, Michael Serafini, Alex Ander, and Steve Farias.

Earl and Larry, owners of Spin, help ring in their second year.
Photo by Terry Gaskins

Oscar night at Spin (left to right) Ralph, Daisy Mae, and David Barrick. Also hanging out at Spin's Oscar night (left to right) Jamie Kowalski, Xviar Snow and Armando Gutierrez.
photos by Terry Gaskins

In January 2012, Real Housewives of New Jersey's Melissa Gorga, along with hunky husband Joe Gorga, judged the DRAGZILLA amateur drag competition. In April 2012, Sharon Needles from Ru Paul's Drag Race (RPDR) appeared at Spin. Other drag queens from RPDR at Spin included Ongina and Jade.

After a change in ownership, two straight men, Jason Zilberbrand and Jordan Zabinger, tried making it a straight bar named Chloe's/Whiskey Trust. It's ownership then reverted to Gassman.

The bar closed in 2014.

This was the location of VII, Den, Eons, Foxy's, the second incarnation of Manhole, Whiskey Trust.

Spitz's
7149 S. South Chicago Ave.
Circa: 1976

Splash Chicago
3339 N. Halsted St.
Circa: 2018-2021

According to *Gab Magazine*, Splash was a "Narrow, dimly lit gay bar with a diverse crowd open late & serving mixed cocktails & dancing."

Spot
4437 N. Broadway
Circa: 2007-2009

A straight gay-friendly bar comprising two floors, three bars, and two stages. *Time Out* described the bar, "With its three distinct barrooms, this Uptown oasis is custom-made for the indecisive patron. An imposing wine rack and wafting surf-and-turf scents give the ground floor an air of fine dining, while the upstairs plays host to a weekly improv competition on Thursdays and stand-up on Tuesdays and the basement sports lounge boasts a 130-item bloody mary bar with brats and Italian sausages for your next bro-down."

Spy Bar/Millenia X
646 N. Franklin St.
Circa: 1997-present

The grand opening of Millenia X Tuesday gay nights was December 23, 1977. Popular DJs include Hugo, Jonathan Montiero, and Mark Hultmark.

Spyners Pub
4623 N. Western Ave.
Circa: 2007-present

A "sporty dyke" bar. Many sports teams head to Spyner's after the game. The bar hosts a variety of community benefits. On June 4, 2020, more than 100 patrons and community members gathered in front of the pub to protest owner and general manager, Maureen Sullivan's, alleged racist Facebook posts and past racist comments toward numerous bar patrons. During the 2020-2021 pandemic, the bar shut down for renovations, but reopened.

Stage 618
618 N. Clark St.
Circa: 1976-1977

According to Richard Pfeiffer's column in *GayLife*, Friday, April 16, 1976, the bar was owned by Charles "Chuck" Renslow, using staff from his recently burned-down disco Zolar. However, Renslow says that although he helped start the 618, it was run by Ira Jones. One patron, who declined to be identified, claimed it was "syndicate owned." He was probably referring to "owner" Nick Argiris, who also owned the Ranch. The bar closed in October 1977 when it failed to renew its liquor license.

In Richard Cooke's Discovery column in *Gay Chicago Magazine*, "As you might recall, Stage 618 was a sleazy, dimly lit, sweaty, perverse bar on Clark Street that was one of my favorite places."

This was also the location of Upper Class.

Stages Music Hall
3730 N. Clark St.
Circa: 1980

Stages took over when Charles "Chuck" Renslow's Center Stage went under. Although Renslow was not involved any more, Stages hosted his seventh annual White Party there in August 1980. *GayLife* wrote, "Now known as Stages Music Hall and no longer operated by Renslow, the three-story former theater premises were the scene of performances by Chicago's Gay Pride Band, the New Wave band Stranded, and Chicago-born disco singer Loleatta Holloway during the evening.

"The main spectacle of the evening was the crowd itself, composed mostly of men but including some women, and nearly all dressed in white costumes that ranged from nondescript street clothes to white tie and tails, tutu and toe shoes (worn by an actual dancer – male), uniforms, designer jumpsuits, shorts and vests, or less. Many Indian feathers and leggings were in evidence, as were many faces not commonly seen in Chicago gay nightspots.

"Politicians who appeared during the evening included State Reps. Susan Catania, William A. Marovitz, and Elroy C. Sandquist, Jr., sponsors of gay rights legislation.

"Business clients of Renslow's management firm who helped to host the party were the Gold Coast bar, Man's Country baths, the Machine Shop bookstore, and *GayLife*."

Other LGBT entertainers who performed at Stages were Cris Williamson, Tom Robinson, Meg Christian, Lori Noelle, and Trish Alexander.

This was also the location of Centerstage, Smart Bar, and Metro.

Star Bar
2934 N. Halsted St.
Circa: 1994

Stardust Ballroom
35 W. Galena Blvd., Aurora
Circa: 1981-1983

Star Gaze
5419 N. Clark St.
Circa: 1997-2010

Originally opened as Café Ashie in April 1996, it was renamed Star Gaze in 1998 and became a fixture in the lesbian community. When it closed, owner Mamie Lake cited burn-out. In 2010 it was the sole remaining lesbian bar – as opposed to mixed gay/lesbian – in Chicago. During its heyday, Star Gaze hosted a "Funny Chix Night" with lesbian comics Jessica Halem and Tracey Rose. In September 1998, Valerie James and 20 other performers help Minerva Rex become Miss International Gay Rodeo. In February 2003, Michelle Malone

Being Sassy at Star Gaze. Photo by St Sukie de la Croix

performed. Other performers over the years included the Chicago Kings, Ripley Caine, Sean Wiggins, Commonbond, and Trish Alexander. Benefits were held for Gerber/Hart Library, and Lesbian Community Cancer Project, among other agencies. On weekends it was a gathering spot for women's sports teams after their games.

Stargazer
4153 W. 26th St.
Circa: 1960s

Also at this location were La Cueva and Dolly's.

Stars
61 W. Hubbard St.
Circa: 1976

This was also the location of Roadhouse.

Stars
3209 N. Halsted St.
Circa: 1989–1990

The grand opening of Stars was held in July 1989 with featured entertainers Darrol Rierson, Stardust, the Lebeznik Sisters, and Kenned & Carl. The bar was advertised as, "Halsted's only piano bar where everyone's a 'Star.'" The owners were Mark LaValley and Sam Marsala. Other performers during the bar's short existence were, Michael James, Marna – the Last Lady of Song, and the zany Darryl Nitz.

This was also the location of Happy Hours, Pangea, and Guzzlers.

Steppin' Out
162 S. Broadway, Aurora
Circa: 1984–1985

This was sometimes listed as the Outer Limits I and II. The grand opening was in January 1984 with Quincey Gaines as the featured performer.

Steve and Eddie's Saratoga
1123 N. State St.
Circa: 1983

This was a gay-friendly restaurant and piano bar.

This was also the location of No-Name.

Still of The Night
Division St. and Clark St.
Circa: 1965–1966

Stop 65
65 E. Illinois St.
Circa: 1985–1987

An ad in May 1986 read, "STOP 65, 65 W. Illinois, is now open at 7 a.m. with your host, Big Sugar.".

Stop & Drink
742 N. Clark St.
Circa: 1992

Storm
State St.
Circa: 1962-1963

Jerry C recalled, "It was dark with Christmas tree lights all around. It was called the Storm because when you went inside, they played music like there was a storm outside, with lightning going on and thunder."

Tony Simes played the piano at the Storm. He also played at Kitty Sheon's Little Club.

Student Prince
4639 N. Damen Ave.
Circa: 1970

Studio 69
3474 N. Clark St.
Circa: 1981

The grand opening of Studio 69 was in January 1981, with Daisy, Danelle, Dolores, Tonette, Miss Factory (China), and TaTa. Ralph Mitchell was one of the bartenders.

This was also the location of Zo-Ran, the Factory, Christy's on Clark, and Party Party.

Subterranean
2011 W. North Ave.
Circa: 2005-2019

Subterranean was a mixed gay/straight bar that has hosted many LGBT events, including the Estrojam Festival in August 2003, the Sissy Butch Bros. present "One Bad Ass Burlesque Show in November 2002, Pussy-Whipped parties, and Queeroke! In July 2009, gay punk band, Pansy Division, performed there.

Suds Club
7301 W. Forest Preserve Dr.
Circa: 1983

Sue and Nan's
3920 N. Lincoln Ave.
Circa: 1975-1977

Sue and Nan's was a lesbian bar with drag shows, buffets and raffles, but gay men were welcome. Sue was Sue Hughes.

Rose remembered, "It was all black, floor, walls, ceiling, windows, everything. They had a huge dog. It was a really tough bar ... they had to know you to let you in and I went there with my first lover, and they referred to her as 500, because she was from Indianapolis. Not only did you have to know somebody, but you had a name."

Sugar Shack
436 N. Clark St.
Circa: 1971-1972

Other bars at this location include Big Basket, Baton Show Lounge, Queen's Surf.

Sunday's (Child/Children)
430 N. Clark St.
Circa: 1973-1981

The owner was Allan Rodman, the bar opened as Sunday's Children in 1973, the word Children was changed to Child and then dropped completely. DJs started around 10 p.m. each evening and played until 4 a.m. (5 a.m. on Saturday).

Michael Triner was a regular DJ. Popular bartenders include Karen Ross – later head typesetter for *Gay Chicago Magazine* and Chuck Rodocker – now the owner of Touché.

In October 1977, Dennis and Sam Gibson were the new operators at Sunday's.

Nancy Reiff recalled, "At Sundays, Allan collected antiques, so there was a lot of church type of stuff, huge light fixtures hanging down that were out of churches, church pews, and the ceilings were very high and almost cavernous over the bar. It's hard to explain."

Sunday's, located in what is now known as Chicago's River North, was described in an October 1975 issue of *GayLife*, as having a large dancefloor and an exciting light and sound system. The club was known for its upside-down Old Style beer sign outside and two speakers hanging over the dance floor.

This was also the location of the Baton Show Lounge, Loft, Ramrod, Annex 2, Punch's.

IN HONOR OF THE POPE JOHN PAUL II and his visit to Chicago. A special party is being arranged to be held at Sunday's 430 North Clark Friday, October 5th, starting at 10 p.m. Everyone welcome!

Suzie B's
1829 W. Montrose Ave.
Circa: 1987-1992

Suzie B's grand opening was on November 5, 1987. It was owned by Barb Slockbower and Deb Stewart. It was a lesbian bar.

Deb reported, "I opened it in 1987, the Lady Bug closed and I graduated from Columbia with a degree in photography and took off to Europe and I was just going to take pictures and become a famous photographer, and then I came back four months later. I wasn't a famous photographer. I didn't know what to do with myself, so a friend of mine, Barb Slockbower, she hated her job, so she quit. So, we both had no jobs and didn't know what to do with ourselves, so we just thought that maybe we should open a bar. Mainly because we didn't know where to go. The Lady Bug wasn't there, and Paris [Dance] was too fancy for us. We just wanted a regular old bar.

"The bar before was called Rocky and Angie's Time to Remember, and it was a straight bar with a bunch of old neighborhood alcoholics in it. It was really run down. During the construction of it, we just put a stage in the front, we didn't really have a plan for it ... for some reason I just said, 'Let's put a stage there.' There was a piano already there, so we put the piano up on the stage, and for our opening night, this girl Marsha Wilkie came in, and she was a comedian, new in town, and she headed up this whole Women in Comedy thing. So, then Paula Killen played there, and we started doing a lot of different performances, open mic, poetry readings, and we had a different artist on the wall every month. We didn't do a lot of advertising because we didn't have a big budget. It wasn't like we went into it with a lot of money or anything, we were scraping just to get it open, and it was always just trying to keep it open. We were there for five years."

This was also the location of Off the Line, Ravenswood Tavern, Wee Frog, and Scot's.

Swan Club
3720 N. Clark St.
Circa: 1981-1986

The grand opening of Swan Club was held on April 15, 1981. Paté was the star bartender at this popular lesbian gathering spot. Anita remembered, "It was very small, very smoky, you walked in and there was a small dance floor, a bar ... I think most people went there to drink and meet women."

Maria, a bartender at Swan Club, explained the closing at the height of its popularity, "Dolly [Kaly, the owner] passed away, and Dolly and Anna were really very private people. Anna was encouraged by many friends to have some kind of public memorial, and she agreed to do that. I think it was really important for a lot of people, because Dolly touched the lives of a lot of people. I remember the week she died, I went out every night to the bars and I would just lend an ear to women who felt they had been touched by Dolly in some way, or by the

Swan Club. People just wanted to tell stories about the Swan Club and their coming out."

Lauryn Kushner recalled, "At the Swan Club there was 'some' disco music, and there was Vanessa Davis, she's a blues singer, and she was just putting out singles, and a couple of her songs were on the jukebox. It was not like the Lost and Found with 'God Bless America' stuff on there. That was not 'happening.' George Thorogood, a little harder rock 'n' roll more than disco."

This was also the location of Teddy's Lounge and Raw Bar.

Photos by Mark DeSanto and Dan Di Leo
Any reason for a party. Above, a capacity crowd helped the Swan Club mark its second anniversary.

Sweet Alice
1056 N. Damen Ave.
Circa: 1992

This was also the location of Ten 56

Sweets
3477 N. Clark St.
Circa: 1983-1984

This was also the location of Little Hercules Disco and ? (Question Mark).

T

Take It Easy Inn
3325 N. Halsted St.
Circa: 1975-1976

The Take It Easy Inn opened on July 9, 1975. The bar was managed by Frank Leonard and Ron Hawbaker. A notice in the *GayLife* read, "A new gay bar on the scene is Take It Easy Inn with a free bottle of champagne given away every Friday and Saturday night." In September 1975, the bar hosted an Astrology and Numerology Party with Homer Lathrop (Astrologer) and Sandra Hansen (Numerologist). In October 1975, patrons were invited to body paint a go-go boy. In November 1975, the bar closed for renovation. In 1976, the Mr. Take It Easy Inn contestant for the Mr. Windy City contest, Steve "Missy" Allman's bio read, "Steve, at 24 years and weighing 165lbs, is one of Chicago's top bartenders. Regularly employed by Cheeks, Steve shows off his 'bluebird tattoo' in the Cheeks ad." The bluebird is on his ass.

Steve Allman remembered, "That was the weirdest place. There were extension cords everywhere. The guy that owned it lived across the alley from there, and he had all these extension cords going to his house for the electricity. It was weird."

Take One
2570 N. Clark St.
Circa: 1983-1988

Take One was a neighborhood bar. The grand opening was on December 14, 1983, and the bar was owned by Michael Glenner and William Lane. In 1985, the TV show *Brothers* was shown weekly in the bar.. Also extremely popular was the bar's *Dynasty* night.

Take One closed in February 1988.

This was also the location of Bughaus, K's on Clark, Robert's Lounge, and Molly's Follies.

At Mr. Take One contest (from left) are Ralph Paul and Dan DiLeo, publishers of 'Gay Chicago'; 'Windy City Times' publisher Jeff McCourt; and Chuck Renslow, whose Bistro Too bar will open soon.

SOUND...

& VISION

Join Us Aug. 1 for
"Liquid Sky" at 8pm

TAKE ONE

2570 N. Clark   929-4540

Tambourine
200 E. Chestnut St.
Circa: 1980s

Tambourine was a theater bar with an open mic night.

Tania's
2659 N. Milwaukee Ave.
Circa: 1996–1997

Circus was gay night at Tania's with DJs Teri Bristol and Julius Oliver. In April 1996, the Association of Latin Men for Action presented Noche de Gala 96 with Cuban food and salsa dancing to the rhythms of Tania's live orchestra.

Taverna 750
750 W. Cornelia Ave.
Circa: 2010–2015

Taverna 750 was a restaurant and after-hours cocktail lounge. In March 2012, it hosted a T750 Lounge Launch with Candis Cayne of ABC's *Dirty Sexy Money* and *Nip/Tuck* and famed fashion designer Traver Rains.

This was also the location of Cornelia's.

Teddie's
3160 N. Clark St.
Circa: 1985–1986

Teddie's grand opening was February 19, 1985, with a Mardi Gras masquerade with Cajun food, DJ Mark Stephens, and prizes for best costumes. This was also the location of Annex 3, Shakers on Clark, the 3160 Club.

Teddy's Lounge
3720 N. Clark St.
Circa: 1976

This was also the location of the Swan Club and Raw Bar.

Temptations
10235 W. Grand Ave., Franklin Park
Circa: 1990–2012

The grand opening was on June 20, 1990. The co-owners of Temptations were Michael Torres, George Grivas, and his wife, Bessie. In 1996, Sherry West was the manager. The bar was geared mostly toward lesbians, but there were events for men, like Sarabia's Stud Puppy Tuesdays – there was a "Big Basket" and "Best Butt" contest. Temptations hosted many events over the years, including a Hawaiian Beach Party and Limbo

EROTICA

Friday Night
June 21st

Featuring...

Jade Dragon Tattoo Booth

Sexy and Safe "S&M" Fun

Hot Madonna Videos

Playful Whipping, Candle
Wax Excitement, Spankings
and more...

The word
"Temptations!"
takes on a
whole new
meaning!

Temptations Nightclub
10235 W. Grand Ave. Franklin Park, IL
847-455-0008 • www.TemptationsNightclub.com

Contest in 1997, Miss Tee's Tacky Tuesdays in 2000, and the Black Bra party in 2010.

Several comediennes performed at Temptations, including Lea Delaria in July 1996 and Ellen DeGeneres in June 2000. Also, bands such as Stewed Tomatoes, Halcyon, and the Cathy Richardson Band.

Having fun at the popular "Black Bra Party"
Photo by St Sukie de la Croix

Ten 56
1056 N. Damen Ave.
Circa: 1998

This was also the location of Sweet Alice.

Tenement Square
247 E. Ontario St.
Circa: 1974-1975

In the *Chicago Gay Directory 1974-1975,* Tenement Square was described as "semi-gay."

This was also the location for Dingbats.

Texas Ranch
2409 N. Mannheim Ave., Franklin Park
Circa: 1998

A straight bar with Friday as gay night.

This was also the location of Moda VIP.

Thumbs Up
3127 N. Clark St.
Circa: 1989

The grand opening of Thumbs Up was held on April 13, 1989; by May, it was no longer listed in the bar guides.

This was also the location of Windy City Bar & Grill and Clubhouse.

Thurston's
1248 W. George St.
Circa: 1999

In December 1999, all-women rock band Evil Beaver celebrated the release of its 4-song Christmas EP *Smells Like Christmas Spirit.*

Tilt Inn
2626 N. Halsted St.
Circa: 1972-1973

This was also the location of Noche de Ronda and Prodigal Son Bar & Grill.

Tiny and Ruby's Gayspot Lounge
2711 S. Wentworth Ave.
Circa: 1954-1955

"Tiny" Davis

"Tiny" Davis and her lover, drummer, pianist, and bass player, Ruby Lucas (Renee Phelan). The club opened on June 17, 1954. The opening night featured Tiny Davis and her Hell Divers and from Kansas City, Tiny's daughter, Dorothy Davis, on bass, and Evelyn Twine on piano. The following month tenor saxophone player Paul Bascomb played there, also lesbian Vi Burnside, but by October 1955, the club was sold.

Tip Top Tap, Allerton Hotel
701 N. Michigan Ave.
Circa: 1940–1961

Like most hotel bars, the Tip Top Tap had a discreet gay clientele. This was augmented by the fact that, when the hotel first opened, it had fourteen floors of small apartment-style rooms for men (and six similar floors for women). Police at the time used to joke about, "The Tip Top Tap, where the fairies fly up to the bar."

The Tip Top Tap closed in 1961 and was converted to a ballroom when the structure became a standard hotel.

TJ's on Oak
46 E. Oak St.
Circa: 1986–1993

TJ's on Oak was originally owned by Ken Killian and Tony Williams, but in late 1988, Bob and Harriet Goodman became the new owners. The bar opened in February 1986, and the staff that night were Jay Kirkpatrick, Laird Brandin, and Joe Archambeault.

TJ's on Oak bartenders Joe Archembault and Tommy Almada with manager Laird Brandin during the bar's "Nuts and Bolts" party. *Frank handed out the nuts and bolts during TJ's on Oak "Nuts and Bolts" party.* Photo by Tom Granzow

In April 1986, there was a Vodka and Video Party with DJ Mark Hultmark. Charlie Oliver was a popular bartender there. In September 1988, Jerry Goudy was the manager.

TJ's on Oak closed in 1993.

This was the location of Loading Zone and Scalawags.

Togetherness
61 E. Hubbard St.
Circa: 1972-1973

The bar was owned by civil rights attorney Ralla Klepak and managed by Marge Summit. Artesia Welles recalled performing at the bar, "The dressing room was on the third floor, and there was a freight elevator that we had to take, and that scared the shit out of me. We didn't want to drink too much there; we didn't want to end up flying down the elevator shaft. It was actually a pretty tacky place; the back of the stage was all done in mirror tiles, but it was a place to work."

Tocci's
46 154th St., Calumet City
Circa: 1968-1971

A lesbian bar.

Touché
2825 N. Lincoln Ave.
Circa: 1976-1990

Originally opened in 1976, by Fred Wasser and Wally Thomas, owners of King's Ransom. Thomas bought out Wasser a year later and operated it as a leather bar. He sold to Chuck Rodocker in 1977, because of family commitments. Rodocker was a bartender at Sundays and Redoubt. David Boyer and Jerry Musleve were the bar's managers.

In the March 5, 1976, issue of *GayLife*, columnist Richard Pfeiffer wrote, "Check out a new bar, Touché, on Lincoln. Timmy of the King's Ransom is now bartending there."

Events over the years have celebrated those with a fetish for boots (February 23, 1981), and rubber (April 7, 1989) and even held an annual Easter egg hunt. On June 26, 1977, Touché held a Turkish Party featuring shish kebob, Turkish vodka, and pasha. Monthly Full Moon parties usually feature a tan line contest, and in December/January 1988-1989, there was a black-out party. On January 27, 1988, Touché held a special banana night. If you had a banana in your back pocket, you got 50c off the price of cocktails all night long.

Tim Cagney remembered, "There was a bathtub, which was not connected to anything. It was there for a specific purpose if you knew the environment."

In a November 1985 *Windy City Times*, Tracy Baim wrote: "Four men arrested Aug. 11 at Touché were given short periods of court-ordered supervision Oct. 29. All pleaded not guilty to the charge of public indecency. But charges against the bar, located at 2825 N. Lincoln, were dropped. A bar employee had been arrested and charged with being the keeper of a disorderly house. The attorney for the four men, Larry Rolla, said each entered a technical plea of not guilty and of the four supervision sentences, none was more than six months.

"According to the police report on the Aug. 11 arrests, which took place about 10.45 p.m. Two citations were issued for no liquor license, one person was charged with being the keeper of a disorderly house, and the four men were charged with public indecency. Police entered Touché allegedly in response to a citizen's complaint received by the office of Chicago Mayor Harold Washington. According to the police, officers observed a number of 'lewd' behaviors."

Touché's Lincoln Avenue location was destroyed by fire on Saturday, March 3, 1990, between 5:00 and 6:00 a.m. The fire broke out in a storage area for the heating and electrical systems, then spread to an area for alcohol inventory. When the alcohol exploded, the bar's roof caught fire and was destroyed.

Touché
6412 N. Clark St.
Circa: 1991-present

After the original location burned, Chuck Rodocker bought a building in Rogers Park and reopened Touché. The atmosphere is much the same as the original. Among the groups holding events at the bar were the Windy City Gay Naturists (September 2000), The Chicago Hellfire Club (April 2006), Great Lakes Bears (March 1996), in 1997, the Zoo BBS celebrated its 9th birthday. In August 2002, Fallen Angel Steve Cannon celebrated his birthday at Touché, and in May 1998, there was a Full Moon Fattest Ass contest. In April 2005, "Leather Eye for the Preppy Guy," a makeover contest took place at the bar.

**M.A.F.I.A.
CLUB NIGHT**
Friday the 13th

Touché
CHICAGO'S LEATHER BAR
6412 N. Clark Street
(At Ashland and Devon)
Open till 4 a.m.   Saturdays till 5 a.m.

WELCOM

**THE MEN O
RODEO
17'**

DECEM
4 · 5

Op
5 pm we

Here's Looking at You

Photos by Mark DeSanto
Members of Cin City Cycle Club were guests club members at a Black and White themed party at Touché last week. Included in the night's festivities was a wet Jockey shorts contest.

AND MY BROTHERS
ARE MINE

Touché

*Join the
Greatest Show
on Earth
at*

Touché
2825 N. Lincoln Ave.

Touché
6412 NORTH CLARK STREET
CHICAGO'S LEATHER BAR SINCE 1977

BLUE MOON
January 31st
**SUPER BOWL
SUNDAY**
&
**MR. UNIONSUIT
1999**

ce $100⁰⁰ Cash

g At Midnight

Touché
Chicago's Leather Bar
Clark Street @ Devon
- Plenty of Free Parking -
/MC/AmEx/Discover Cards

Photo by Jack Sitar/GayLife
"Boys in the Sand" star Casey Donovan (in leather harness) joins Touché owner Chuck Rodocker (rear) and staff members to celebrate the bar's eighth-plus anniversary.

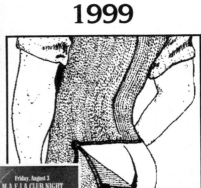

Friday, August 3
M.A.F.I.A CLUB NIGHT
Saturday, August 4
**BEAR NIGHT WITH
GREAT LAKES BEARS**
Premiere of Cyberbear's
'Hairy Hole Bar' Part 1
Free copies of Bear Party Magazine

CyberBears

Sunday, August 5
BEER BUST
50¢ Bud and Bud Light Drafts
After the Beach Raffles 4-8pm

Touché
6412 N. Clark Street
www.touchechicago.com

Tovia Disco Club
6018-6020 W. Belmont Ave.
Circa: 1980

Town & Country
Palmer House Hotel, State St. and Monroe St.
Circa: 1950s-1980

Another hotel bar frequented by gay men. Bob Egan remembered, "It was in the basement of the Palmer House hotel. It was a cocktail lounge next to a restaurant. About 4 p.m., five days a week, it got packed. A lot of people coming in on business, and they all knew what bar to go to. It obviously wasn't advertised as a gay bar, but those were the people who came in. ... There would be a lot of people you didn't know until you went there a lot. The same people would be there night after night. Everybody was there in a shirt and tie. They were all coming in after work, or they were traveling through. It was a small bar, and sometimes it was so crowded, you could hardly get through it. Contact-wise, you might be sitting next to somebody, and their knee would be up on the barstool, and you put your crotch on top of their knee, but you didn't let the bartenders see that. You could talk to people, come in and shake hands with people you knew."

Township
2200 N. California Ave.
Circa: 2013

Alcohol-free dance space, first Thursday of the Month was the gay night, called Nut & Bolts.

Trace/Refuge
3417 N. Clark St.
Circa: 2003

Refuge was this straight club's gay night featuring underground house with DJ Kenny Ray.

Trade and Flavor
422 S. Wabash Ave.
Circa: 1994

Trade Winds
Rt 66A, Joliet
Circa: 1965-1966

Transfer
2851 N. Halsted St.
Circa: 1975

The grand opening of this gay disco juice bar was December 5, 1975. It closed two days later.

Transit
1431 W. Lake St.
Circa: 2001-2020

Transit was a straight club that hosted gay events. In August 2001, the Hearts Foundation presented "Hearts in Transit 2," a tea dance with DJs Mark Vallese and Neil Lewis with proceeds benefiting Hearts Foundation's Take Pride in Yourself program. In May 2015, Transit hosted the Nuts to Butts dance party, celebrating 21 years of Bear Pride with DJ Jesse Mercado and DJ HAZMAT. And in June 2002, Chix Mix Productions' Freedom dance party with sexy dancers and bartenders, DJs Harry T and Solange.

Traveler's Rest
1138 W. Granville Ave.
Circa: 1990-1999

This was also the location of the Eagle's Nest.

Trianon
3150 N. Halsted St.
Circa: 1984-1986

Trianon was a dance club owned by Bruce Kuntz, Fred Hands, and Dale Sapper. A popular DJ there was Mark Vallese. Trianon held many events. Among them, a July 1984 fundraiser for the Frank M. Rodde III Memorial Building Fund, featured an auction of Mister Windy City Contestants.

In September 1984, Stardust, a female vocal trio specializing in music from the 1930s, '40s, and '50s, gave a benefit concert for the Chicago Gay Men's Chorus. Disco diva Linda Clifford recorded a music video, "A Night Out with the Boys," at the club. In May 1985, Sheryl Lee Ralph, recording star of Broadway's *Dreamgirls*, performed. In April 1985, Men in Leather presented Tuesdays with your hosts, Terry Hunter, Damien, Tim Henley. And in June 1985, Robin Dupree presented a COMMAND PERFORMANCE, a Night of Royalty, starring Cherine Alexander (Miss Gay Continental 1985), Sherri Payne (Miss Gay Illinois), Chili Pepper (Miss Gay Continental #1). This was also the location of Club La Ray.

Farewell to Trianon's Jerry Carlson as he leaves Chicago for much warmer weather. Jerry (center) seen here with two of the many friends and well wishers Andy Sanders and Fred Schramm, who showed up for his going away party.

Trip
27 E. Ohio St.
Circa: 1968–1976

The Trip opened on September 8, 1967. It was owned by Dean T. Kolberg and Ralf L. Johnston.

It was a popular men's bar, three floors comprising a dining room, cocktail lounge, and cabaret room. In October 1968, Mattachine Midwest hosted an event at the bar. The speaker was Dr. William Simon, who conducted a survey of homosexuality for the Kinsey Institute. On March 19, 1974, Glen Mansfield beat out 26 other contestants to become Mr. Trip 1974 in the Mr. Windy City contest. In September 1976, Pudgy and the Sam Hill Trio performed. In July 1976, the Trip was under new ownership.

Fred Steinhauer remembered, "The Trip in 1973 was very colorful, very lively, a lot of people, very friendly ... it was more of a community center than it was a place to pick up people."

Jan Dee recalls, "Laurie Lynn sang and played the piano. The bar was like walking into family; when you walked in, everybody was friendly, the guys were friendly, the girls were friendly, everything was family from the first day ... the Trip was a trip."

In June 1968, the Trip was raided for the second time, and its liquor license was suspended pending appeal. On March 27, 1969, the Illinois Supreme Court ordered the return of the liquor license to the Trip. The court declared unconstitutional the section of Illinois liquor laws allowing the City of Chicago to keep taverns closed while license revocations were being appealed.

The Trip

Level I — Fine Cuisine
Chef Kevin features a different special every day — serving fresh vegetables, potatoes, soup du jour and fine desserts 6 PM to midnight — Monday through Saturday — SUNDAY BRUNCH 1 to 5 PM

Level II — Entertainment Lounge
Something special everyday. Monay through Firday: Cocktail hour / Cheese Bar. Wednesday through Sunday: Live Entertainment / Tommy Oman at the piano bar Wednesday and Thursday evenings / Susie Heenan andthe Sam Hill Trio Firday, Saturday and Sunday.

Level III — Newly Remodeled
Live Disco D.J. — Larger Dance Floor
Seven Days A Week!

— Dining Room • Cocktail Lounge —
Twenty-Seven East Ohio Street • Chicago, Illinois

Open Daily 4 P.M.   467-6330   No Cover

"I was there the night they raided it," Charlie Tuna told the authors, "It was the week before the Democratic National Convention; they raided a lot of the bars, if not all of them. That raid (at the Trip) was live on TV, Channel 5, I believe. It was a set-up, the cops arrived along with the 10 o'clock news, and it was broadcast live."

"They charged through the door, and it was clear their No 1 target was the membership list, because it was, at least nominally, a membership club at the time. The owner dropped the box down the dumb waiter shaft and then sent the dumb waiter down. So they never did find it.

"Anyway, they dragged out a bunch of people who were quite well-known, and some were quite wealthy, and the whole thing was covered live on TV; their faces were on TV. There was a hell of a lawsuit, and everybody settled up, the city settled up on behalf of the police."

This was also the location for Harlow's.

Tripp
Rush St. and Division St.
Circa: 1973

This was a two-level bar.

T's Bar & Restaurant
5025 N. Clark St.
Circa: 2001-2018

In 2012, the *Chicago Reader* chose T's as the best lesbian bar in Chicago. This was a popular gathering spot for women's sports teams after a game. It had a small sidewalk patio, and they served food – the burgers were especially popular. T's front room was the restaurant area and bar. The back room had a jukebox, pool table, and a smaller bar.

This location was also the Gold Coast. The property was sold, and the building demolished.

The Meeting House Tavern is now located at this address.

Tunnel Chicago
809 W. Evergreen Ave.
Circa: 1997-1998

DJ's at this dance were Abel, Earl Pleasure and Lego.

This was also the location of Dragon Room.

Tutsie Johnson's
2464 N. Clark St.
Circa: 1980

Tutsie Johnson's was owned by Norma Pearson. An ad read, "For an experience you'll never remember."

Tweets
62nd St.
Circa: 1970s

Dion, AKA Diana McKay, remembered, "The first bar I performed in was called Tweets on the South Side on 62nd St. That was a Black bar. But I thought to myself, that I wasn't going to make it on the South Side because nobody was going to come there to see me, so I moved to the North Side."

Twelve West Nightclub
12 W. Elm St.
Circa: 2012

In December 2012, the Chicago Black Gay Men's Caucus held its holiday soirée at the Twelve West Nightclub.

Twilight
1924 W. Division St.
Circa: 1999

On March 28, 1999, Twilight hosted a "Queer Beat Science Dance Party" that was ethnically and genderistically all-inclusive. Resident queer DJs Bathsheba and Gigglebyte spun hip-hop, drum 'n' bass, R&B, and House music.

Two Way Inn
3935 N. Broadway
Circa: 1980

The Two Way Inn opened in July 1980 with a free buffet and guest DJs. Customers were invited to share their talents at the open mic. On September 6, 1980, George Vaughn Lowther, a hypnotist, entertained at the bar.

U

U-Bahn
3406 N. Sheffield Ave.
Circa: 1989

The grand opening was on May 10, 1989. An ad read, "U-Bahn goes the '50s and '60s for a Sock Hop," and in September 1989, ACT UP held a dance party with DJs Galen Davis, JR Garcia, and Teri Bristol.

Ultimate Oz
7301 W. Roosevelt Rd., Forest Park
Circa: 1997-1998

The Hideaway II was briefly renamed Ultimate Oz before being renamed Club 7301.

In June 1998, the Berwyn Gay Block Party took place at the Ultimate Oz bar. The party included a dinner buffet, dancing with DJ, and reduced-price drinks, all for $10. Popular DJ was Dan Badea.

Underground
56 W. Illinois St.
Circa: 2007-present

Union
3101 N. Sheffield Ave.
Circa: 1989

Sunday was gay night and known as BVD (Being Very Decadent) with dancers, the Rockets.

Up North
6244 N. Western Ave.
Circa: 1971-1976

Up North was one of the most active establishments in supporting the gay community at the time. The restaurant's owner, Jack David's support of the *Chicago Gay Crusader* kept the early gay press alive. The 1st issue of the eight-page *Chicago Gay Crusader* was published in May 1973. The only bar that advertised in that issue was the Up North.

Good evening and Welcome to the Up-North restaurant!

Your dinner is prepared especially for you. Please allow us the time to prepare it properly.

SHRIMP COCKTAIL   1.75

Entrees

NEW YORK STRIP STEAK	4.75
Twelve ounces ot thick, tender beef garnished with mushroom caps or onion rings.	
THE UP NORTH STEAK SPECIAL	3.95
"CHICAGO" PRIME BUTT STEAK SANDWICH	3.25
Eight juicy ounces of Prime beef on toast.	
STEAK TERIYAKI	3.50
Tender young beef marinated in the Up North's own Oriental sauce and delightfully garnished.	
BEEF BROCHETTE	3.75
Hearty, tender beef chunks broiled to a turn with fresh garden vegetables and mushrooms served on a skewer.	
ADAM'S RIB	3.95
Meaty, juicy baby back ribs bar-b-qued in a delicate sauce.	
COUNTRY FRIED CHICKEN	2.15
Golden, tender young chicken fried for that "down home" taste.	
SOUTH AFRICAN LOBSTER TAIL	Ask waiter for price
Succulent and meaty served with drawn butter, lemon, and onion rings.	
GOLDEN FRIED PERCH	1.75
Boneless and tasty served hot w/ tartar sauce or lemon butter.	

All of the above dinners include Soup du jour; Baked Potato with sour cream, chives or bacon bits; or Cottage Fries; Garden Salad with your choice of dressing (Roquefort 25¢ extra); Hot Rolls; and Butter.

THE "JD" SPECIAL
One half pound ground sirloin steak broiled especially for you, served on dark rye, or english muffin garnished heartily with lettuce & tomato, served with choice of cottage fries or potato salad.
1.50

A DELIGHTFUL ARRAY
OF DELICATELY TOPPED BURGERS

SWISS MISS	1.75
Swiss cheese melted on top.	
LITTLE BOY BLUE	1.75
Tangy blue cheese on it.	
WISCONSIN QUEEN	1.75
Mild cheddar.	
DALE'S DELIGHT	1.75
Smotherd in mushrooms.	
THE ASPEN LADY	1.75
Cream cheese and crispy bacon bits	

All of our sandwiches include your choice of breads – light, dark, or toast; and lettuce , and tomato. Your choice of french fries, cottage fries, or potato salad.

HAM SANDWICH	1.25
BACON, LETTUCE, TOMATO	1.25
GRILLED CHEESE WITH HAM	1.30
GRILLED CHEESE	1.00

Our desserts are home-made and different each day - 50¢ to 1.00

Our own Cheese cake	.75
Ice Cream	.50
Coffee	.25
Tea	.25
Milk	.25
Hot Chocolate	.25

We sincerely hope you enjoy dining with us-we are pleased to have you here. We like to consider you as a personal friend. May we suggest you ask your waiter's name. As a "for us - by us" place, we are dedicated to providing only the very finest for everyone in this special world of ours!

And - may we call your attention to our daily specials and ● invite you back everyday!

Thank you, and have a very good evening!

● MONDAY
1.50
Dinner Special

● TUESDAY
50¢
cocktails
Zodiac birthday party
(last Tues. of month)

● WEDNESDAY
50¢
cocktails
and
$1.99 International Dinner

● THURSDAY
couples' night
David at the piano

● FRIDAY
raffle – giveaway

● SATURDAY
party night
!!!

● SUNDAY
champagne brunch
(Sept. thru May only)

SOMETHING SPECIAL
EVERYDAY

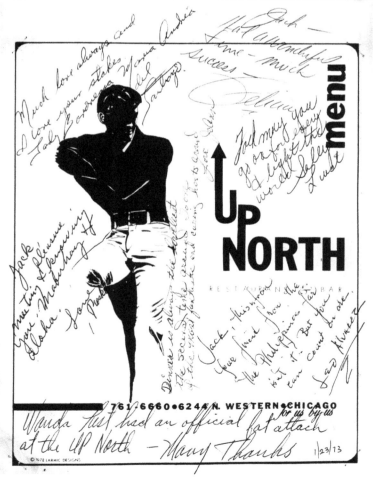

Events for a Halloween party in 1975 included a "Deep Throat" banana swallowing contest and a marshmallow-stuffing competition (The winner wedged 30 marshmallows in his mouth).

Jack David recalled, "We had a Mr. Up North contest. I think that was something every bar did, and there may have been some sort of city-wide contest. There may have been a half dozen contestants. I know that I was afraid there wouldn't be enough contestants, so I said to someone I had become very close to, 'I don't care, you're going to have to get up there.' and he said, 'But I don't have any briefs.' So, I said, 'Do it in your underwear.'

"There were judges. I know that Jim Flint from the Baton, and Roby Landers, from the House of Landers, and also Wanda Lust, acted as judges for a number of things that we had, Halloween parties and that sort of thing."

"It seems to me that there was one gay restaurant/bar that predated our opening, and that was called the Trip on Ohio. In the beginning, it was mostly men, but after being in business for a while, we began to draw a number of women in who felt comfortable in a mixed situation. But that's because my concept of the Up North was always a restaurant with a bar, not a bar with a restaurant. The restaurant to me was always a significant part of it."

Up North was forced to close when its lease with Z Frank auto dealer next door ran out. It closed on April 24, 1976.

Upper Class
618 N. Clark St.
Circa: 1975

This was also the location of Stage 618.

Ups and Downs
606 Stateline Rd., Calumet City
Circa: Unknown

This was also the location of Mr B's.

Uptown Underground
4707 N. Broadway
Circa: 2015-2018

Up Your Alley Lounge
5748 Chicago Ave.
Circa: 1967-1970

US Studio Warehouse
326 N. Michigan Ave. (lower level)
Circa: 1980

Black dance club.

VII
3200 N. Halsted St.
Circa: 2016

This was the last incarnation of this property as a gay bar. After a short-lived attempt at making it a straight bar named Chloe's/Whiskey Trust, it became the second incarnation of Manhole in the basement and upstairs was known as the Den.

Previously this was the location of Foxy's, Spin, Whiskey Trust, Den, Manhole, and Eons.

Valley of The Dolls
7502 S. Exchange St.
Circa: 1982

Valley of the Dolls was a lesbian bar.

Velma's Lounge
6342 Cottage Grove Ave.
Circa: 1956

Lesbian trumpeter, Tiny Davis, played at Velma's Lounge in May 1956.

Velvet Rope
728 W. Lake St., Oak Park
Circa: 2008-2012

The Velvet Rope was owned by Frank Elliot. Events at the bar included Bottoms up Bingo with Tajma Hall, Salsa Lessons with Anna Marie, and Half Price Champagne in the Champagne Lounge with live jazz. In December 2009, the Velvet Rope hosted the House of Divas drag show with Cee-

Cee LaRouge, Francheska Friskey, Myka Myleah, Keisha Foxx, and Mercedes Andrews, and Patty Paige.

The bar rang in New Year's Eve 2010 with a party featuring Miss Foozie with a countdown of the hottest dance tracks of 2009, hosted by Dave Tripper from Fusion Radio.

The bar closed after burning down from suspected arson.

Victor Hotel
311 N. Sangamon St.
Circa: 2007

Wednesdays at Victor Hotel featured music by DJs Dhanna and Pete Augusta. Hosted by Danielle Bumpsey and CT Couture.

Vinyl
1615 N. Clybourn Ave.
Circa: 1996-1998

Saturday was gay night, and the club hosted some gay events.

Virgo Out
642 W. Diversey Pkwy.
Circa: 1974-1976

Virgo Out was a leather/Levi bar owned by Fred Wasser and Wally Thomas. The bar opened in October 1974.

On April 28, 1976, a farewell party was held before moving to the Clark St. location.

This was also the location of Big Red's and Boys at Sea.

Virgo Out
2546 N. Clark St.
Circa: 1979-1980

At this location, Virgo Out was more of a cabaret bar than leather/Levi. In November 1976, *GayLife* wrote, "The Virgo Out opens at noon every day and closes at 2:00 a.m., except on Saturdays when it stays open until three. There are always special events going on at the Virgo, like the monthly zodiac parties honoring those born under the sign of that month. (The Sagittarius Party will be held on December 8th). On the first and third Fridays of every month the Tradewinds Motorcycle Club meets at the Virgo for fun and games. And on the second Friday of the month the Cossacks meet for their monthly club night. On Wednesdays from opening to closing there are special drink prices for people who wear Virgo Out patches, tee-shirts, jackets or club colors."

Winning music at Virgo Out marathon

Participants at the marathon included (from left) Bob Moreen, Virgo Out owner Fred Wasser, Tom Oman, Paula Karol, Rep. Danny O'Brien, Karen Burns, Chris Clason, Lou Brousek and John Eskola.

Some of the performers at Virgo Out were Sheila Ceaser and Dick Gallagher, Mary Lynn Morrison and Bill Muzzillo, Laurie Lynn, and Billy Prewitt and Dana Clark.

In December 1979, Fred Wasser called it quits and sold the place to Wes and Bob Middleton, who renamed it Checkmate II.

This was also the location of the Inner Circle, and (Paul's) Checkmate.

CHICAGO'S *Different* BAR!!

Thursday, Nov. 6th — 7 PM til 2 AM
Italian Dinner
Lasagna & Mostacholi—Salad & Garlic Bread
Chianti Wine—50¢ per person

**1st ANNIVERSARY PARTY
SUNDAY, NOV. 16th
ALL DAY — ALL NITE
PRIZES EVERY HOUR**

Turkeys — Booze — Plus Surprises

NOW OPEN   NOON DAILY

EVERYDAY SPECIAL PRICES Til 7 PM
MONDAY (all day) Bar Drinks—Beer—Wine 50¢

642 W. DIVERSEY ⑪ CHICAGO

* *PHONE 248-4832*

Vision
3432 W. Irving Park Rd.
Circa: 1991-1996

The grand opening of Visions, a mostly lesbian bar, was on November 9, 1991, with band Fantasy, playing country rock, blues and ballads. Jake Cohn remembered, "You had to be buzzed into the bar. The first few times there, they did not allow men in the bar."

On September 16, 1996, Visions hosted its 4th annual celebrity auction for the Chicago Gay and Lesbian Hall of Fame. Celebrity auctioneers were Trish Koch of Diversity Radio and David Boyer of Chicago's Original Country Dance.

In August 1995, Visions hosted Chicago Leatherwomen Night every Monday.

This was also the location of Friends Pub.

Vision Nightclub
632 N. Dearborn St.
Circa: 1989–2010

Vision Nightclub was owned by Freddy Hoffman and his son Mark. This is the sister-bar to Excalibur at the same address at the same time. The club hosted the 2009 and 2010 Nuts to Butts Bear Pride closing party with DJs Jose "Spinnin'" Cortes and Jesse Mercado.

This was also the location of Limelight, and Sanctuary.

Vista Hermosa
3702 N. Halsted St.
Circa: 1977–1978

A Latin bar with a regular Mexican buffet.

This was also the location of Aloha Bikini Lounge, Cell Block, and Loading Dock.

Vix
2814 N. Halsted St.
Circa: 1998

Volli-Bal
2124 N. Clark St.
Circa: 1950s

The Volli-Bal started out as a drag bar, then became a lesbian bar. In St Sukie de la Croix's book, *Chicago Whispers*, he wrote,

Exterior of the Volli-Bal. Circa 1950s

"The Volli-Bal had an oval bar at the front, a dance floor, though same-sex dancing was illegal, and a small stage where Volli Charles did his one-man show. Charles lasted a year, then left abruptly after crossing a gangster. That's when the Volli-Bal went lesbian. … Prior to being the Volli-Bal, the location witnessed one of Chicago's most famous events; it was next door to the S-M-G Garage, scene of the St. Valentine's Day Massacre. In the 1950s, when the Volli-Bal was in business, the bar owner's father often took customers into the back of the old S-M-G Garage to view the crime scene. Bic Carroll remembered putting his fingers in the bullet holes. 'He was an old timer,' explains Carroll, 'who told us wonderful stories about the old days of the Mob.'"

Rose told the authors, "It was right next door to the Scarlet Ribbon, which was the guy's bar. Up on Clark Street. Lots of big fat women, big fat dykes … major, major."

Voltaire
3441–3443 N. Halsted St
Circa: 2000–2001

This restaurant bar was short-lived. It opened in May 2000. Among those who performed there were Judy Tenuta, Spider Saloff, and Sapna Kumar. In June 2000, Phyllis Diller performed there in a benefit for the AIDS Memorial Quilt. In

October 2000, Voltaire held a fundraiser for US Rep. Barney Frank and State Rep. Larry McKeon. And Bea Arthur dropped in one night to see the show and to sing a couple of songs.

The hilarious Charlene Unger hosted the Sunday Brunch.

This was also the location of Halsted's Bar & Grill, Lark Lounge and Madam B.

Volume I
1608 N. Wells St.
Circa: 1977

This was also the location of Willoughby's.

Voo Doo Nightclub
601 Mall Dr., Schaumburg
Circa: 2005

Vortex
3631 N. Halsted St.
Circa: 1990–1996

Vortex had its grand opening on August 29, 1990. It was owned by Ben Pohl, Pat Kasaras, and Jeff Tessler. The club was a multi-level complex featuring a large dance area and numerous lounges. It was known for its lavish parties and celebrity performers. Among them, Judy Tenuta, Loleatta Holloway, Holly Woodlawn, Crystal Walters, Martha Wash, Lypsinka, Thea Vidale, Lea Delaria, Marky Mark & the Funky Bunch, RuPaul, and Jimmy Somerville of Bronski Beat. It also hosted fundraisers such as an "Art & Antique Auction" to benefit the Dan Di Leo PWA Fund – the event was sponsored by *Gay Chicago Magazine*, with guest auctioneers Chuck Renslow and

Owners and guests celebrated the opening of Vortex, Chicago's newest night time diversion on North Halsted. From left to right, Susan Tessler joins co-owners Ben Pohn, Jeff Tessler and Pat Kasaras.

3631 N. Halsted
975-6622

VORTEX

Fri. Feb. 17th

Alexandra Billings

brings her unique comic stylings and vibrant vocal talents to the BallRoom!

2 performances midnight and 1:30am

Thom Dombkowski. Also, the Chicago Gay Men's Chorus' annual fundraiser party.

Club kid Silky Jumbo presented "Burp the Baby ... a totally infantile experience!" upstairs at Vortex, with Jeff Free and Jo Jo. Some of the popular bartenders include, John Parisot, Jeff Pool, Michael Kerrigan (Bar Back), and Benedict J. Michalowski.

Vortex closed in October 1996.

This was also the location of Rhumba Room and Fusion. The building was eventually demolished, and condos were built on the lot.

W

Waldman's
164 N. Michigan Ave.
Circa: 1930s

The bar had two white grand pianos in the window.

Walton Street Water Works
933 N. State St.
Circa: 1984-1986

The Walton Street Water Works cocktail lounge opened on April 8, 1984. Ralf Johnston was the owner. He co-owned the Trip. Johnson died from natural causes in July 1986.

This was also the location of the Night Life Lounge.

Wang's
3317 N. Broadway
Circa: 2010-present

According to Wang's website, "Our greater mission at Wangs is building and connecting an influential community around music and live performance that we find inspiring and talented. On a day-to-day level, we worship creativity by the thoughts we hold, the company we keep, and the improvements we make here at Wangs and beyond."

In January 2010, Wang's DJ Jacob Meehan was spinning anything from Italo Disco to Chicago House. In January 2014, Wang's hosted Pleasure, a new drag experience featuring JoJo Baby, Banjee Report's Mr. Wallace, Precious Jewel, Ruby Dee and hosted by Pearl.

In March 2020, Wang's came under fire for not serving women during peak business hours.

Warehouse
738 W. Randolph St.
Circa: 1991

This was also the location of Club Voyage.

Warehouse
206 S. Jefferson St.
Circa: 1976-1980

Open Saturdays only, the club started as a series of parties held at various locations by Robert Williams and his friends. US Studios AKA the Warehouse, opened at its renowned location in 1976. It is the origin of "house" music as popularized by Warehouse's resident DJ Frankie Knuckles. Knuckles first spun there in early 1977. In 1980, he developed a partnership with the IRS Record Pool and its Imports Etc. storefront. His progressive mix of new wave and import tracks with underground disco and occasional sound effects drew a younger, crowd.

Knuckles' playlist in April 1981, as published in Brett Wilcots' column in *Gay Chicago Magazine*, featured everything from Nick Straker and People's Choice to Brian Eno & David Byrne and Yoko Ono. Knuckles often received records before any other DJ in the city, introducing his audience to new, obscure music.

One of Knuckles' signatures was playing a recording of an express train, moving the sound through the club's sound system. "It scared the shit out of people," Knuckles related in a 1990 *Sun-Times* article, "But they came back, hoping to hear it again."

A members-only after-hours club, the Warehouse opened around midnight on Saturdays and kept going strong until after sunrise. In a 1981 article for *GayLife*, Albert Williams enthused, "Most DJs, if they're any good, have a following. Frankie Knuckles has believers – people who religiously save themselves up for late Saturday night."

Joan Jett-Blakk remembered her days at the club, "The Warehouse was all about the music because it was an after-hours club.

"We'd go to the Warehouse at three in the morning, the music was funkier, the dancing was sweatier, and it was a smaller place. It was mostly Black, but it wasn't all Black. A place that hip, you couldn't keep white people out if you tried. And besides, there would always be one or two white queens on the North Side that could sniff that out, and they would come running down there, and word spread that way. That's how I got down there; I would never have gone if my white friend hadn't taken me there. It was all about the music and dancing. And you felt totally hedonistic because it was one of the first places that was open at four or five in the morning, where you could go after you'd imbibed whatever it is that you imbibed that would keep you up until four in the morning."

James, a dancer at Coconuts, shared similar memories, "The Warehouse was a trip. It was hi-energy and it was just about the music. Medusa and Frankie would get people in there and make them crazy, take them on this musical journey. If I remember right, there was a little bit of drugs going on down there too. I remember the acid punch. We used to go there, and it was like church. In fact, we used to call it church. We'd go there about three or four in the morning, and everybody would be in make-up and outfits, then you'd roll out of the place at noon on Sunday, as everyone was going to church downtown."

Watergate
LaSalle St. and Van Buren St.
Circa: 1976–1977

A *GayLife* article in October 1975 summed up the bar as, "A new gay club called Watergate opens at LaSalle and Van Buren. They have disco dancing, live bands, and steak sandwiches and omelets at midnight." The Watergate was open Wednesday through Saturday.

THERE IS A PLACE . . . THERE IS A TIME

watergate

LaSalle and Van Buren   427-8234

Saturday Midnight Brunch
Omelettes • Steak Sandwiches

DISCO DANCING
WEDNESDAY
•
THURSDAY

LIVE BAND
FRIDAY
•
SATURDAY

WEEKDAYS 9 P.M. to 2 A.M. • SATURDAYS 10 P.M. to 3 A.M.

Waterhouse
3407 N. Paulina Ave.
Circa: 2014

Straight bar with gay events. In March 2014, Waterhouse hosted a Gayco Open Bar Party celebrating intelligent comedy and achievements such as gay marriage.

This was also the location of Ye Old Mill Lounge.

Water Tower Inn
800 N. Michigan Ave.
Circa: 1966–1976

By 1973, this was gay only during cocktail hour.

Watra Night Club
4758 S. Pulaski Rd.
Circa: 2012

Thursdays was LGBTQA night with DJ Fuego and drag performances.

Wee Dee's
2101 S. Fairfield Ave.
Circa: 1972-1975

Wee Frog
1829 W. Montrose Ave.
Circa: 1993

This was also the location of Off the Line, Ravenswood Tavern, Suzie B's, and Scot's.

Welcome
22 E. Chestnut St.
Circa: 1974

Wells Street Depot
1311 N. Wells St.
Circa: 1973

A bar and restaurant.

Wet
209 W. Lake St
Circa: 2004-2006

Wet was a straight club that held gay events. In June 2006, it hosted a fundraiser with a live jazz band and DJ Quad called "United in Pride" for Windy City Black Pride.. This was also the location of Leatherneck.

What's Up
65 W. Illinois St.
Circa: 1984-1985

The grand opening of What's Up was June 15, 1984.

This was also the location of Redoubt.

Where the Boys Are
955 W. Fulton Mkt.
Circa: 1979

In the October 12, 1979, *GayLife* an ad reads, "Arnie and Associates invites you to see for yourself WHERE THE BOYS ARE Friday, October 12, 1979. come sweat the night away in Chicago's only private late-hour, fantasy danceland ... Time 11:01 PM to 7:01 AM. Punking the box Gene White & Michael Ezebukwu, plus the hottest trade in the city. Donation: $4 with plugger, $5 without. Admit bearer & 3 guests."

Whiskey Trust
3206 N. Halsted St.
Circa: 2014

In August 2014, Whiskey Trust hosted Red Light Riot, an evening of provocative stage performances by Shotglass Sally, Mia D. Vine, Dizzie Lizzie, Queerella Fistalot, Madame Envy, and Tamale Sepp.

This was also the location of Foxy's, Eons, Spin, Den, the second incarnation of Manhole, and finally VII.

Whisky River
1997 N. Clybourn Ave.
Circa: 1992-1993

Whisky River was a mixed straight/gay country and western bar with David Boyer and DJ Ron Goodman on Sundays.

White Elephant Bath Lounge
114 W. Hubbard St.
Circa: 1976

This was also the location of Ozone, White Elephant Bath Lounge, Druids, IC Station, and Oz Again.

Wilde Bar and Restaurant
3130 N. Broadway
Circa: 2007-present

More restaurant than bar, it serves as a gathering place for the few LGBT folks who still live in the area.

Wild Pug
4810 N. Broadway
Circa: 2008-2010

The Wild Pug was owned by Steven Milford and Brian Wells who also owned Crew, a couple of doors down. The bar hosted literary events and potlucks, as well as open mics and theme parties. Its most popular event was Dog Days, Saturday afternoons when folks were welcome to bring their dogs to the bar.

In November 2009, the Wild Pug hosted its monthly Prose, Poetry and Pints at the Pub with readings by Terry Oldes, CJ Laity, and Anthony Fleming. Asians and Friends met at the bar to play Mahjong.

Willie's Lounge
8105 S. Cottage Grove Ave.
Circa: 1985

This was also the location of Amen Corner.

Willoughby's
1608 N. Wells St.
Circa: 1974

This was also the location of Volume I.

Wind Blew Inn
116 E. Ohio St.
Circa: 1922

The Wind Blew Inn was a prohibition cafe that was raided many times by the police. It was a bohemian gathering place run by circus performer Lillian Collier and her "friend" Virginia Harrison. In February 1922, it was raided and forty people arrested. *The Chicago Tribune* reported that one of them, Theodore Strehlow, a student at Northwestern University, was "prominent in dramatic circles at the university, having taken the leading feminine role in last year's annual play of *The Hermit and the Crow*." The charges were dismissed. It was raided again a month later.

Then on April 23, 1922, the *Chicago Tribune* headline read, "Hobohemia's Temple Burns." ... "Art treasures, the work of a coterie which finds its mission in life to be 'self expression' were destroyed yesterday morning when the Wind Blew Inn went up in smoke. The place was a rendezvous for long-haired and bobby haired real and near bohemians."

Windup Lounge
669 N. State St.
Circa: 1944-1949

The Windup Lounge was run by the Allegretti brothers, Jimmy and Tony, and Tony's wife Florence Ramsey, all members of the Guzik-Capone gang.

Frank W., a bartender who worked at the bar, told the authors, "The Windup was a converted storefront property. Double wide storefront and the space that was the window area on the south side front was the coat check space. It was a very plain and tacky interior with a horseshoe-shaped bar with the back to the north side. That had a small bandstand platform and there was a trio or piano player for entertainment most of the time. The police raided it and closed it down a few days after New Year's Eve and used it as a start to crack down on crime in Chicago. We had had a good holiday season and no trouble, so when they hit on the Saturday after the Eve, we were surprised. Captain Harrison, head of the Vice Squad at the Chicago Avenue Station at the time, came a little after midnight and went around talking to a few people. I was running the '26' dice table that night and he came over and asked me to write my name on a slip of paper for him as he wanted to 'be sure he had it'; I did so, and then signaled one of the floor men over to ask what was going on. He pointed out that we had been under arrest for over an hour (this was about 1:30 AM) and pointed out that there were plainclothes officers at the door who were letting people in but not letting anyone leave. Everyone was taken to the station in 'black marias' and it was a very messy night for all.

"All of the newspapers had photographers covering the front door as we were led out one by one to the wagons and it was

terrifying. All of the other near north side gay bars closed when they heard what was happening and the patrons and a few of the employees from the other places came over to see what was going on. Over 87 men were taken in and booked that night and several committed suicide as a result, because of their fear over what the publicity would do to their families and their careers."

The next morning the headline on the front page of the *Chicago Tribune* read, "File Charges Against 87 in Vice Net."

One observer of the court case said, "One by one the men appeared before Judge John Griffin. News photographers were standing at the front, and to the side of the judge's bench, another group was standing at the back. When the cameras were raised at the front, the arrested men looked back to avoid being photographed, and then the newsmen at the back would snap away, and as they turned, the cameras at the front would get them."

All the charges were dropped, but everyone's name had already been printed in the paper, so careers were lost, and families split up.

Bar token from the Windup Lounge, circa 1944. These tokens were used to gamble in a dice game called 26. Women were employed to keep score and they were called, 26-Dice Girls. The game was played using tokens. This got around Chicago gambling laws.. The tokens could then be exchanged for drinks and money.

CAPT. HARRISON JAILS 24 IN WAR ON DEGENERATES

In a drive against degenerates infesting vice and clip joints, Capt. Thomas Harrison of the E. Chicago av. station early yesterday arrested 15 men and nine women in taverns on the west side of N. Clark st., between Chicago av., and the river.

Accompanied by six detectives and a patrol wagon, Harrison questioned hundreds of patrons in taverns, sent degenerates to the police station for investigation, and broke up couples who had newly met.

After being processed thru the police bureau of identification, all 29 were charged with disorderly conduct. Most were freed on bond. The women will appear in Women's court today, and the men will appear in E. Chicago av. police court.

Ten With Police Records

Ten of the men have minor police records, and one, James Burns, 34, of 619 Madison st., has a record showing more than 50 arrests, half of them in Chicago. He once served a prison term in Arizona for burglary, the records showed.

Harrison, who last week arrested 93 men in a raid on the Windup lounge, 669 N. Clark st., a hangout for perverts, condemned degenerates for the recruiting of adolescents.

Dr. Harry R. Hoffman, Illinois state alienist, agreed, and added

that homosexuals should be incarcerated in institutions "for the protection of society."

18,000 In Chicago

Capt. Harrison said that Chicago probably has at least 18,000 sexually maladjusted men, all potentially dangerous.

Boys as young as 12 have been approached, Capt. Harrison said, and unless they have been forewarned by parents, friends, or church leaders, might easily fall victim.

Many homosexuals, Capt. Harrison said, maintain luxurious apartments where they entertain young, unsuspecting "recruits" with food, music, liquor, and obscene literature.

"That's the beginning of the downfall of many boys and young men," Capt. Harrison said. "All families with boys should warn them early to beware of strange men at all times."

Unofficial information received by Harrison indicated, he said, that most of Chicago's degenerates are members of a national organization run by a man named Brown living in or near Miami.

Dr. Hoffman said that for years he has campaigned against the problem. In his opinion, he said, the degenerates "are born and not made."

"Cure is secondary," Dr. Hoffman said. "They should be taken out of society as the first step."

CONTINUE HEARINGS OF 86 MEN ARRESTED IN POLICE VICE RAID

Hearings for 86 men arrested early Sunday in a police raid on the Windup lounge, 669 N. State st., a hangout for sexual degenerates, were continued yesterday to Jan. 21 by Judge John Griffin in E. Chicago av. court. Seven minors also were seized.

The delay was asked by Atty. Milroy Blowitz, who called the raid "a disgraceful action." The wholesale arrests were made by Capt. Thomas Harrison in his avowed drive to suppress vice and clip joints on the near north side. Police said the Windup is operated by a segment of the Guzik-Capone mob. Its license is in the name of Paul Medor, 33.

Principal defendants are the manager, Anthony Policheri, 45, alias Allegretti; the floor manager, Jack S. Kaplan, 29, and the bartenders, Frank Woods, 21, and William Ramsay, 29. Charles W. Taylor, 35, of Winfield, in Du Page county, was incorrectly booked as a bartender, and will be booked as an inmate of a disorderly house.

Judge Griffin reduced the bond of Kaplan from $1,000 to $400. Police files show that Kaplan, alias Sol Kaplin, was sentenced Nov. 4, 1939, to Riker's Island, New York, for impairing the morals of a minor and in June, 1943, in Cook county, to jail for a year for contributing to the delinquency of a minor.

3 BARTENDERS FINED AS RESULT OF RAID ON WINDUP LOUNGE

Three bartenders in the Windup lounge, 669 N. State st., arrested in a raid on the tavern Jan. 9, were fined yesterday by Judge Oscar S. Caplan in jury court as inmates of a disorderly house. They were among 93 persons arrested in the raid. The tavern, notorious hangout for degenerates, subsequently lost its liquor license. The bartenders, addresses they gave, and their fines were: William R. Ramsey, 24, of 1454 E. Marquette rd., $45 and costs; John A. Giacakette, 34, of 701 S. Hoyne av., $25 and costs, and Oscar L. Ferner, 23, of 162 W. Oak st., $25 and costs.

DIVE KEEPERS ON N. CLARK ST. GET WARNINGS

Capt. Walsh Personally Visits Vice Region

Near north side saloon operators who have been operating "clip joints" and other dives in violation of the law were personally warned early yesterday by Capt. John J. Walsh of the E. Chicago av. police district to quit violating the law or quit business.

Acting in the wake of THE TRIBUNE'S disclosures of the vicious knockout drop racket on N. Clark st., Capt. Walsh told the honky-tonk operators that he was sent into the district last Monday by Police Commissioner Prendergast and Mayor Kennelly to "clean it up."

News of Capt. Walsh's trip apparently preceded him. No women were present at any of the places which employ hostesses to solicit drinks. He warned, however, that their return would bring license revocations and also ordered that windows be cleared so that interiors of the barrooms can be viewed from the street.

Wars On Degenerates

"Scrape the paint off or take down the venetian blinds if you have to," Walsh told the operators, "but fix the windows so we can see thru them." He then assigned detectives' and policewomen to patrol the district nightly.

Walsh also ordered the cleanup of other saloons in the area which cater to degenerates. It was pointed out that many men who infest the saloons which thrive on the business they bring are morally depraved.

They make no effort to conceal their depravity. In fact, they proudly display the earmarks of their trade, the waved hair, the mincing walk and feminine make-up. And since their activities are illegal, the dives in which they congregate wink at the law altho police beatmen patrol the streets where the saloons' gaudy neon signs make red patches in the night.

Hangout Is Notorious

The situation—which has existed under police noses for many months—came forcibly to public attention early yesterday when two men caught by park police in Lincoln park fled from the squad in an automobile traveling 80 miles per hour. When the fleeing car—under police fire—hit a street car, it knocked the public vehicle off the track and shook up 40 passengers.

The two men said they met at the Windup lounge, 669 N. State st., a known hangout for the degenerates. It is licensed by the city and the licensee's name is Paul Medor. In both 1947 and this year, police have received many complaints of indecent singing, indecent exhibitionism, and solicitation in the Windup, but no action has been taken.

In the late evening hours, when the N. Clark st. dives are soliciting the city's visitors, the immoral crews congregate in many other saloons in addition to the Windup. And the dim lit, smoky barrooms are jammed with shrill voiced men, customers who go to be approached, and the merely curious.

Gambling Also Reported

The license of the club at 7 W. Division st. is issued to Carlo Lamark. In addition to the unsavory morals of many of its patrons, police also list gambling complaints against it.

Perhaps the prize exhibit of the area is the Shanty Inn, 716 N. Clark st., a shoddy saloon licensed to Sid Rosenthal and Jerry Abraham. It was closed briefly in 1947 by police, but it soon reopened. It has a long record as a center for degenerates and even murderers. A Negro, Tyree Soree, was slain there on March 25, 1947.

Next door, at 714 N. Clark st., the Green Lantern club, licensed to Helen Benedict, is a dive. Other dives are The Sewer, 620 N. State st., a saloon with a record for immoral entertainment and serving liquor to minors, and a saloon at 5 W. Erie st. known variously as the Glass pub and the Jungle club.

The Sewer's license is issued to Joseph Cohen, and the Jungle club's is issued to Abby Davis. There are many more.

6 ARRESTED IN VICE RAID ON N. STATE ST. DEMAND JURY TRIALS

In a four hour court session 72 defendants arrested by police on Jan. 9 in a raid on the Windup Lounge, 669 N. State st., paraded yesterday before Municipal Judge John J. Griffin in the Chicago av. police court. Of that number 23 were discharged, two were fined, six demanded jury trials and 41 were ordered examined at the court's psychiatric unit, 1121 S. State st.

Capt. Thomas Harrison charged that the lounge was frequented by homosexuals. The police raid was conducted shortly before midnight on Jan. 9 after police had investigated the place for some time.

Those demanding jury trials were Anthony Allegretti, 39, of 2200 W. Campbell Pk., John Grachetti, 24, of 701 S. Hoyne av., Clyde Miller, 23, of 48 W. Goethe st., Bill T. Ramsey, 24, of 1454 E. Marquette rd., Frank Woods, 21, of 1246 N. Dearborn st., all bartenders; and Jack S. Kaplan, 47, of 927 Wilson av., floor manager. Allegretti and Kaplan also were charged with operating a disorderly house. Other defendants were tried on charges of frequenting a disorderly house.

Nearly · $200 were contributed to the March of Dimes fund by those who were discharged after a suggestion from Judge Griffin.

Windy City Bar & Grill
3127 N. Clark St.
Circa: 1985–1988

Windy City Bar was on the second floor of the corner of Halsted and Clark. The piano was located at the apex of the triangle-shaped room, with piano bar seating and cabaret tables. At the opposite end of the space, the base of the triangle was a dance bar and beyond that, there was a kitchen. Pianist Joe Kregor usually led sing-alongs or accompanied people during the open mic segments. Later Kregor was replaced by Harry Campagna. It closed in October 1987 and opened two weeks later under new management, then closed permanently less than a year later. Near the end of its run, the focus shifted to a dance bar with male strippers. The building has been demolished and there's a shopping development there now.

This was also the location of the short-lived Thumbs Up and Clubhouse.

NEW WINDY CITY BAR
(SOON TO BE THUMBS UP)

75¢ WELL, WINE, DRAFT
MONDAYS 8 PM–CLOSE

AND

$1 WELL, WINE, DRAFT
FRIDAYS OPEN TO CLOSE
($2 cover 10 PM–CLOSE)

3127 N. CLARK 4 PM–4 AM EVERYDAY 348·3458

Winners
4530 N. Lincoln Ave.
Circa: 1995–1997

Winners was a sports-themed lesbian bar. In February 1996, there was a Leftover Lesbian Post-Valentine's Bash at Winners with a kissing booth and DJ Red. A $5 donation went to the Lesbian Avengers.

This was also the location of the Rainbow Rooms

Wooden Barrell Pub
2326 N. Clark St.
Circa: 1972–1974

In the July 1973 issue of the *Chicago Gay Crusader*, there's a coupon for a free drink at John Britt's Wooden Barrell Pub. The paper describes John Britt, who operates the bar, as "a short version of Burt Reynolds" and the bar described as, "A small dark bar, perhaps too dark" and "A tavern with a quiet atmosphere." Britt also owned/managed Boys at Sea.

Britt Top's
WOODEN BARRELL PUB
248-4511
2326 N. Clark
Chicago

XYZ

X–TE–C
5415 W. Irving Park Rd.
Circa: 1998

In May 1998, Thursdays were gay Latin night with DJs Mark Grant and Oscar McMillan.

Y
224 W. Ontario St.
Circa: 2004

With DJs Chris Eterno and Luis M.

Ye Old Mill Lounge
3407 N. Paulina Ave.
Circa: 1975–1976

An article in *GayLife* on December 3, 1975, stated that the bar was "going gay." In January, it began advertising in the gay press and reopened in January 1976 with a regular show by the Playgirls, who were Pearl Diamond and Laura Merrill, with guest artists every week. On July 2 and 3, 1976, one of the guests was Tillie (The Dirty Old Lady).

In the March 5, 1976, issue of *GayLife*, Rhonda wrote in her Round 'n' Round column, "Hearts and fairies ... Valentine's weekend was certainly something else. All the parties were great, but one has to be singled out as spectacular. And that, of course, was the glorious red, white, and pink cloud atmosphere created by Donn Abbinanti for Ye Old Mill. The sweet table was loaded with red and white goodies, including some erotic cookies that melted in your mouth."

By November 1976, the bar went back to being a straight bar.

This was also the location of Waterhouse.

Yellow Unicorn
868 N. State St.
Circa: 1976

A listing in the gay press in July 1976 reads, "At the magnificent Yellow Unicorn, a gay bar on Monday and Tuesday evenings, singer Colette performs at the piano. Her repertoire ranges from Martha and the Vandellas 'Jimmy Mack' to the new theme from *Mahogany*."

One paper wrote, "For a while, it seemed the piano bar was a fast-fading treat, but at the Yellow Unicorn it had become a welcome and warm home."

This was also the location of Foster's Little Club.

Your Place
3196 N. Milwaukee Ave.
Circa: 1995

Your Place was a straight bar with a Thursday gay night.

Yvette
311 S. Wacker Dr.
Circa: 1998

Yvette was a piano bar/cabaret. Honey West and Nan Mason performed there.

Zack's
5400 S. Cicero Ave.
Circa: 1979

Zack's was a gay men's disco.

Zack's
24 W. Van Buren St.
Circa: 1965-1971

Ken told the authors, "Zack's was predominantly white, but the Blacks went in for trade ... There wasn't much in the way of entertainment in the bars. They had a jukebox and you just sat around with friends and met other people."

Zentra
923 W. Weed St.
Circa: 2003-2005

A straight bar that hosted a number of LGBT events, including the Mr. Latino contest, and Windy City Black Pride's "Blue Party." DJ Eclipse played house, salsa, bachata, cumbia, and Spanish rock. Other DJs there included DJs Anton and Thickdick.

Zolar
936 W. Diversey Pkwy.
Circa: 1975-1976

Zolar opened on October 23, 1975. In the October 29, 1975, issue of Chicago *GayLife*, columnist Christopher wrote, "The Preview Party at Zolar, Chuck Renslow's new disco-bar at Diversey and the 'El' Stop, was a real madhouse. Be sure to look up at the ceiling too. Above the frescoed cut-out ceiling is a freak-out treatment that goes with the name of the place. Back further is the flashing light dance floor. Further back yet is a beer bar and game room, with genuine mechanical games to play. Upstairs at Zolar is the real disco scene, however, with the sound system that brings to mind the Bistro. Of course, the dancefloor is smaller, but the lights. Wow! With the music and crowd noise, I never did hear an el train pass by."

Chuck Renslow told the authors, "It was the House of Landers, then they went out and I turned it into a disco, Zolar. Our motto was 'Zolar, it's Magic.' Then it burned down, everybody started saying, 'Zolar, it's tragic.'

"It was small, but it was beautiful, and we did a lot of work on it. Once again, it was what we had. When we moved in it was very art deco and, instead of taking that stuff out, we just added to it. We put in the first-ever Plexiglas dance floor with lights underneath it, ¾ inch Plexiglas, it was very small, it was about 10'X10' but it was striking.

"Here's the shame of Zolar. It was next to the elevated tracks, and we couldn't get fire insurance. There's a program the state has when you can't get fire insurance, and we had applied for that. It was going to kick in in 30 days, and it burned 15 days later. [on March 21, 1976] I lost a fortune on that one. We had electrical wiring that some prior people had done upstairs, and the whole room burned off."

Jim Edminster reported that he believes the art deco décor that Renslow refers to dated back to when the bar was owned by Al Capone.

Zo-ran
3474 N. Clark St.
Circa: 1986

In April 1986, the bar held its grand opening, featuring La Faye Elliot in the piano bar. The bar's owners were Bob Randall and Peter Zagrafos, who owned the Factory Disco.

This was also the location of Christy's on Clark, Party Party, Studio 69, and the Factory.

SHARED SPACES

Chicago's liquor laws are quirky to say the least, and the enforcement of them often depends, as so much does in Chicago, on who you know. Until recently the liquor licenses were connected to the address, not the individual operating a bar. That meant that bars were often sold with a liquor license assigned to the property and the bar operated under a D.B.A. (Doing Business As) agreement. Sometimes the owner of the property rented out the space and allowed a business to operate under his/her liquor license. If the bar failed, the owner simply rented the space and liquor license out to someone else. Consequently, we discovered that many locations were home to several gay bars and clubs. Here's a list of clubs by address.

7 E. Chestnut St.
Foster's, Punchinello's

27 E. Ohio St.
Harlow's, Trip

41 S. Harlem Ave., Forest Park
Adron's, Bus Stop Lounge, Nutbush City Limits.

46 E. Oak St.
Loading Zone, Scalawags, TJ's on Oak

61 W. Hubbard St.
Roadhouse, Stars

65 W. Illinois St.
What's Up, Redoubt

111 W. Hubbard St.
Belfry, My Brother's Place/Oasis

112-114 W. Hubbard St.
Druids, IC Station, Oz Again, Ozone, Ranch, White Elephant Bath Lounge

118 E. Jefferson St., Joliet
Continental Club East, Maneuvers

200 State St., Calumet City
Bank Vault, Double RR Lounge, Kismet Club, Ms. Behavin

209 W. Lake St.
Leatherneck, Wet

308 W. Erie St.
Buzz, Club Inta, Cuveé

247 E. Ontario St.
Dingbats, Tenement Square

318 W. Grand Ave.
Funny Firm, Karma

430 N. Clark St.
Annex 2, Baton, Loft, Ramrod, Punch's, Sunday's (Child/Children)

432 N. Clark St.
Jock's, Marilyn's

436 N. Clark St.
Baton Show Lounge, Big Basket, Queen's Surf, Sugar Shack

440 N. Halsted St.
Club Flamingo, Clubhouse, Jokes on U, Red No. 5, Redoubt, Rialto

440 N. State St.
Downtown Bar & Lounge, Gentry on State

520 N. Clark St.
Bus Stop, St. Regis

551 E. 79th St.
My Place, Other Bar, Ronny's

606 Stateline Rd., Calumet City
Mr. B's, Ups and Downs

611 E. 63rd St.
Jerry's Place, Kitty Kat Club

618 N. Clark St.
Stage 618, Upper Class

632 N. Dearborn St.
Excalibur, Limelight, Sanctuary, Vision

642 W. Diversey Pkwy.
Big Red's, Boys at Sea, Virgo Out

644 N. State St.
644 Club, CC's

661 N. Clark St.
Ms., O'Banion's, PQ's, Saturday's (Girl)

674 W. Diversey Pkwy.
Cesar's, Cocktails & Dreams, Dickies, Piggen's Pub

706 Stateline Rd., Calumet City
Bells, Club, Our Way (Gallagher's)/Our Place

720 N. Wells St.
720 Club, Cairo

744 N. Clark St.
Chatterbox, George's

750 W. Cornelia Ave.
Cornelia's, Taverna 750

809 W. Evergreen Ave.
Dragon Room, Tunnel

811 W. Lake St.
Club Reunion, Rooster Blues

868 N. State St.
Foster's Little Club, Yellow Unicorn

905 W. Belmont Ave.
905 Club, Dago Rose's Hideaway, Jimmy's 905 Club, Nine-O-Five

933 N. State St.
Nite Life Lounge, Walton Street Water Works

936 W. Diversey Pkwy.
House of Landers, Zolar

954 W. Newport Ave.
Club Lower Links, Crawlspace, Houndstooth

959 W. Belmont Ave.
Avalon, Showcase One

1015 N. Halsted St.
Powerplant, Riverside Club, Rockers

1056 N. Damen Ave.
Ten 56, Sweet Alice

1110 N. Clark St.
Gold Coast, New Jamie's

1113 W. Lawrence Ave.
Mike's Aragon Lounge, Sharon's Side Track

1123 N. State St.
No Name, Steve & Edie's Saratoga

1137 W. Granville Ave.
Granville Anvil, Hi-Ho Terrace, Mike's Terrace Lounge

1138 W. Granville Ave.
Eagle's Nest, Traveler's Rest

1177 N. Elston Ave.
Bridge, Fire Island, Scooter's

1355 N. Wells St.
Carol's Speakeasy, Den One, Our Den

1415 E. New York, Aurora
Galaxy, Odyssey

1437 N. Wells St.
Butterfly, Our Way on Wells

1502 W. Jarvis Ave.
Chalmer's, Charmers, Pepper's

1516 N. Milwaukee Ave.
Artful Dodger Pub, Dreamerz

1608 N. Wells St.
Willoughby's, Volume I

1620-22 Plainfield Rd., Joliet
A Frame, Club Illusions, Continental Club West

1640 N. Damen Ave.
Amadeus, Mad Bar

1665 W. Fullerton Ave.
Factory Disco, Liar's Club, Music Factory, Risque

1675 N. Elston Ave.
Krush, Prop House/Rails

1744 W. Balmoral Ave.
Joie De Vine, Nobody's Darling

1770 W. Greenleaf St.
Greenleaf, Oz

1829 W. Montrose Ave.
Off The Line, Ravenswood Tavern, Scot's, Suzy B's, Wee Frog

1840 N. Wells St.
Hugo's, Place

1932 E. Higgins Rd., Elk Grove Village
Hunter's, Phoenix Bar & Nightclub

22nd St. & Washtenaw Ave.
Cookie & Shirley's, Jo-Jos

2350 N. Clark St.
Hoots, Neo

2409 N. Mannheim Rd., Franklin Park
Moda VIP, Texas Ranch

2479 N. Clark St.
Meat Rack, Park West Lounge, Pepper & Salt Lounge

2500 N. Southport Ave.
Lite Factory, Bird's Nest

2519 N. Halsted St.
Carol's Coming Out Pub, Little Bits

2546 N. Clark St.
Checkmate, Checkmate II, Inner Circle, Virgo Out

2548 N. Halsted St.
Grapevine, Julie's, Mother's Other, Redford's

2554 W. Diversey Pkwy.
QWEST, Ranch de Luna, Caribe

2559 N. Southport Ave.
Déjà vu, Petunia's

2568-70 N. Clark St.
Bughaus, K's on Clark, Molly's Follies, Pourquoi Pas?, Robert's Lounge, Take One

2626 N. Halsted St.
Noche de Ronda, Prodigal Son, Tilt Inn

2628 N. Halsted St.
Carnival, Pits, Snake Pit

2683 N. Halsted St.
Company, El Dorado, Harlequin's

2828 N. Clark St.
Allegro International, Century Disco, Siegelman's Allegro

2838 N. Broadway
Ann Arkees, It's Here, Le Troll's

2848 N. Broadway
Paradise, Paradome, Phoenix

2856 N. Broadway
Bedrock, Bubbles

2914 N. Broadway
Avenue Tavern, Big Daddy's, Bulldog Road

2917 N. Sheffield Ave.
Backstreet, Baskets, Frog Pond

2959 W. Irving Park Rd.
Kitty's Korner, Lost & Found

3019 N. Clark St.
Big Red's, Jock's, Locker, Minkees

3060 W. Irving Park Rd.
Lizard's Liquid Lounge, Lost & Found

3127 N. Clark St.
Clubhouse, Thumbs Up, (New) Windy City Bar & Grill

3150 N. Halsted St.
Club La Ray, Trianon

3153 N. Broadway
Club Victoria, Crystal's Blinkers, Other Side

3160 N. Clark St.
3160, Annex 3, Shakers on Clark, Teddie's

3169 N. Halsted St.
Inner Circle, Irene's Diamonds, Lucky Horseshoe

3200 N. Halsted St.
The Den, Eons, Foxy's, Manhole, Whiskey Trust, Spin, VII

3209 N. Halsted St.
Guzzlers, Happy Hours, Pangea, Stars

3231 N. Clark St.
BJ's, Odyssey Bar, Ruthie's

3320 N. Halsted St.
Bugle Boy, Bushes, Carr's Halsted Street Cabaret, Gentry on Halsted, G-Spot, Niteline, Rocks, Scarlet

3341 N. Halsted St.
Felt, Mini Bar

3359 N. Halsted St.
Cocktail, The Loading Zone, Men's Room, Progress Bar

3401 N. Sheffield Ave/3400 N. Clark St.
(The building had two entrances.)RDeeks, Normandy, Palace (Palacio)

3407 N. Paulina Ave.
Waterhouse, Ye Old Mill Lounge

3420 W. Grace St.
Abbey Pub, One More Time

3432 W. Irving Park Rd.
Friends Pub, Visions

3439 N. Halsted St.
Buck's, Replay Lakeview

3441-43 N. Halsted St.
Halsted's, Lark, Madam B, Voltaire

3445 N. Halsted St.
Lady Bug, Rick's Retreat

3458 N. Halsted St.
Christopher Street, Hydrate Nightclub, Manhole

3474 N. Clark St.
Christy's on Clark, The Factory, Party Party, Studio 69, Zo-Ran

3477 N. Clark St.
Little Hercules Disco, ? (Question Mark), Sweets

3501 N. Halsted St.
Little Jim's, LJ's

3510 N. Broadway
Broadway Kunfusion, Carol in Exile, Garland's

3631 N. Halsted
Fusion, Rhumba Room, Vortex

3641 N. Halsted St.
Circuit/Rehab, Fantasy Night Club, Halsted Street Café, M7

3700 N. Halsted St.
Halsted's, Kit Kat Club, LA Connection

3702 N. Halsted St.
Aloha Bikini Lounge, Cell Block, The Loading Dock, Vista Hermosa

3714 N. Clark St.
Broadway Lady, Cherry Tree, F Beat

3720 N. Clark St.
Raw Bar, Swan Club, Teddy's

3724 N. Clark St.
Giovanni's, Macho/Chicago

3726 N. Broadway
Augie and CK's, Charlie's, Darche's

3729 N. Halsted St.
Augie's, Big Red's, Bobby Love's, Dandy's, In Between, Norma's

3730 N. Clark St.
Center Stage, Metro, Smart Bar, Stages

4096 N. Broadway
Foster's on Broadway, Jacquelyn's

4153 W. 26th St.
La Cueva, Dolly's Place, Stargazer

4400 N. Clark St.
Erotica, Lolita's

4530 N. Lincoln Ave.
Rainbow Room, Winners

4636 N. Broadway
Office, Quenchyurs

4923 N. Clark St.
Different Strokes, Sofo Tap

5006 N. Clark St.
Chicago Mining Company, Rage

5015 N. Clark St.
Bistro Too, Chicago Eagle

5025 N. Clark St.
The Gold Coast, Meeting House Tavern, T's

5244 N. Sheridan Rd.
Dancers, Mr. T's

5246 N. Broadway
Coconuts, Normandy

6301 S. Harlem Ave.
Escapades, Inn Between, Scorpie's

6319 W. Roosevelt Rd., Berwyn
Angel's Palace, Antronio's

6341 N. Clark St.
Badlands, Dan's on Clark, Parlour on Clark, Pelican

6403 S. Martin Luther King Jr. Dr.
Edye Room, Sculpture Room

6406 N. Clark St.
Jackhammer, JJ's, Numbers

6920 N. Glenwood Ave.
Rogers Park Social, Sidecar Bar

7300 S. Cottage Grove Ave.
Another Place, Bitter End

7301 W. Roosevelt Rd., Forest Park
Club 7301, Hideaway II, Ultimate Oz

7414 W. Madison St., Forest Park
Blue Max, Hardwood

7740 S. Stoney Island Blvd.
Burning Spear, Club 77, High Chaparral

8105 S. Cottage Grove Ave.
Amen Corner, Willie's Lounge

8710 Golf Rd., Des Plaines
Charlie's Angels, Club Bolero

13101 S. Cicero Ave., Crestwood
Hitching Post, Ranch

13126 S. Western Ave., Blue Island
131 Club, Clubhouse Players, Club Krave, Edge

INDEX

Creating a workable index for this project proved to be a difficult task. In pre-Stonewall days people often went by first names only or had "bar names" which were completely different from their given name. Then there was the case of performers of various types who had stage names, often many different pseudonyms, that could be spelled differently from different sources.

We have chosen to alphabetize drag queens by the first letter of their name, similarly to that of a band (Sly & the Family Stone, would be listed under Sly, not Stone). For example, Butter Scotch instead of Scotch, Butter. However, in the case of transgendered individuals we follow standard alphabetization Billings, Alexandra. We are aware that in many cases, some (not all) drag queens then went on to later identify as transgendered. We have done our best to honor the chosen name and identity of as many individuals as we could, but many of these names and identities are no longer able to be tracked down.

Similarly, we identify DJs by their stage name, following the same format as above, and identify them as a DJ. Often their stage name was all that was available. Sometimes the stage name is the same as their given name. Therefore, they are all alphabetized by the first letter of their stage name, whether that is A-Alex (DJ), or F-Frankie Knuckles (DJ), or P-Psycho Bitch (DJ).

Bartenders also, were very often identified only by their first name or a nickname. In these cases, we have listed them by the first name and indicated the bar with which they were affiliated. For example, Casey (Meat Rack).

ACKNOWLEDGMENTS

This book started when somebody was trying to remember the name of a gay bar from their past and Rick Karlin came up with the answer. Then somebody said to him, "You should write a book about Chicago's gay bars!"

As the entertainment editor for *Gay Chicago Magazine*, and the publication's gossip columnist, Karlin had the inside info on the city's gay bar scene from the late 1970s until he left Chicago in 2013. Rick thought about the idea for a while and decided he needed to work with someone who had a stronger connection to the history of the Chicago's LGBT community prior to the 1970s. He immediately thought of St Sukie de la Croix, his friend of many years. Sukie moved to Chicago in 1991 and became fascinated with the city's history. His Chicago Whisper's column ran in several LGBT publications and websites. He interviewed hundreds of community members about their memories of Chicago's LGBT scene. Of course, many of those memories were made in Chicago's gay bars and other LGBT friendly haunts. They decided to pool their resources and create this book, an encyclopedia of sorts.

Karlin and de la Croix first decided to restrict the area geographically to bars in the Chicago area, ruling out nearby cities such as Rockford, Peoria, or Champaign. They did allow for bars in Hammond, Indiana, across the street from Illinois. The establishments included are bars, nightclubs, and taverns, although a few restaurants that functioned as bars after dining hours are included. Some bars, which featured a gay or lesbian night are also included as are primarily straight bars that were/are known to be accepting of the LGBT community. Of course, most bars pre-Stonewall were not officially gay or lesbian, but were still well known within the community. Many were owned and operated by straight proprietors who either actively courted a gay clientele or turned a blind eye. And, of course, many bars were operated by the mob who were happy to take money from "queers" and "dykes" in exchange for a modicum of protection from the police.

In compiling the information in this book, the authors are grateful for the cooperation of John D'Emilio, Bobby Torsvik, Byrd Bardot, David Cunningham, David Velasco, Steve Plambeck, Brent Cooper, Mike Midgette, DJ Psycho Bitch, Scott Free, Dave Awl, Lee A. Newell II, Stacy Bridges, Tracy Baim, Andrew Davis, Kirk Williamson, Brian Boulineau Hagen, Karen Ross, Dan Neniskis, Cody Las Vegas, Art Johnston & Pepin Pena, PattyDukeEllington Pritikin, Toni Armstrong Jr., Gerald Myers (Rhodesia), Mamie Lake, Charlie Brown, Tamara Lee, Kevin Bernal, Matthew Scott Dontje, Crystal Kimmey, Gregg Shapiro, Gary Ward, Miss Foozie, and Ron Ehemenn. The authors would also like to thank the hundreds of people interviewed by St Sukie de la Croix over the years. Additional thanks to Art Smith and his website GayBarchives.com for his support and sharing of materials and information.

The authors also offer their gratitude to the elders in our community who lived the life this book documents and for those who survived and shared with us, Art Johnston and Pepe Pena, Marge Summit, Jim Flint, Mark Hunter, Gary Chichester, and Michelle Fire. They are also indebted to the hundreds, if not thousands of bar owners, bartenders, barbacks, DJs/VJs, management folks, and all the others who made each bar a home for its regulars. To the employees, publishers, and producers of Chicago's gay press which provided a wealth of materials upon which they were able to draw: *Chicago Gay Crusader*, *GayLife*, *Gay Chicago Magazine*, *Windy City Times*, *Outlines/Nightlines*, *Chicago Free Press*, LesBiGay Radio, *Boi Magazine*, *Nightspots*, and *Grab Magazine*.

The authors would like to thank Ian Henzel, Managing Publisher at Rattling Good Yarns Press, for his painstaking restoration of hundreds of bar ads and photos and patience through this mammoth project.

Finally, the authors hope that this book inspires writers from other cities to record the history of their own LGBT-friendly taverns, hangouts, and haunts, for that is where much of the LGBT community's history can be found.

ABOUT THE AUTHORS

Rick Karlin is a playwright ("Witches Among Us," "Spin Cycle", "As Time Goes By" and "Seuss on the Loose"), novelist (*Show Biz Kids, Tales of the Second City, Death on the Rocks*), free-lance journalist (*Chicago Free Press, Bay Area Reporter, Windy City Times, Chicago Tribune's Metromix* and OutTraveler.com) and was the Entertainment Editor for *Gay Chicago Magazine* for 10 years.

A community activist, he was inducted into the City of Chicago's LGBT Hall of Fame in 1997. He founded the popular charity fundraisers, "Night of 100 Drag Queens" and *Gay Chicago Magazine's* "After Dark Awards." In his stage personae, Charity Case and Helen Highwater, he is renowned for his quick wit and snappy repartee as a performer and emcee for charity events and shows.

His memoir, *Paper Cuts: My Life in Chicago's Volatile LGBTQ,* published by Rattling Good Yarns Press, is a fascinating account of his experience working in Chicago's stormy LGBTQ press community.

He was also an award-winning teacher. Rick is the proud father of his adult son, Adam. He is currently the Food & Travel Editor for *South Florida Gay News*. He lives in Fort Lauderdale with his husband, the award-winning poet and writer, Gregg Shapiro, and their dog Coco.

St Sukie de la Croix has been a social commentator and researcher on Chicago's LGBT history. He has published oral-history interviews; lectured; conducted historical tours; documented LGBT life through columns, photographs, humor features, fiction and local LGBT history. He has had columns in local publications or online news and entertainment sources such as *Chicago Free Press, Gay Chicago, Nightlines/ Nightspots, Outlines, Blacklines, Windy City Times,* and GoPride.com, as well as numerous others outside the city. In 2008 he was a historical consultant and an on-screen interviewee for the WTTW television documentary *Out & Proud in Chicago*. In 2005 and 2006, he had two of his plays, *A White Light in God's Choir* and *Two Weeks in a Bus Station with an Iguana,* performed by Chicago's Irreverence Dance & Theatre Company. A popular and engaging lecturer, he has spoken at various venues from Chubb Insurance to Boeing and from Horizons Gay Youth Services to the Chicago Area Gay and Lesbian Chamber of Commerce. His crowning achievement came in 2012 when the University of Wisconsin published his in-depth, vibrant record of LGBT Chicagoans, *Chicago Whispers: A History of LGBT Chicago Before Stonewall*. The book received glowing reviews and cemented de la Croix's deserved position as a top-ranking historian and leader. In 2012 de la Croix was inducted into the Chicago LGBT Hall of Fame.

His other works of nonfiction include *Out of the Underground: Homosexuals, the Radical Press and the Rise and Fall of the Gay Liberation Front* and *Chicago After Stonewall: A History of LGBTQ Chicago from Gay Lib to Gay Life*. With historian and author Owen Keehnen he edited, *Tell Me About It: LGBTQ Secrets, Confessions and Life Stories, Tell Me About It 2* and *Tell Me About it 3*. His works of fiction includes, *The Blue Spong and the Flight from Mediocrity*, a novel set in 1924 Chicago, *The Orange Spong and Storytelling at the Vamp Art Café, The Memoir of a Groucho Marxist,* and *St Sukie's Strange Garden of Woodland Creatures,* illustrated by Roy Alton Wald. His latest novel is *Twilight Manors in Palm Springs God's Waiting Room*.

He lives in Palm Springs, CA with his husband.

CPSIA information can be obtained
at www.ICGtesting.com
Printed in the USA
LVHW061056120123
736975LV00004B/168